AF387964

JERSEY BOSS

JERSEY BOSS

The Rise of Mafia Power Jerry Catena

SCOTT M. DEITCHE

BLOOMSBURY ACADEMIC

NEW YORK • LONDON • OXFORD • NEW DELHI • SYDNEY

BLOOMSBURY ACADEMIC
Bloomsbury Publishing Inc, 1359 Broadway, New York, NY 10018, USA
Bloomsbury Publishing Plc, 50 Bedford Square, London, WC1B 3DP, UK
Bloomsbury Publishing Ireland, 29 Earlsfort Terrace, Dublin 2, D02 AY28, Ireland

BLOOMSBURY, BLOOMSBURY ACADEMIC and the Diana logo are
trademarks of Bloomsbury Publishing Plc

First published in the United States of America 2026

Cover design: Sally Rinehart

Bloomsbury Publishing Inc does not have any control over, or responsibility for,
any third-party websites referred to or in this book. All internet addresses given in this
book were correct at the time of going to press. The author and publisher regret
any inconvenience caused if addresses have changed or sites have ceased
to exist, but can accept no responsibility for any such changes.

A catalog record for this book is available from the Library of Congress.

ISBN: HB: 978-1-5381-9460-7
           ePDF: 979-8-8818-6592-4
           eBook: 978-1-5381-9461-4

Typeset by Integra Software Services Pvt. Ltd.
Printed and bound in the United States of America

For product safety related questions contact productsafety@bloomsbury.com.

To find out more about our authors and books visit www.bloomsbury.com
and sign up for our newsletters.

CONTENTS

ACKNOWLEDGMENTS

As always, my first thanks go to my wife for her love and patience while I wrote this (and all of my books). She is my biggest supporter.

I want to thank my family for their continued support. Thanks, as always, to my literary agent, Gina Panettieri, who is always there with advice, guidance, and the ability to make things happen. Thanks to Sarah, Becca, and all the staff at Rowman & Littlefield for their hard work in bringing the book to print.

A special thanks to Eugene Giufurta and Robert Petrin Jr. for sharing family stories and giving me a glimpse inside the Catena family.

Extra thanks to Michael Weisman for his insight into Longie Zwillman and for introducing me to several sources and Ronald Eskesen for bequeathing to me a massive trove of never-before-seen NJ mob materials.

For personal stories and photos of Jerry Catena, thanks to Myron Sugerman for sharing all your stories, photos, and the history of Runyon Sales; Chris Franzblau for his insight from his years representing Catena; Michael and Jaime Schutz for the Doc Stacher stories; Danny Williams III for sharing his grandfather's stories; Jeff Berger for the latter Runyon years; Kevin Connors for anecdotes from his father's storied FBI career; Glenn Wichinsky for sharing items from his father's career; Saverio for the inside view of things; Kevin Steinbach on the Zwillman family; and Andy Aldi for his recollections and the inside scoop on The Arch.

For help with references, sources, and stories, I'd like to thank former Broward Sheriff Al Lamberti, Sammy "The Bull" Gravano, Joel Turner, Xavier Eboli, Kathy Hennessy-Riley at the NJ SCI, Matthew Beddingfield & George Leopold, The Black Hand Forum crew (especially Eboli), Emily Sweeney, Casey McBride, Joey Nat from the FB group NJ Underworld, Paul Novack, Amma Osei, Joe Pappalardo, OC Shortz, Michael Greene, Eric Grabowsky, Professor

Michael Green, Paul Camacho, Tony Distefano, David Uslan, David Schwartz, Paige at the Newark Library, staff at the Mob Museum in Las Vegas (especially Jonathan Ullman, Geoff Schumacher, Ashley Miller, Jackie Apoyan, Gillian Riggleman, Sabine Von Hemming), and all my other "sources."

For anyone I forgot, I'll catch you in the next book!

PROLOGUE

The week of April 11, 1965, was busy for Jerry Catena. Like any corporate executive, his days were often meetings after meetings. Some planned well in advance. Others were on the spot, putting out fires that seemed to come from every side. Jerry was adept at handling the intricacies and subtleties of negotiating within the confines of organized crime. He deftly worked with political contacts but could also deal with political adversaries. He was also able to make sound business decisions that led to profitable growth for the myriad of companies in which he was invested.

He started the week with hearing about the fallout from a police raid of a craps game in east Newark. One of Catena's contacts in the Newark Police Department was picked up. Catena met with two trusted soldiers, Johnny "Coca-Cola" Lardiere and Joseph "Joe Peck" Pecora. He grew up with both; they were close friends and business associates. Jerry knew that they could handle whatever their police contact needed to stay out of trouble. And if the cop needed a reminder that if he did get in trouble, he should keep his mouth shut, Joe Peck and Coca-Cola could also deliver that message.

Catena met with Harry Summers, a contact at Gold Medal Packaging Corporation the next day. Their Utica plant was scheduled to be demolished, and the firm was set to receive at least $400,000 from the federal Urban Renewal Program. A commission was set up to assess the true value of the Gold Medal property and settle on a final monetary sum. Summers told Catena that he had the head of the Program in his pocket, intimating that Catena and Summers would get a little slice off the top of the Urban Renewal Funds.

On April 15, 1965, Catena again met with Johnny Coca-Cola and gave him $2,750 to distribute to one of the capos in the crime family. He then discussed a recent issue with a Passaic County political leader, Joseph Bozza, who ran a numbers operator out of Paterson, New Jersey. That numbers operator was affiliated with some of Catena's associates. Joseph Bozza was attempting to put the squeeze on the mob. He wanted 50 percent of all the illegal gambling action in the County to guarantee police protection from both local and state law enforcement. Catena balked, telling John Lardiere that Bozza was crazy. But Catena had an upcoming grand jury appearance, so he did not want to be directly involved. He left it up to Lardiere and another soldier, Daniel Polidori, to deal with as they saw fit. Jerry knew when to delegate. Within that one week, Jerry deftly moved between criminal rackets, politics, legitimate business ventures, and personnel management.

Authorities described Jerry Catena in dozens of reports as the most powerful racketeer in New Jersey. He wasn't described as a gangster or a wiseguy. Even the most ardent investigators of Catena's illegal empire realized he was different. In many ways, he was the opposite of what most people think of when they think "mob boss." Jerry Catena was cut from a different cloth.

Jerry's story is the story of organized crime, business, and politics in twentieth-century America. He grew up in the rackets as the mob itself grew. But Jerry also saw the opportunities in business, more than many from the underworld. Jerry Catena extended his reach across vast sectors of American life. And he was a witness to some of the most pivotal events in the history of the American Mafia.

1

Beginnings

The story of Gerardo Vito "Jerry" Catena begins like many of his contemporaries. It's partly the story of the great wave of European immigration to America at the turn of the twentieth century. It's also a story of opportunities denied, and opportunities found, and how many of the early generation of organized crime figures would, under different circumstances, have been captains of industry, business leaders, or successful entrepreneurs. It's also the story of a man who did not fit the generally accepted mold of a crime boss. In many ways, as echoed by others, Catena broke that mold, instead falling somewhere between the robber barons of the late 1800s and the new generation of CEOs and entrepreneurs that guided America's growth into the new millennium. His story is a story of business success. But make no mistake, Jerry Catena was also a student, practitioner, and teacher of the intricate politics and policies of La Cosa Nostra.

Jerry Catena's story starts in the tightly packed streets of Newark, New Jersey. The wave of Italian immigration to New Jersey, specifically Newark, echoed the overall immigration trends into the United States. From 1880 to 1920, over five million Italian immigrants came to America, primarily from the southern regions of Italy, where poor economic conditions made the three-month ship passage across the Atlantic seem like the only option to escape poverty. In Newark, the Italian population went from under a thousand at the turn of the twentieth century to over 27,000 in 1920. Newark had one of the largest Italian populations outside New York City at that time.

Most Italians lived in the First Ward, clustered around 7th Avenue, with St. Lucy's Roman Catholic Church the center of the community. When Jerry was born, however, the Catena family were living in another prominent Newark Italian neighborhood, the Ironbound. Also known as "Down Neck" due to its proximity to a neck in the Passaic River, the Ironbound was a thriving immigrant enclave encompassing four square miles by the time Francesco Catena arrived. Now known primarily for its large Portuguese population, the neighborhood attracted many European immigrants in the late nineteenth and early twentieth century, including a large Italian population and a large diaspora of Black Americans during the Great Migration. The neighborhood was both a source of work, with many factories, breweries, and the nearby railroads providing job opportunities, as well as a tightly knit community.

Two members of that Italian community were Francesco Catena and Donata Speziale. Francesco Catena was born on August 7, 1875, in Salerno, Italy. Francesco immigrated to the United States in 1897. Like many immigrants, his route went through Ellis Island, where he arrived on the SS *Fulda* on October 28, 1897, with only $2 to his name. He listed his intended destination as Newark, where his father, Antonio, already lived. As a single young man with little formal education, he found work as a laborer and as a mason. Francesco listed his height as medium and build as slender, with brown hair and brown eyes.

Donata was born in New Jersey in November 1883. Her parents came from Campania. Francesco and Donata lived near each other in Newark, which is likely how they were introduced when she was still a teenager. They married in 1898.

Shortly after their marriage, the newlywed Catenas moved into their first home, at 290 Van Buren St. in the Ironbound. It was a brick multi-family complex in a predominantly Italian area, with several Italian businesses, markets, and social clubs dotted around the neighborhood. They were right near East Side Park,[1] one of the few recreational green spaces in the heavily industrial neighborhood. Donata's parents and siblings also lived nearby.

Gerardo "Jerry" Vito Catena was born in this apartment on January 8, 1902. Francesco and Donata had four other children in the small walkup: Leonard (born in 1899), Eugene (born in 1904), Mary (born in 1908), and Frank (born in 1909). By all accounts, the family blended well in the tight-knit community, among other Neapolitans and Sicilians who made Newark their new home.

By 1910, the family, bursting at the seams with five kids, moved a couple of doors down, within the same building complex, to 284 Van Buren St. This was also the building where Donata's parents and sister lived, bringing the larger Catena clan under the same roof. Two more children followed the move to 284: Antonio (born in 1913) and Sadie (born in 1915).

Little is known about Jerry's early life. His father worked a lot, and the family stayed close to the neighborhood. The Ironbound was lined with shops and markets, so the family didn't need to travel outside the neighborhood for daily necessities.

However, when it came time to attend elementary school, Jerry went to Charlton Street Elementary School, located on the corner of Charlton and Waverly Avenue, now known as Muhammad Ali Avenue. The imposing three-story brick structure[2] was a block from the Third Ward Political Club, the epicenter of political power in the Ward, and a place whose members would come to forge business alliances and partnerships with Catena in the coming decades.

The Charlton Street school was located in the heart of the Third Ward, which was then a predominantly Jewish neighborhood and what must have seemed a world away from Jerry's home in the Ironbound. Although less than two miles in actual distance, the two neighborhoods were cut off by train tracks, contributing to two distinctly different cultures in each. There wasn't any indication that these differences mattered to Jerry. He was able to blend in well and make friends.

Jerry adapted to his new environment and learned much from his Jewish classmates, two in particular. According to some sources, it was on the grounds of the Charlton Street School that Jerry first met two friends who would help shape his future career, Abner "Longie" Zwillman, and Joseph "Doc" Stacher, who lived nearby the school. Zwillman was two years younger than Catena while Stacher, who emigrated to Newark when he was ten years old, was the same age as Jerry. Catena, Zwillman, and Stacher became fast friends and continued this friendship throughout their lives. Jerry's brother, Eugene, also hung around the group. Other sources say that Jerry's relationship with Zwillman and Stacher occurred when he was a little older.

In the coming years, Jerry's closeness with Jewish crime figures would become a unique feature of his life in organized crime. His cultural connection with them, forged through his formative years at Charlton Street, would become a valuable aspect of Catena's criminal, business, and social life. Jerry's inner circle of close social friends was predominantly Jewish as well. This closeness with Jewish business and criminal associates would also lead to some conflict with other Italians. Still, for the most part, Catena's close ties with Zwillman, Stacher, and others served him well, guiding his rise through the ranks of organized crime and the business world. And the business world, at that time, had limited opportunities for young Italians from the streets of Newark.

The Charlton Street Elementary School went through eighth grade, but Jerry did not continue the school path. Later, he told a United States Senate panel that he went to two years of night school in lieu of high school but never finished. He attributed his interest in crime to a lack of formal education. However, for whatever formal education he lacked, Jerry was very literate and had a mind for numbers and business, two attributes that would serve him well as he entered the working world.

Kids leaving school early to work and help provide for their family was not unusual back in the 1910s. But while most worked regular jobs, Jerry supplemented his income with some early street-level criminal activity. While Jerry gravitated toward the street to make his way, it was not from the emulation of his upbringing. His father, Francesco, was not involved in organized crime. Like most first-generation immigrants of that time, he found employment in the trades, working as a laborer and a mason's assistant, among other things.

When Jerry was 15, his brother Leonard died, the day after Christmas 1917. He was buried in the Holy Sepulchre cemetery in East Orange. Shortly after, in January 1918, Donata died. The family was devastated, especially Jerry's father. Two years later, the Catena family moved to a single-family home at 176 Oliver Street,[3] a few blocks from their prior residence on Van Buren. While Jerry still lived at home, Eugene moved out, although he stayed close, living a block away at 207 Oliver Street.

At the time, Jerry and his brothers Gene and Frank worked as laborers at Port Newark[4] during the day, Frank eventually becoming a hiring boss for longshoremen. These ties to Port Newark and the Longshoremen's union were valuable building blocks for the Catena brothers' deep infiltration of union activity decades later. By fostering relationships early on, Jerry was able to leverage these ties to his advantage, bringing many of the powerful unions that worked in and around the Port under his influence.

After work, Jerry and his brothers spent time at some of the underground gambling dens that dotted the city. While never known as a big gambler or bettor, Catena enjoyed casual gambling. But found it much more lucrative to run games. One of Jerry's first jobs in the gambling industry was working as a watcher over craps games run by Jake "Mohawk" Skuratofsky, a one-time boxer who was also part of the Minutemen group that defended Jewish neighborhoods in Newark against American members of the Nazi party in the years leading up to the Second World War. Jake was also "the greatest bookie of Newark, whose reputation was impeccable."[5] Mohawk had the games in Linden and Catena served as a young pit boss, standing on a ladder to make sure he could see across the craps table and keep an eye on the game.

Illegal gambling was already big business for crime by the time Jerry came on the scene. Almost every tavern, saloon, and back room of a store had gambling machines, took bets on sporting events, or hosted craps and card games. Betting on horses was another popular pastime. The ubiquitous nature of gambling funneled staggering sums of money through the underground economy, which in many cases wound its way to police, judges, and politicians. Many regarded gambling as a victimless crime—even in cities where numbers games and backroom casinos prospered, the penalties were light. Others railed against the pervasive influence of gambling, especially on how it affected men's livelihoods. Stories of suicides and losing family fortunes were commonplace in newspapers of the time.

The movement against gambling also corresponded to the rising temperance movement in the United States. Preachers, newspapermen, and temperance groups often lumped the evils of drinking and gambling together, linking the two through their presence in bars frequented by fathers, husbands, and brothers. Newark has an estimated 1,400 bars, and the Newark-based Anti-Saloon League was working to vice check every one of them for gambling activities. More often than not, however, money was exchanged, and the gambling joints continued to offer games of chance. And for Jerry, this was the way he wanted it.

Jerry Catena's first arrest occurred when he was 21 years old, on August 11, 1923. Jerry was caught by Newark police, running a craps game in the back of a Newark storefront. It was his first offense, and a minor infraction. Catena received a suspended sentence, which did little to dissuade him from gambling business ambitions. A few months after his craps arrest, on December 9, 1923, he was arrested again for running a gambling game in Newark. This time he was fined $2, which he promptly paid.

In late October 1924, police responded to reports of a man being assaulted on Ferry Street, the main drag through the Ironbound. When they arrived, they found Jerry and two of his young crew, Jacob Lordi, a stick-up man well known to Newark police, and Victor Troycasco. When the police attempted to arrest the trio, Catena lashed out and bit the patrolman on his right hand while his associates came to his aid. All three were quickly subdued by police backup and placed under arrest while the cop went to the hospital for treatment. Catena was charged with interfering with an officer. In January 1925, he was placed on two years' probation. He was fined an initial $50, then $1 a week for the rest of the probation period. It was a rare show of temper from the usually mild-mannered Catena. His disposition was his strength. After this incident with the Newark cop, there were very few instances of Catena letting his emotions get the better of him.

But trouble was still around for the young gangster. He was brought in as a material witness to an armed robbery in Harrison, New Jersey in the summer of 1926. Catena was accused of robbing a resident of $32 on his front doorstep. Released on $750 bail, Catena was formally arrested the next month and charged with robbery. Catena denied the charges but was found guilty and served a short sentence.

This late 1926 sentence took Catena off the streets for only a short time, putting little dent into his operations. At that time Catena was involved with not only gambling, but another racket that Catena was beginning to realize the potential of—hijacking trucks. Jerry wasted no time returning to the game after his release on the robbery case. The truck hijacking racket was growing, and Jerry dove back in with a crew of local neighborhood toughs, some of whom went on to long criminal careers.

As mentioned previously, Jerry and his brothers worked at the nearby Port Newark facility. With so many ships bringing cargo into the Port, the trucking industry that developed to transport the cargo across the region became a target both for robbery and infiltration by organized crime. The tangential businesses that were dependent on the Port's cargo traffic generated significant revenue, and local crime figures from Newark and Elizabeth were only too happy to take advantage of the situation.

Jerry's gang of truck thieves was one of the more active groups engaged in hijacking trucks from the Port. From late 1926 through early 1927, his gang hijacked a dozen trucks from various businesses, including the New Jersey Tobacco Company and the Royal Cigar & Candy Company, both located in Newark. The gang made off with over $75,000 worth of goods.

Although not explicitly stated in contemporaneous reports, Jerry was the head of the gang. Among his closest confidants was his brother Eugene. While Jerry preferred quiet power, his brother Gene was the opposite. He had a more fearsome reputation that sometimes manifested itself in ways that caused trouble for both brothers. Their younger brother Frank was tangentially involved in their activities. Other members of Jerry's gang included Joseph "Happy" Bellina, who in 1982 became a soldier in the Philadelphia Mafia, as a member of their Newark crew.[6] Another gang member who rose to prominence as a Philly mob's Newark crew member was Anthony "Tony Bananas" Camponigro. Jerry often worked in tandem with the Pecora brothers—Thomas, Edward, and Joseph (Joe Peck). Another member of Catena's gang was Victor Marsillo, who in the ensuing years would become a close associate of Jerry and Eugene and a noted boxing manager for Sugar Ray Robinson and Jersey Joe Walcott, among other fighters.

Jerry's hijacking crew had kept the cops at arm's length for the latter part of 1926, even during Jerry's stint in prison. While they were sometimes close to being arrested, they always avoided their pursuers.

The big break for law enforcement came one afternoon in January 1927, when three detectives were given cigars at a store in Newark. They noticed that the cigars had no bands and the boxes they came in were unlabeled. As true cigar aficionados, the three detectives also realized that the cigars were "too classy for the place they were in."[7] They realized that the cigars were likely stolen, so they searched the store. That led them to buy even more of the merchandise on the hijacked trucks. Working from that, they were able to track down and arrest twelve members of the hijacking gang, including Jerry Catena. During his arrest, one of Jerry's long-term aliases was uncovered: Jerry Allen.[8]

While he was hijacking trucks, Catena was also working with them in a far more lucrative racket, one that would make many gangsters' fortunes, while leaving others in the ground, bootlegging. The passage of the 18th Amendment to the U.S. Constitution, more popularly known as Prohibition, brought new opportunities for a young, ambitious man like Catena. And for a city dotted with breweries, now closed, and access to one of the largest ports in the United States, the allure of illegal alcohol smuggling was too much to resist.

Prohibition was a boon for gangsters in New Jersey. Nestled conveniently between New York City and Philadelphia, with hundreds of miles of coastline, estuaries, and creeks, perfect for the Jersey Skiff, a specialized boat favored by Jersey rumrunners to evade the Coast Guard, the Garden State became known as the "Booze State" from 1920 to 1933. The vast distilling, smuggling, trafficking, and distribution networks from the rural northwest corner of the state, all the way down to the Shore, supplied speakeasies, jazz bars, and underground gambling clubs with all the hooch they could handle.

Newark was at the crossroads of the bootlegging industry. Dotted with dozens of shuttered breweries and warehouses, the city's backstreets were well-traversed by trucks carrying barrels and cases of imported liquor that arrived across the Atlantic. Ships carrying illegal alcohol would drop anchor twelve miles offshore, in international waters. From small coves in Raritan Bay, Jersey Skiff would head out to meet the supply ships out of reach of law enforcement. In the rare instance when they were interrupted by Coast Guard cutters, the skiffs could easily outrun the aging Coast Guard fleet, at least early on during the Prohibition year, before the Coast Guard upgraded their fleet. Still, the amount of intercepted booze paled compared to the amount that made it through and back on shore, where fleets of trucks would be waiting to transport that hooch to warehouses.

The profit from liquor was enormous. A case of whiskey that went for $20 in Europe could easily fetch three to four times that amount on the streets of New York City. Millions of dollars of liquor were held offshore on the transport ships. It was clear why this racket was so desirable to many in the underworld. Liquor was served at hundreds of speakeasies and hidden bars across the state. Newark was dotted with them. Right in the heart of the City was Charlie Charlie's Saloon at the Four Corners—the intersection of Market and Broad Streets. The Palace Chop House and Ludwig Achter-Stetter's Restaurant, advertised as the "largest and most popular restaurant in the State," were also gathering spots for politicians and gangsters.

Newark's advantage was twofold. It had a large industrial base, so the hundreds of factories and warehouses that dotted the waterfront were perfect hiding places and headquarters for bootlegging gangs. Distillery operations supplemented the high-quality European liquor with homegrown hooch. Although not as high quality and sometimes downright poisonous, the "bathtub" gin was an essential part of the Prohibition-era liquor supply. It also helped spur the creation of cocktails that utilized sweeter ingredients to hide the often-unpalatable flavor of the liquor product.

Another advantage was the waterfront. Newark sits at the convergence of the Passaic River, Hackensack River, and Newark Bay. This estuary was vital to Newark's growth, primarily due to its protected location, which served as the ideal location for dredging a shipping channel and eventual construction of the Port terminals in the 1910s. With the construction of Newark Airport in 1927, Newark became one of the busiest transport hubs in the northeast, a perfect cover for bootleggers and their illicit cargo. Smaller creeks and dock facilities surrounding Newark also provided easy cover for the Jersey skiffs that were bringing the cargo to land from the offshore ships. In many ways, Newark was the ultimate bootlegger's paradise.

The liquor transport system relied on reputable drivers and men who were loyal to the bootlegging gangs. Paychecks of $100 per week sweetened the deal.

This was too good an opportunity for a young guy like Jerry Catena to pass up. He already had his hands in gambling and truck hijacking. Moving into bootlegging and transportation of illegal liquor was a natural progression. More importantly, Catena had a strong ally at the top of the Newark bootlegging racket, his friend, Abner "Longie" Zwillman.

The press dubbed Zwillman the "Al Capone of Newark," and he did little to dissuade the comparison. He assembled a crew of like-minded compatriots, all dedicated to maximizing the revenue stream of illegal alcohol smuggling, transport, and sales. Zwillman's reach extended far beyond Newark. In addition to the offshore ships carrying liquor from Europe, Zwillman supplemented his supply with overland and sea routes bringing liquor from Canada. He partnered with Canadian liquor barons to keep New Jersey and New York as wet as possible in the face of the ascending temperance movement and their partners in law enforcement.

Longie first worked with Jerry Catena in 1927, bringing Jerry and his crew of truck hijackers into the Third Ward Gang operations. Catena started off as a driver and gunman on some of the truck routes that crisscrossed Essex County. They were not only concerned about police and federal law enforcement, but other rival mobsters looking to take the cargo.

Zwillman and Catena employed a fleet of Mack AC cargo trucks built initially for use in the First World War. Nicknamed the Bulldog, the Mack AC trucks were known for their durability and strength, which was helpful for the occasional need to crash through a police roadblock or push through the closed gates to a warehouse. The trucks would unload liquor along Newark Bay's docks and a pickup spot that Zwillman controlled in Long Branch, further down the Jersey Shore, along the Atlantic. The trucks would bring the liquor to warehouses along Prince Street, which ran through the Jewish Third Ward, where Zwillman held court at the Prince Street Café.

Jerry Catena worked his way up to become Zwillman's right-hand man, and the operations grew exponentially. Frank Reitman, another successful Newark-based prohibition figure, described competition with Zwillman and

Catena as friendly and it never descended into the violence that plagued other competitors. However, although he had never dealt with them, he maintained that their reputation was one of the best in the business.

Zwillman had let Jerry into his organization and saw the potential in his friend. Now joined, the two men would take their business to the next level, both in the illegal world and branching into legitimate industries. With Zwillman as his mentor, Jerry was about to harness his natural business mindset and start on a path to financial success that few others in organized crime could achieve. But the path was not a smooth one. Rivalries threatened to upend everything Catena and Zwillman worked for. It was time to fight for what was theirs.

2

Rise of the Racketeer

Gene Catena was on the run. Jerry's brother found himself in an unenviable position. On the night of November 10, 1929, Grant Patterson, a fireman from Lyndhurst, was called out to an alarm. He was disappointed that he had to cancel the date he had set up for that night. After the call, after midnight, he joined some friends at a bar in downtown Newark, the Picadilly Night Club.[1] Gene Catena worked as a doorman/bouncer at the club that night.

One of the club owners, George Pallitto, a one-time boxing manager, was in the restroom when Patterson entered. Patterson and his friends were getting a bit rowdy, and according to Pallitto, when Patterson encountered him in the restroom, they got into an argument that turned physical. Patterson returned to his friends with a black eye, and things escalated. The men went after Pallitto, and Gene Catena stepped into the fray.

As the free-for-all continued, five shots rang out, two of which embedded themselves in the walls of Piccadilly, while the other three hit Patterson. He died on the floor of the club. Catena fired the shots. He ran off into the night before the police arrived, which was not long after as the club was just two blocks from the Newark Police Department.

Newark police fanned out across the city looking for Catena. Gene had reason to run. In June 1927, he was arrested for assault and battery with intent to kill and served a year in the Essex County Penitentiary. Police found his gun near the club, but Catena managed to slip through the dragnet. By the following day, the Lyndhurst Fire Department, where Patterson worked, issued a call to the Governor demanding a state investigation into the murder and greater resources to capture Catena.

Police brought Pallitto and the other co-owner of the club, Joseph Schilling, the nephew of the Newark Police Chief, in for questioning. Pallitto called the shooting an act of self-defense. Although they were no closer to catching Catena, their eight-hour interrogation of Pallitto and Schilling did net some positives. Both men admitted they were running a liquor smuggling operation, and police found 200 beer kegs in a warehouse owned by the men. Not a good look for the police department.

Determined to find Gene Catena, the police offered a $1,000 reward. This substantial incentive failed to produce any immediate results, prompting the police to broaden their search. By spring 1930, Newark detectives had traveled across the United States to Italian neighborhoods in Chicago, New York, and San Francisco. They even extended their search to Italy, "where police in Naples, Palermo, and other cities were scouring the underworlds in an effort to capture Eugene Catena."[2]

After the trail had gone cold, the police received a tip in the spring of 1931 about a "retired" poultry farmer in Springfield, Massachusetts, who resembled the 27-year-old Gene Catena. In August 1931, the police arrested Gene outside an apartment building in Springfield and brought him back to Newark to stand trial for the Patterson killing. Gene was scheduled to go to trial on October 5, 1931. Instead of going to trial, Catena entered a no-contest plea and was sentenced to eight years.

While Eugene was "on the lam" in Springfield, Jerry moved deeper into the Zwillman's Third Ward Gang. He often worked with Doc Stacher. Jerry forged relationships with others in Zwillman's orbit including Charles Haber, James "Niggy" Rutkin, Max "Puddy" Hinkes, Samuel "Big Sue" Katz, and Abe Green.

Abe Green was one of Jerry's closest friends in the Third Ward Gang. Abe was tall and good-looking but had an air of calm about him. Although he could crack skulls with the best of them, he was described as soft-spoken and kind to those who knew or interacted with him. He rarely raised his voice and kept his cool demeanor even when things got heated. He worked his way up with Zwillman and became one of his trusted associates. But Abe was also very close to Jerry and Eugene. They naturally gravitated toward each other, and Abe Green became an essential part of Jerry's business life in the years to come.

Catena's persona changed. Under Zwillman's tutelage, he moved away from street-level crimes that had dominated his early forays into crime. Catena was smart enough to realize that he needed to develop a more innovative approach to move ahead, both financially and within the political landscape of organized crime. Longie already had a savvy business acumen and grew more dependent on Catena's support as a driver, bodyguard, and mentee. And to Catena, Zwillman's power and how he used it served as a guide to how he saw his future. He did not need to be a gangster who bit cops' fingers and hijacked trucks. He needed to be smarter about how he operated.

Catena gave up on hijacking trucks. Instead of stealing from the Port, he started developing relationships with union officials whose fellow union members worked the Port, from laborers to truck drivers to stevedores. Jerry backed away from small-time gambling games and went from operating craps games in the Ironbound to overseeing large, luxury gambling dens in Bergen County. While Catena was firmly a New Jersey guy, he made the trip into the city to build strategic partnerships with organized crime figures there, understanding the benefits of mutual collaboration and teaming. And above all, Catena saw how successful Longie became with his legitimate business investments. Jerry emulated Zwillman and followed in his footsteps.

Zwillman diversified his interests outside bootlegging and gambling. His businesses ranged from vending machines to restaurants, to a bowling alley, a brewery, and a furniture company. And, when Prohibition ended in 1933, Longie went into business with his old bootlegging partners in legitimate liquor distributorships. This was a model that Jerry could follow.

One of Jerry Catena's early legitimate investments was in the Public Service Tobacco Company. Public Service Tobacco was incorporated in September 1932 by William Lillien, who, with his brother Al, controlled a huge rum-running empire out of the Atlantic Highlands in New Jersey. Public Service Tobacco was headquartered in the township of Hillside, just outside Newark. Public Service provided cigarette vending machines to bars and restaurants throughout the state. At its height, Public Service had over a thousand machines in operation, generating significant income for Lillien and his partners.

The vending business was eyed as a lucrative way for organized crime to invest and launder money. The post-Prohibition years saw many organized crime figures get involved in the vending machine industry. It was not relegated to New York and New Jersey. From Chicago down to Tampa, gangsters moved their money into the business, coinciding with the overall vending business's revenue increase.

With that potential, Catena and Doc Stacher eyed Public Service Tobacco as ripe for a takeover. William Lillien didn't have the muscle that his brother had during Prohibition because his brother was murdered in March 1933. There was an opening to make a move. Catena turned to Longie Zwillman. Longie ordered Puddy Hinkes to soften Lillien up. Hinkes was a former boxer and all-around tough guy who was not afraid to use his fists, as he did against Nazis who marched through Newark in the years leading up to the Second World War. Hinkes went to visit Lillien, supposedly shoving Lillien into the trunk of a car and not letting him out until he agreed to sell.

Lillien relented, and in November 1936, Jerry, along with New York mafioso and close confidant of Charlie "Lucky" Luciano, Mike Lascari, purchased the firm. Along with Lascari's wife, the three named themselves as directors of the company on November 25, 1936.

The minutes of that meeting reflected the fact that the stockholders had voted by ballot for the directors. The only three stockholders were Catena and the Lascaris. The minutes also reflected William Lillien's immediate resignation.[3]

Although Doc Stacher's name was not on the ownership documents, Mike Lascari later testified during a Senate inquiry that Stacher definitely owned a piece of the company. Also, in a separate testimony to Congress, Longie defended Lascari against accusations that Mike was involved in the rackets: "He came to Jersey and worked all day and night on the Public Service thing. Certainly, that does not spell out an underworld man who works 20 hours a day."[4]

Catena brought Zwillman into Public Service in 1939. The company was generating massive profits. By 1949, Public Service Tobacco was grossing over $1.4 million a year. This was from the one company alone, not counting the myriad of other business ventures that Catena and Zwillman had invested in, and the illegal gambling operations that they oversaw throughout North and Central New Jersey.

While Zwillman and Catena were quietly expanding their empire, across town another up-and-coming underworld power was starting to flex its muscles. Ruggerio Boiardo, a.k.a. Richie The Boot, grew up in the First Ward, the Italian neighborhood north of the Third Ward. Boiardo started his criminal career working with the Mazzocchi brothers, Dominic, John, and Frank. The Mazzocchi brothers were big bootleggers and also ran still operations in abandoned warehouses and backrooms across the First Ward.

The Boot was a character in his own right. He dressed flashy, wearing diamond-studded belt buckles and the latest custom suits. He had no issue with drawing attention to himself. He amassed significant political contacts in the First Ward. By 1928, The Boot was breaking away from the Mazzocchi brothers. Boiardo felt that their leadership was constraining him. He wanted to forge his own path and move on to bigger rackets.

The Boot antagonized the Mazzocchis when he set up a bar up the street from their headquarters. From there, physical confrontation was only a matter of time. The Boot and his guys hit first, and they hit the hardest. On August 19, 1929, two Mazzocchi gunmen were ambushed by Boiardo's men. Agostino Dellapia was shot twice in the chest, twice in the stomach, and once in the back. Vincenzo Follo was shot three times in the chest.

The next to go was Frank Mazzocchi. He was talking with friends when a car drove by spraying Mazzocchi with machine gun fire. He died at the hospital. His brother John was killed in March 1932. With John's death the Mazzocchi brothers were done. Boiardo had wiped away the remnants of the organization. The First Ward was all his now.

But there was another rivalry that Boiardo was getting swept up in, between his First Ward Gang and the Third Ward gang of Zwillman and Catena. Boiardo believed that Zwillman had backed the Mazzocchi brothers and rather than come talk with Zwillman, Boiardo started making incursions into the Third Ward and Ironbound. Zwillman and Boiardo started exchanging gunfire and beatings of each other's men. One story that made its rounds during the heyday of the feud concerned two Boiardo hitmen who dressed up as women and came to see Zwillman at his headquarters, the Riviera Hotel. The hitmen were taken upstairs to Zwillman's room, where they were "unmasked" and threatened. Longie reportedly told them, "I'll give you a number. You tell Boiardo if he doesn't call it in 24 hours, you're all dead. My people will clean every one of you rats off the streets of Newark. Now, get out of here."[5] It's unknown if the story is true, but it is now a part of the Boiardo–Zwillman feud lore.

What is true is that after some back and forth between the two gangs, Boiardo invited Zwillman to a three-day conclave to sign a truce between the two factions, ending the war. The meeting took place at the Nuova Napoli restaurant in October of 1930. The lavish feast was the talk of the town. Photographs of the meeting appeared in local newspapers and accounts landed in the gossip columns. The era of celebrity gangsters was officially in full swing.

Catena attended the banquet with Zwillman and other representatives of the Third Ward Gang. Zwillman and Catena left the meeting feeling that peace was achieved and they looked forward to partnering with Boiardo. But things almost went completely sideways a month later. Boiardo was stepping out of his bulletproof limousine in front of his apartment at 242 Broad Street in Newark on November 26, 1930, when an unknown gunman fired from a window across the street from where Boiardo was exiting the car. Eleven bullets tore through Richie's body, six hitting his torso, and five hitting him in the head. Police said that two men rented the room a week prior. This was a planned hit.

His associates immediately drove him to the hospital. While he was being brought into the hospital, he remarked, "They got me." Detectives asked for more details, but Boiardo remained tight-lipped. Although seriously wounded, Boiardo made an amazing recovery. Initial speculation was that the recent truce had broken down. But there was no indication from Zwillman or Catena that things had turned sour between the Third and First Ward Gangs.

Suspicion for the attempt on Boiardo fell to Dominic "The Ape" Passelli, a bootlegger and one-time associate of Boiardo. Passelli had fallen out of favor with The Boot. He was suspected of initially being aligned with Zwillman and may have had a hand in the shooting of some Boiardo men in September 1930. Boiardo declared him *persona non grata*, which irritated the gangster.

On the evening of November 2, 1930, Passelli showed up at Newark General Hospital with cuts and bruises on his face. He told the nurses that he had been in an accident, having fallen out of a moving car. They patched up his bruises and stitched his cuts. But The Ape did not want to leave. He convinced the staff to let him pay for his own private room. They agreed.

A few hours after Passelli settled into his private room, two men walked into the hospital and up to Dominic's room. Witnesses described them as a stout man and a slender man—not good enough for conclusive identification. But one nurse did identify Jerry Catena as one of the two men and said he had a gun under his coat. Whether it was Catena or not was unclear. The men spoke with Passelli for a while, then left.

On the evening of November 3rd, two other men came to the hospital. They walked up to The Ape's room and opened fire. The two gunshots hit Passelli in the head and neck. He died in his hospital bed. In the commotion after the shooting, the two men walked back out the front door and into a car they had parked at the ready. The Ape was dead, and some felt that Boiardo's shooting was avenged.

Within days police arrested four suspects in the Passelli shooting: Ralph Russo,[6] Harold Corrbitt, Tony Bove, and Ernest Fiumara.[7] All four were known Boiardo crew members and once reported to Passelli. On November 17, 1930 Jerry Catena was brought in by police as a material witness to the shooting, due to the identification of him by one of the nurses. He was turned over to prosecutors, but nothing came of his ties to the Passelli killing, and he was released.

Catena was back on the street, and Boiardo was recovering from his shooting. Catena and Boiardo became closer, although in later years there was much speculation that Boiardo always had a deep distrust of Catena, stemming from Jerry's close association with Zwillman. Boiardo forgave, but he never forgot.

Boiardo's headquarters was the Vittorio Castle, an Italian restaurant in the heart of the First Ward.[8] The Vittorio became a popular eating establishment for local officials, politicians, celebrities, sports stars, and many of Boiardo's fellow Jersey criminals, including Jerry Catena.

The young, 20-something Catena was rising fast. It was only a decade ago when he was still earning a living as a laborer and starting his gambling career watching games for Jake Mohawk. Now, aligned with Longie Zwillman, Jerry Catena was ready to take the next step up the ladder of organized crime.

3

The Delmore Connection

Jerry's sphere of associates expanded geographically during the Prohibition era. He began partnering with Italian mobsters in other parts of the state as well as New York City. His Newark-centric business and crime focus was turning outwards.

One of the key alliances he made during Prohibition was with Nick Delmore—like Catena, an up-and-coming mobster who hung around the Third Ward Gang, despite living in Elizabeth. Delmore was the uncle of future crime family boss Sam DeCavalcante. His Prohibition activities connected him with Zwillman's Third Ward Gang.

One of Delmore's bootlegging partners was Max Hassel, known throughout northern New Jersey as one of the top liquor smugglers. Hassel, along with his bodyguard Max Greenberg, was gunned down in 1933 at the Elizabeth-Carteret Hotel. Hassel was killed by two Italians, Joseph Troia and "Frankie" Carbo, who later went on to become the mob's point man in the boxing industry. After Hassel's death, Delmore, Catena, and Zwillman assumed Hassel's businesses.

One of the businesses that Hassel partnered with Delmore was the Rising Sun Brewery in Elizabeth. The brewery operated before Prohibition, so it was an easy transformation to go from making legal beer to bootlegging "real" beer post-Prohibition. The brewery was known to law enforcement, and there were several raids dating back to 1923. Sightings of Rising Sun Brewery trucks were commonplace throughout northern New Jersey. They sometimes had men dressed as police officers driving the trucks to avoid suspicion. People would see a truck driven by a cop and think it was spoils from a raid, headed to the police station.

On September 19, 1930, a team of six federal agents left Philadelphia with warrants to raid and search the Rising Sun. On the way to Elizabeth, the men were sideswiped by a car. This gave them pause. What if the brewery was tipped off? Did they have a leak in their ranks? They continued on anyway, arriving in Newark. When they entered the brewery, they found several employees working. The agents, led by John G. Finiello, gathered the employees in the boiler room. Unbeknownst to the six agents, several men were in a building across from the brewery. While Finiello and the agents were questioning the employees, the men moved from across the street and into the brewery, slowly working their way to the boiler room.

One of the agents, Robert Young, was surprised from behind by the bootleggers. They disarmed him and made the other five agents drop their weapons. One of the bootleggers recognized Finiello, and said "get him" to his compatriots. A series of shots rang out, hitting Finiello eight times. He slumped to the floor, dead. The gunmen ran off into waiting cars, according to witnesses, avoiding a convoy of police vehicles that descended upon the brewery after Finiello was shot.

Based on eyewitness accounts, police suspected Nick Delmore was one of the gunmen almost immediately. They went to his apartment above the brewery, but Nick was gone. The living space was decked out with all types of wires and buzzers that were connected throughout the brewery, basically an alarm system that would alert Nick when they were being raided. This likely is how the men across the street were warned that the federal agents had entered.

Within days, federal agents were tracking Delmore across the region. They sent out feelers to past associates and detailed Delmore's prior activities to the newspapers. Some of Delmore's associates defended him to reporters. "Delmore is definitely not of the gangster type. Public print and public hysteria are attempting to pre-judge his character in a way that is unfair and un-American."[1]

The intense focus on Delmore and his crew resulted in significant disruptions to the Delmore/Catena/Zwillman bootlegging operations. Some of the brewery operations were shut down. Raids continued. But Delmore was still nowhere to be found. Police did not question Catena, but police brought in many shared contacts, both as witnesses and potential accomplices.

One of the main witnesses to the shooting was August Gobel. He was working as an engineer at the brewery and was on the scene when Finiello was shot. After the Rising Sun incident, he got a job as a fireman for a company in Newark. On November 7, 1932, a patrolman was guarding Gobel at his place of employment. The cop, Adolph Weigand, was talking with Gobel in front of a boiler. Gobel walked around the corner to an open courtyard, out of Weigand's field of vision. Within seconds, Gobel cried out that he had been hit. Weigand went around the corner and saw two men firing on Gobel. He returned fire at them, but was hit in the arm and body. The men fled the scene.

Even though the key witness was dead, the police kept building the case against Delmore and his accomplices. This was all done while Delmore was still "on the lam." Police initially believed that Delmore had fled the country. He had the means and opportunities. Delmore, although he maintained that he was born in San Francisco and not Italy, still had deep connections back in the old country.

Police also kept close watch over Delmore's associates. They pressured a few to give up Delmore's location, but most held firm. Jerry Catena was arrested on November 3, 1933, for loitering. This move was designed to keep the pressure up on Catena to see if he would flip and let police know Delmore's whereabouts. He received a sixty-day suspended sentence for a loitering charge.

However, as it turned out, Delmore stayed close to home, literally inside his house. On October 19, 1933, police found Delmore asleep in his Berkeley

Heights home. Police received some tips that Delmore was at his house and was looking to surrender to the prosecutor. When police arrived at his house, Delmore reacted calmly, saying that he would be happy to follow them downtown and surrender. He was tight-lipped on where he was holed up before federal agents found him, adding a bit of a mystery to his whereabouts and who else may have assisted him during his time in hiding.

Delmore was charged with first-degree murder for the death of Agent Finiello. His trial was scheduled for November 20, 1933. The trial lasted eight days. No one expected the jurors to turn it around so quickly when they went in for deliberation. Within two and a half hours, they came back to the courtroom with a verdict. Delmore was acquitted of the murder of Agent Finiello. His elation was short-lived. As soon as he was acquitted for the Finiello murder, federal agents arrested him in the courtroom. They charged him with conspiracy, resisting a federal officer, and assault with a deadly weapon.

This second trial was scheduled to begin in January 1934. Delmore, probably feeling that his efforts against a witness in the first trial were a big factor in his acquittal, reached out for some assistance on this go-around. He didn't need to get rid of a witness; instead, Delmore asked for help bribing a juror. Jerry Catena was happy to assist.

Alonzo Chambers Applegate was selected in January 1934 to be part of the Delmore jury. Four men approached Applegate at his home. The men were Jerry Catena, George A. Kent, William "Squawk" Reilly, and Jack S. Costa, a police officer in Toms River. The men told Applegate that if he voted to acquit Delmore, they would pay him $500. Catena paid Applegate $100 on the spot to sweeten the deal, with the balance due when Delmore was acquitted.

Appelgate immediately went to the court to inform them of the bribe. Police then set up a sting operation. They had Applegate ask for a meeting with the four men at Jack Costa's home. When all four men showed up for what they thought was a discussion with Applegate on the acquittal plan, they were arrested by state troopers. They were transported to Trenton and arraigned in front of a federal judge They were charged with "aiding, abetting, and tampering with a federal juror."[2]

The four men pleaded not guilty and were released on bond. Applegate turned the $100 bribe over to police. Prosecutors were confident that they were going to convict Delmore this time. Nick did not even need the bribe. He was acquitted at trial for a second time and released back to the streets of Elizabeth. This episode also strengthened ties between Delmore and Catena.

On March 12, 1934, all four men changed their plea to guilty. Costa was sentenced to a year's probation and fined $350. But his co-defendant Kent got off even lighter, receiving only a $150 fine and a year's probation. Catena and Reilly were sentenced to three months and a $500 fine. This was the longest prison sentence Jerry ever served at that point.

Less than a month later, on April 3, 1934, Jerry's father, Francesco, passed away. It was another loss for Jerry, who had already seen his mother and older brother pass. While that part of his life was slowly slipping away, Jerry was ready for his own family.

In the fall of 1936, Jerry married Catherine McNally, whom everyone called Kay. He had met her a few years earlier. She was born in Brooklyn and was a showgirl in New York City when Jerry met her.[3] They were married in Newark, where they lived in a rented single-family home in the Weequahic section of Newark, moving to their first purchased residence in Montclair a few years later. They would have four daughters and a son.

Around this time, Jerry began working with Guarino "Willie" Moretti, a Bergen County-based gangster. Moretti was a member of the crime family led by Charlie "Lucky" Luciano, often referred to as one of the architects of the modern Mafia, bringing it out of the old system of small families and heritage-based groups, and organizing a more integrated system with a core focus on making money.

Moretti operated gambling dens with Longie Zwillman. Hence, Jerry entered that sphere of influence. It was here that Jerry, while working under

Zwillman, started to gravitate toward working under made Mafia members. Moretti was only six years older than Catena, but had already become the capo of the crew, with some sources saying he may have served as underboss for a time in the late thirties/early forties.

Under Moretti, Catena's career continued on an upward trajectory. He was seen as an earner who could bring money to the organization. He also had his business interests, which generated a sizable salary for his growing family. He caught the attention of higher-ups in the crime family, including Luciano, and another high-level member, Frank Costello. They saw potential in the Newark recruit.

Jerry Catena became a made man in the Luciano crime family in December of 1943. He was made along with Richie Boiardo and Nick Delmore in the same ceremony. One of the prerequisites at that time for new recruits into the Mafia was that the candidate must have killed someone, or "made their bones," as one expression went. Although Jerry certainly found himself in some scrapes and acts of violence in his younger years, there has not been any conclusive evidence to show that Catena ever killed anyone. He very well may have, but if he did, that story is lost to time.

While Catena, Boiardo, and Delmore were made into the Luciano family, at some point soon after, Delmore moved over to the Elizabeth Mafia family, eventually becoming the boss. It wasn't the only interesting switch that occurred around that time.

Philadelphia Mafia boss Joe Bruno championed Angelo "Gyp" DeCarlo, who also went by Ray, and William "Si" Rega to be made into the Luciano family, Rega and DeCarlo were also in Willie Moretti's crew, like Catena. He went ahead and inducted DeCarlo and Rega himself and immediately transferred them back over to Moretti. DeCarlo recalled the induction. "How do you think we got in? When they made Ritchie, Jerry Catena, and Nick Delmore. Joe Bruno hollered like a S.O.B. He said 'what's the matter with Ray and Si?' he said 'what's the matter with those two guys? You're making these guys!' So we got made a few months later."[4]

The early 1940s saw Jerry Catena start venturing to a locale that would become pivotal to him and his family in the years to come—Florida. The Catenas vacationed there regularly, escaping the cold winters of New Jersey for some sunshine. Coincidentally, Florida was also becoming a destination of choice for many of Catena's underworld colleagues. The destination of choice was South Florida, more specifically for Catena, Miami Beach.

The cities of Miami and Miami Beach—in fact, the whole South Florida region—were unique outposts for organized crime as they were recognized as "open" or places where no one mob family held sway. The Tampa Mafia oversaw a large area of west central Florida, and although they also had a presence in South Florida, they were just one of many crime families and independent associates operating in the region.

However, the area was becoming a popular tourist destination as well. During those early years of travel to Miami Beach, the Catenas often stayed at the Hotel Raleigh, an iconic art deco hotel built in 1940. The Aqua Cabana Club pool is a Miami Beach landmark, looking the same in 2025 as it did in 1942 when Jerry's wife and three daughters were photographed for *The Miami Herald*. Other hotels that became regular stops for Jerry, both with and without his family, were The Singapore Hotel (a favorite of Meyer Lansky's), the Eden Roc, and the iconic Fontainebleau.

The Crime Commission of Greater Miami also noted Jerry's frequent trips to Florida. In 1948, Commission director Daniel P. Sullivan released a list of gangsters in the region, and Catena's name appeared as Zwillman's chief lieutenant. Apparently, Sullivan did not receive the memo that Catena was, by then, a made member of the Mafia. Other crime commissions were also on the case. The Chicago Crime Commission reported observing Zwillman and Catena meeting in Miami.

The Crime Commission also noted that Jerry procured gun permits from law enforcement. They used this to support their assertion that Jerry was a major political fixer. Access to firearms is a crucial component of a criminal enterprise. Guns were never uncommon among organized crime figures who obtained them through various channels. For Catena, he found a supplier in an unlikely place—the police. Asbury Park policeman Frank Rowland became an unusual source for several crime figures seeking weapons. From 1931 to 1938, the cop purchased over two dozen revolvers and then transferred them to underworld figures, including Doc Stacher and Jerry Catena. Two of the other guns that were moved in New York City were used in gangland murders. Rowland was charged for the gun purchases, but Catena and Stacher avoided any legal ramifications from the case.

In December 1946, there was supposedly a grand meeting of major Mafia figures and Charlie Luciano in Havana, Cuba. Luciano, who had been deported to Italy in February 1946, flew to Cuba in the fall of 1946 for a six-month stay. It was then that this grand Havana conference was to be held. I've written previously about the conference and the appearance of crime figures like Santo Trafficante Jr. However, more contemporary analysis shows that there was not one large conference but rather a series of smaller meetings between Luciano and visiting mobsters from the US.

The meetings were likely related to Havana gambling and the rise of casino operations on the island. There were concerns about constructing the Flamingo hotel in Vegas and Benjamin "Bugsy" Siegel's role in project management. But the most pressing issue was that with Luciano never able to set foot in America and ruling the family from Naples, would he be amenable to stepping down and appointing a successor?

Among the various groups that traveled to Havana in December 1946 were Meyer Lansky and Frank Costello. They flew down first on December 1 for two days. After they left, Vincent Alo and Joe Adonis flew down. After they left, Willie Moretti, Vincent Mangano,[5] and Jerry Catena flew down on December 13, flying back to Florida on December 18. The next day, Frank Costello, Joe Adonis, and Vincent Alo flew back down.

Moretti recounted the trip a few years later.

Mr. Halley: Who did you go with?

Mr. Moretti: Myself and two other fellows.

Mr. Halley: Who were they?

Mr. Moretti: Vincent Mangano and Gerry (*sic*) Catena.

Mr. Halley: How long did you stay there?

Mr. Moretti: About five or six days.

Mr. Halley: When you were there did you see any other people besides

Lucky Luciano?

Mr. Moretti: Mo; just a couple of Cubans—couldn't even talk to them.

. . .

Mr. Halley: What was Gerry Catena doing on the trip?

Mr. Moretti: He knows Luck well too. We happened to be in Florida,

and I took him along with me. I wanted to see Charlie Lucky, so they

volunteered, just on a friendly basis.[6]

Catena also later recalled the Havana trip, noting that he, Moretti, and Mangano met with Luciano over dinner at the Nacional, along with a couple of Cuban contacts whom Catena did not know. When pressed if he was involved with any business discussions with Moretti and Luciano after their dinner, Catena said he "just went around out in the outside, like any other visitor of Cuba."[7]

Based on the succession of flights, which continued into February 1947, it is more likely that there were multiple small meetings to discuss the organized crime business rather than one set meeting. Most importantly, the first wave of fellow crime family members and close associate Meyer Lansky dealt with the lines of succession. Lucky Luciano agreed to step down, and Frank Costello became the crime family's boss.

Things were looking up for the crime family in the 1950s. Now a fully fledged mafioso, Jerry Catena was enjoying the fruits of his labor, vacationing often with his family, and running a successful business alongside his growing criminal portfolio. As organized crime in general expanded across the country, some in Washington, DC, were watching. And they were about to use a new medium—television—to show the country just what these gangsters were doing.

4

Kefauver Comes Calling

The wedding was one of the biggest ever seen in Newark. St. Lucy's Catholic Church, a neoclassical marvel in the heart of the Italian First Ward, was overflowing with family, friends, well-wishers, and everyday residents of the neighborhood. On April 30, 1950, over 2,000 people filled every available bit of floor and pew space in the sanctuary, which only had seating for 750. Forty-three ushers were needed to keep things under control. People were sitting two to a seat. The crowd filled every space, forcing the bride and groom to stand up on the altar for their vows. Authorities estimated another 15,000 people spilled out of the church onto 7th Avenue and down Sheffield. A police contingent of twelve officers kept the street clear. The onlookers hoped to catch a glimpse of the bride and the groom as they walked out of the church.

Although it rained heavily earlier in the day, by 6 p.m. the rain had tapered down, and the temperature hovered at 50 degrees. Inside the church, the ceremony began at around 6:30 p.m. After the flower girls squeezed through the crowded church, down the aisle, they were followed by the best man and matron of honor, Jerry Catena and his wife, Catherine. Jerry waited until his wife was able to work her way next to the bride before he joined her. As they ascended the altar and found a small space for each other to stand, Jerry stood next to the groom, Anthony "Tony Boy" Boiardo, the son of Richie the Boot.

Four priests and twelve altar boys oversaw the ceremony. The service was quick, and before long, the bride and groom showed themselves to waiting throngs before entering their limousine, while the guests left for the Essex House, where the reception was held. The Essex House was a thirteen-story brick building, originally built as an Elks lodge in 1923, but by the time of the Boiardo wedding, it was a hotel and nightclub. Thankfully, the Essex was large enough to hold the 600 guests who came for the cocktail hour, swelling to over 1,500 guests for dinner.

Catena held court at his table, surrounded by politicians, businessmen, and mobsters from as far away as Chicago. The tables were supplied with bottles of bourbon, brandy, and champagne. Among the politicians were Ralph A. Villani, the then-mayor of Newark. Joining Villani was U.S. House representative Hugh J. Addonizio, who would become mayor of Newark twelve years later. Various local and state politicians were also among the crowd in Essex.

The bride and groom sat at a table:

banked with especially made sweets and fruit and flanked with displays of snapdragons, roses, carnations, and stephanotis. Honeydew melons, pineapples and cantaloupes were fashioned as baskets to hold assorted fruits and nuts. On the right side of the display a four-foot heart was carved from a block of ice. The left side of the table was decorated with a large basket, also carved from ice. The basket was filled with assorted flowers. The guests were able to pluck ripe olives that had been inserted outside the basket as a decorative measure.[1]

The fact that Catena was the best man at the wedding of the son of his one-time rival showed how far the dynamics of the New Jersey underworld had shifted since the end of Prohibition. Catena and Tony "Boy" Boiardo had become quite friendly, often playing together in golf tournaments. And with Tony Boy being a rising star in the same Mafia family as Catena, it was an alliance that made sense in the mob political landscape of the time. Jerry would later tell one of his capos that he was also looking out for Tony Boy in addition to forging a friendship.

Jerry's summer of 1950 went without much fanfare, save for his participation in some local golf tournaments. By the fall, though, headwinds were approaching out of Washington DC, in the form of a new Senate Committee convened to investigate organized crime's infiltration of businesses. Dubbed the Kefauver Committee, after Tennessee Senator Estes Kefauver, the Committee announced a series of hearings around the country to pull back the covers and reveal the extent of organized crime's influence on American business and politics.

The Committee announced that New Jersey would be one of the regions targeted, and Catena was among the names they listed as potential targets of their hearings. They described New Jersey as being riddled with illegal gambling operations and a deep reservoir of crime figures who operated with relative impunity. They named Joe Adonis and Longie Zwillman as two other targets.

As September 1950 approached, investigators ramped up their efforts to send out subpoenas. With that news, some mobsters became scarce at their usual haunts to avoid the process servers. Jerry Catena and Joe Adonis were among those who left the state to avoid being called. Others, like Willie Moretti, suddenly fell ill and needed hospitalization. The Committee was forced to acknowledge that they were having a hard time getting in touch with their targets.

Catena's name kept coming up as one of the people the Committee was most interested in talking with for the New Jersey hearings. It had only been a few years since his formal induction into the crime family, and Catena was already considered by the Kefauver Committee as one of the heads of the Mafia in New Jersey, despite not even being a capo at that point. It was recognition that Catena was working at a higher level than other mobsters they investigated.

Over Labor Day weekend in 1950, Jack Elich, a former Tacoma, Washington, police chief and assistant to the Kefauver Committee, rang the doorbell to the Catenas' South Orange home. Catherine answered, and Elrich informed her that the Committee had a subpoena for Jerry. He gave her two phone numbers to call and said that as soon as Jerry came home, Catherine was to give the numbers to him so they could arrange the serving of the subpoena. Upon hearing of this, Jerry assured Catherine that he would take care of it, not wanting to worry her.

Right after Elrich's visit, Catherine and Jerry took a nine-day road trip to New Hampshire at the historic Crawford House. Two days after returning, Jerry told his wife that he needed to go on a business trip and that he would call her when he could. Elrich returned to the Catena home the next day, looking for Jerry. Catherine told Elrich her husband was not home at the time, and she didn't know where he went.

However, Jerry's attempts at evading the Kefauver Committee backfired when the Committee served Catherine a subpoena and forced her to testify. The main Committee member who questioned Mrs. Catena was Jack Halley.[2] Catherine[3] was called in front of the Committee in early October of 1950 at the hearings in Newark. One of the first questions that the Committee asked Mrs. Catena, accompanied by her attorney Anthony Calandra, was where her husband was. She told the Committee that he was on a business trip and was not sure when he would return. It was a familiar refrain for many of the missing gangsters, conveniently ill or out of town when the subpoenas were being served.

After the questions about Jerry's whereabouts, the Committee started drilling down into Catena's varied business interests, both legitimate and illegal. Catherine answered plainly, not drawing out any responses, but not evading the questions either. For a person who had never been "grilled" by law enforcement, Catherine maintained an air of calm and assuredness in the face of the Committee's questions. When asked why she didn't know all about the supposed gambling interests of her husband and associates, she replied that she had her first three children in four years and that she was too busy raising them to take part in anything that her husband was doing business-wise.

Although she remained very tight-lipped about her husband's business ventures, Mrs. Catena opened up a bit more about their social circle. It was apparent that Catherine was friendly with many of the wives of Jerry's partners, noting that they occasionally got together for social visits. It offered an insight into the interconnectedness of the crime family and how it intersected with the "regular" family. The Zwillmans visited a few times a year, as did the Morettis. She noted that Frank Costello came to their house in the mid-1940s for a big party the Catenas were throwing, and that she was friendly with the Dotos, whom she met through Jerry after they married. One particular answer of Catherine's showed their fondness for some of New York City's well-known restaurants. When asked where she was introduced to gambler Frank Erickson, she replied that it was in a restaurant in the City during one of their nights out: "It could have bene either Moore's or Shaw's or Gallagher's, or any one of those places."[4]

The Committee let Catherine go after some additional questions from other members. But they did impart one last piece of advice for her, and by proxy, Jerry.

> I think it would be well for you to try to get word to your husband that he is just making it a whole lot harder on himself by avoiding service of a subpoena, that he won't get by with it, and the publicity and the scorn that he will be held in by trying to avoid appearing before this committee will just make it that much worse for him. We have an investigation to carry through. He is a necessary witness. He will have to testify sooner or later.[5]

A few days after Mrs. Catena's testimony, Jerry reappeared and accepted the subpoena at their house. He knew that the resulting media attention would likely be far greater if he didn't testify. And for a nascent mobster on the rise and an already successful businessman, the risk of not showing up was not worth the inevitable fallout and potential damage to his money-making ventures.

But Catena was not quite ready to face the Committee. He decided on another tried-and-true method of avoiding questions—health concerns. The Kefauver Committee agreed to bring Catena in for questioning in December 1950, but the cagey racketeer was confined to his bed for health reasons. According to Catena's attorney, doctors ordered bed rest for a heart ailment. The Committee was not too pleased about this latest attempt to evade their efforts to question Catena, telling his attorney that they were "not very well pleased with the delays that we have in securing his testimony up to this time and that we are not going to put up with any monkey business with his not being here."[6]

After some back and forth between the two parties, Catena finally appeared before the Committee on Valentine's Day 1951. The Committee started off the questioning by asking why Jerry was unavailable for the Committee.

Mr. Catena: I was just roaming around. In the confusion, I was a little confused. My mind cleared up, so I thought I would . . .

Mr. Halley: You mean you were ducking the subpoena in other words, is that what you mean?

Mr. Catena: Well, in a way, you would say that I was, I was just in a state of confusion.

Mr. Halley: What were you confused about?

Mr. Catena: Well about the publicity.

. . .

Mr. Chairman: You had a nice looking wife, she was up here. She couldn't find you at that time. She said she couldn't. So we are glad that you have come back. We are glad that you are here today.

Mr. Halley: Your business partner couldn't find you either, isn't that right?

Mr. Catena: Yes.

Mr. Halley: You just ducked out of sight for a while, is that right?

Mr. Catena: Yes.[7]

The Committee was apparently satisfied that Jerry was at least being somewhat truthful with them on his reasons for evading the subpoena. Catena was then asked about his various legitimate business ventures, opting to answer, albeit with short, curt responses. He was open about his conviction for bribing the juror in the Nick Delmore case, prompting an interesting statement from New Hampshire Senator Charles W. Tobey:

> Pardon me, but all I want to ask you is this. It isn't very often that we run into a man such as you who tried to bribe a juror in a case involving a murder, and you say you did do it and were convicted of it, so it must be true.
>
> The point I make is that you come before us as a clean-looking chap, and we have seen your wife, and she impresses us as being a very sincere and fine woman, and here you stand in the prime of life and tell us that you were convicted for trying to do this, for trying to thwart justice by interfering with justice, and you try to bribe someone to vote a certain way. What is your mental process? You are an American citizen.[8]

However, when the Committee began to dig into businesses outside his legal companies, Catena quickly pled the Fifth. He told the Committee that he wanted to keep matters regarding his income private. When pressed for more information, Catena told them that he had gone legit, but that he "respectfully refuses to answer questions regarding my income."[9]

The Kefauver hearings also provided glimpses into Catena's private life, echoing some of the back-and-forth during his wife's testimony. A line of questioning about Frank Costello revealed some tidbits about Catena's social life. Jerry and his wife often ventured into New York City for dinner or to catch a Broadway show. Jerry testified that they would eat at places like Quo Vadis, an old-school European restaurant that was one of the City's more fashionable spots in 1950. Jerry also frequented Danny's Hide-A-Way, in midtown Manhattan, a popular celebrity hangout known for its steaks, and owner Dante Stradella, who became friendly with Frank Sinatra.

A number of those times Catena just happened to run into Frank Costello, whether at a bar across from the old Savoy-Plaza Hotel or at the Madison Hotel, both located on the other side of Central Park from Frank Costello's luxury apartment. The cocktail lounge at the Madison Hotel was a particularly favorite meeting spot for Costello, which makes it even more unlikely that Catena just happened to run into him at the bar. In May 1950, reporters photographed Costello and underworld figure Frank Erickson at the Madison. When Erickson saw the reporters taking his photo, he dashed out of the restaurant leaving his hat and coat behind. The two reporters were then accosted by a number of men who shoved the would-be paparazzi away from the scene.

Another popular spot for meeting with Costello and other NY-based mobsters was Chalder's Restaurant, on the Upper East Side. Chandler's was reportedly owned by Joseph "Joe the Wop" Cataldo, a soldier in the Greenwich Village crew of the family. Costello and Catena were observed by police eating at Chandler's on several occasions.

Another Catena hangout was the Bleeker Club in Newark. Located on Bleeker Street in downtown, the Bleeker Club was a notorious speakeasy during Prohibition and was supplied by the Zwillman combine. The Treasury agents who raided the Bleeker Club were in the area so often that they had to be transferred out of town because everyone knew them. In the post-Prohibition years, it remained a popular gathering place for underworld figures.

As much as the Kefauver Committee discovered about hangouts and relationships between crime figures, there was still a great deal of information that witnesses were close-lipped about. The testimony of New Jersey figures like Willie Moretti and Catena gave state investigators a jumping-off point for their own inquiries.

As the Kefauver Committee was wrapping up its hearings, New Jersey Deputy Attorney General Nelson Stamler started a probe into illegal gambling operations in Bergen County. The cities of Fort Lee and Lodi were of particular interest to Stamler. He saw those cities as havens for organized crime and gambling, primarily operating under the guidance of Joe Adonis, Willie Moretti, Longie Zwillman, Niggy Rutkin, and Jerry Catena.

Stamler amassed enough evidence to formally indict Adonis, Moretti, and ten others for running illegal gambling parlors in Bergen County. He told the newspapers that he wanted Catena to testify and would be preparing subpoenas. However, Adonis pleaded no contest to the charges, ending the necessity to have Catena testify. Adonis was sentenced to three years in state prison. During his prison stint, federal immigration authorities declared Adonis an illegal alien and proceeded with deportation arrangements. He eventually left the US for Italy in 1956, leaving his vast Bergen County gambling empire to Catena and Zwillman.

The post-Kefauver notoriety did not hamper Catena's rise in the Mafia ranks nor the expansion of his legitimate business interests, but it lifted the lid off his persona enough for keen mob-watchers to realize that Catena was unlike most other wiseguys paraded before the Kefauver Committee. Jerry was a unicorn in a sea of toughs and thugs. There was more to him than the newspapers portrayed.

5

Who Was Jerry Catena?

At his appearance before the Kefauver Committee, some of the members, and press, remarked at how Catena did not fit the mold of the stereotypical organized crime figure. His appearance, more of a professor than a gangster, coupled with his soft-spoken and measured responses, drew favorable comments from the same men who were there to expose the infiltration of the mob. Who was Jerry Catena, the person? You could get one answer by simply looking through the volumes of mentions of him in law enforcement reports or newspaper articles. But the man in the underworld was only one part of Jerry Catena's persona. The way he conducted himself in business showed the entrepreneurial and business-savvy side. In private, as to friends and neighbors, he was warm and kind. Publicly, he often mirrored the kind of person he was in private. And to his fellow mobsters, although he could be treacherous when needed, he often came off as a statesman willing to look for compromise rather than defaulting to violence.

Physically, Catena was 5' 7" with brown hair and blue eyes. He did not necessarily look Italian. Some of his contemporaries remarked that he looked more Irish than Italian. He was often photographed with a wide smile, rarely showing the dour or menacing gazes favored by many underworld figures who found themselves in front of a camera. His appearance was often referred to positively, "always wears the deep tan of an outdoorsman . . . handsome of face and neat in dress."[1]

Sometimes they were not so kind. Ed Reid, whose sensationalist and often muck-raking prose style earned him renown in organized crime writer circles in the 1960s, described Catena unflatteringly as "swarthy and pudgy."[2] By and large, however, Catena's coverage in the media was more even-handed than many other mobsters.

He was described as a "colorful but conservative dresser . . . usually wears expensive casual clothes, with touches such as alligator shoes . . . wears dark-rimmed glasses . . . (and while playing cards) seldom without a big and expensive cigar."[3] His grandson remembers him wearing black and white wing-tipped shoes, always dressed well for any family occasion.

People who knew him described him as a nice, quiet gentleman who got along well with everyone he met. "He came off as a banker or librarian," said Michael Schutz, no 'l' Doc Stacher's nephew. Catena's grandson remembered Jerry fondly, saying he was a true gentleman. Myron Sugerman, whose father would become a key business partner of Catena, described Jerry as a methodical thinker who wielded his power quietly. Myron also recounted his father's impression of Catena, stating that he could have been the head of General Electric. Jerry's long-time lawyer described Jerry as quiet and soft-spoken, avoiding public attention and certainly never drawing attention to himself.

Jerry never finished high school, but he was self-taught. He was an avid reader who always kept current on current events. He could converse with expertise on several topics. Jerry enjoyed playing chess, a testament to how he approached his business enterprises with deliberate consideration. He did not make snap judgments or decisions. Like other contemporaries—Meyer Lansky, for example—Jerry was an above-average intellect who, under different circumstances, may have gone down a different path.

Socially, Jerry was outgoing and cordial. He enjoyed Scotch on the rocks as his go-to drink. He smoked cigarettes when he was younger, switching to cigars as he got older. His cigar smoking ended on a dime when he was diagnosed with lip cancer in the early 1970s. After surgery to remove the cancer from his lower lip, Jerry gave up cigars cold turkey.

Catena was careful not to mix his family with mob business. According to the FBI, Catena had a rule that mobsters could not come to the house and discuss business if his family was there. This must be said, as it differs from many of his contemporaries. Jerry Catena was, by all accounts, a devoted and faithful husband and father. He was involved in his kids' lives and activities. When his daughter took part in a school play, the society page of *The Star Ledger* took note and identified the "Jerry Catenas" of South Orange as the proud parents, taking care not to associate his daughter's achievement with Jerry's frequent mentions in the paper due to his other "family" activities.

While many other mob bosses and contemporaries of Jerry had goomahs (i.e., mistresses) on the side, or in the case of Vito Genovese, particularly volatile relationships when it came to women, Jerry did not engage in any of that. There is no evidence that he was anything but faithful, and the fact that he and his wife were married for over sixty years is a testament to that. Jerry was a devout Catholic and a frequent churchgoer. He also supported many Catholic charities.

He was well-liked in his neighborhood in South Orange. He was "genial but reserved with his neighbors."[4] Catena, "who dressed expensively in dark suits, gives a low-key performance in the suburban community. He speaks with deliberation and his motions are slow. He is genial but reserved with his neighbors."[5]

Few people ever talk about Catena losing his temper. He seemed, by many accounts, to have the ability to remain calm, even when things around him were spiraling. But there were times when he let his façade slip a bit in front of others. Law enforcement often described him with grudging respect, with terms like "a master of the art of union business and political infiltration."[6]

John Connors, one of the main FBI agents in the Newark field office, was a constant in Jerry's life, even if the mobster failed to recognize it. Through several wiretaps that he had planted in various mob clubs and hangouts, Connors could glean a lot of important information about organized crime figures in New Jersey, especially Jerry and his brother Gene. But even Connors, who considered Jerry Catena, like Zwillman, a gentleman and not a thug, saw Jerry turn.

One time my Dad was with another agent and he inadvertently insulted Catena. The blood ran from my father's face when he saw the look in Jerry's eyes. Catena went from a businessman to a stone-cold killer in seconds. There was another agent there with my Dad and I think he realized if he wasn't an FBI agent then he would have been killed.[7]

Connors met Jerry face to face one time after that, under much different circumstances. There was a low-level criminal out in Las Vegas who was throwing Catena's name around and he was saying that he was Jerry's son. Connors went to tell Jerry at Runyon Sales. Jerry said that it couldn't be his son and that his son was right there with him at Runyon's.

Catena also had a charitable side, both to legitimate charities and those in "the life" that were close to him. When Genovese mobster Dominick LaPlaca died suddenly of a heart attack on January 1, 1963, Catena made arrangements to support LaPlaca's widow and kids financially. He did it out of respect for Dominick's father Peter LaPlaca, who at the time was in federal prison for bribery in a 1950 tax case against Longie Zwillman.

Among the charities that Catena supported were ones that dealt with children's health, specifically those with disabilities, like the Crippled Children's Committee of the Rotary Club of South Orange. Another children's charity that was the focus of Catena's giving was The Devereux Foundation. In the summer of 1961 alone, Jerry donated over $1,000 to the Foundation, which works with children with developmental disabilities. Jerry was a big supporter of the Boys Club of Newark, the charity his future business partner Phil Dameo had been instrumental in for decades.

Jerry also supported his friends and "family" when they found trouble. One night, Andy Aldi's father, who became a partner with Jerry in some business ventures, was walking out of the Waldorf Astoria on Park Avenue in New York

City. He was approached by two men who mugged him. Andy's father said that he would give up all his money but that he wanted to keep his money clip, a sentimental family heirloom. The men proceeded to viciously beat him up, taking the money clip. Andy's father was in the hospital for almost a month. Upon his release, he started making some inquiries. His cousin called in some favors in New York City.

Shortly thereafter Andy's father received a call from Newark police. NYPD had called them saying they had found the two men and Andy's money clip. He went down to the police station, identified the men, and walked out. The Newark PD then released the men at around 1:30 in the morning and told them to find their own way to the train station to get back to New York City. Andy's father told Andy later that the men never made it back to New York City, intimating that Jerry took care of them as a favor to his friend.

Andy recalled a similar event a few years later:

> When I was in college, a friend who owned Majestic Amusements called me. He told me that a couple of guys from the Philadelphia mob called him and said that he was going to sell to them. He was scared. He asked me if I could have my father call Abe Green and see if he could help out. My father called and Abe said, "sure I'll meet your friend." So Abe, my Dad, and Jerry went and met with my friend, then went to Philly. They solved the problem.[8]

Although Jerry may have gravitated to more mentally demanding pastimes like chess and reading, he had a passion for sports, specifically golf. Catena played for decades, both for fun and in numerous tournaments around New Jersey and Florida. He was a New Jersey State Golf Association (NJSGA) member. Catena's enthusiasm for the game enveloped other members of organized crime, and Catena was often on the course with some of his mob contemporaries and friends. Jerry played with Longie Zwillman's stepson, John Steinbach. He played with Tony Boy Boiardo, his lawyer Chris Franzblau, and Genovese soldier (and future capo) Pete LaPlaca. Golf was a getaway for

Jerry, a respite from the often-tumultuous world of organized crime. Chris Franzblau recalled Jerry telling him, "Golf's different. That's where we go to relax, to leave the business behind."[9] But even on the course, he dressed to the nines and didn't let his competitive nature get the better of him. He grew to love the game, sometimes more than his day job. "Catena much prefers golf to cracking heads."[10]

In the early 1940s, Jerry joined the Crestmont Country Club in West Orange, New Jersey. The Newark Athletic Club owned Crestmont, whose main headquarters was on Nassau Street in Newark. Crestmont was one of the few clubs that Jerry could belong to back then. Because of several mitigating factors, including his association with organized crime, but also the fact that he was Italian, becoming a member of one of the more prestigious old-money country clubs was not an option at that time. Crestmont members allowed Jerry to join, along with several other associates, including Abe Green and Longie Zwillman.

Every Sunday night the "boys" would play gin at the Club. Longie would often sit in, as would other golfers. Among the gin regulars was Abbey Zurkow, chairman of the Crestmont annual tournament and the owner of Del Clothing Company in East Newark. After one game, as the story goes, Zurkow was suspected of stealing Zwillman's winnings from his locker. After that, Zurkow disappeared and was never heard from again. For years afterwards, public notices appeared in newspapers asking Zurkow to come forward if he was still alive, as part of his relatives having him declared legally dead. Zurkow never responded.

Jerry also golfed at the Jumping Brook Country Club in Neptune and the Nell Country Club in Whippany. Jerry held positions in the Tournament Committee for the Newark and Essex County Golf Association, and around this time, he began playing in tournaments.

Jerry and his partner came in second place at the 1942 annual NJSGA tournament in Bergen County. Later that summer, Catena came in second place again at a tournament, this time playing for the Jumping Brook Club championship. The following year, Jerry, playing for the City of Newark, won his match, enabling the City team to defeat Long Branch.

In June 1945, a one-day PGA Pro-Am event occurred at the Plainfield Country Club, where Jerry and his partner, the legendary New Jersey golfer Danny Williams, tied for third place. A former caddy described Danny Williams as an outstanding golfer and a charming man. Williams first met Catena at Crestmont. They became fast friends. Williams gave Catena lessons, imparting some of his championship skills into the mobster. "It's not a surprise that Catena was good. My grandfather was a legendary teacher."[11]

Danny Williams and his wife were very close to Jerry. The Williams would join Jerry and his wife Catherine in Florida for a few months every year and stay at Jerry's second home there.

My grandmother retired to Florida in the 1980s. We were going through photographs, and she says they were staying with Catena at his house in Florida. My grandfather and Jerry were out playing golf. She was in the house alone. The doorbell rang. She answered the door and a guy is standing there all dressed up like a businessman. He told her that he was looking for Mr. Catena. She told him that no one was home. He said tell him Meyer Lansky stopped by.[12]

In 1947, both Catena and Williams joined the Knoll Country Club. Catena may have gotten Williams the job there. "I remember spending Saturdays at the Knoll in the late 1950s. I met all those guys. It was a who's who of the New Jersey Mafia. Besides Catena you had Tony Boy Boiardo, Pete LaPlaca, and others."[13]

At the Knoll, Jerry gained a reputation among the caddies as a pleasant individual who remained calm during matches and a consistent golfer. "He was a good golfer. Nice guy. He was nice to everybody. He had the bucks. He'd always give somebody, 'here's a buck or five bucks' or whatever. And I remembered guys when they saw him park, they'd always line up to try and caddy for him. He paid the bucks."[14]

Jerry also played for some of the companies he had financial interests in, either above board or as a silent partner. In 1947, he played, along with partner Phil Dameo, for the People's Express golf team. In 1949, Catena played with Myron Friedman in the Mario Morano Memorial Tournament at Crestmont. Friedman was another competitive golfer who, like Phil Dameo, factored into Catena's business ventures, showing up years later as Catena's partner in Las Vegas investments. Catena and Friedman went on to win the Knoll's annual member–guest championship in 1953.

Jerry's golf acumen often made the local newspaper sports pages, but one particular win in 1950 even made *The New York Times*. After a particularly competitive tournament, Catena and his partner, Albert O. Steckman, won the Suburban Golf Club member tournament. "It was Catena who set the pace yesterday for his winning team, getting a birdie on the 16th and one on the 18th with the help of a handicap stroke."[15]

In 1952, Jerry reached the finals of the Member–Member golf tournament at the Forsgate Country Club in Monroe Township. In 1953, Jerry was back at Forsgate, coming in fourth out of twenty-two teams. He also came in the top spot in two other tournaments in 1953, extending his dominance of the local golf scene. In fact, from 1952 through 1957, Jerry's name was mostly in the papers for his golf game, which must have been a welcome respite after the publicity of the Kefauver Committee hearings.

Another club that Catena frequented was the Englewood Country Club. Police described the Englewood Country Club as "a haven for organized crime figures, including the Catena brothers."[16] It was a who's who of Genovese members, including Jack Panels, Gy De Carlo, Richie Boiardo, his son Tony Boy, Tony Bananas Caponigro, Tommy Eboli, and Anthony "Tony Pro" Provenzano. When the FBI requested a list of members from the course, they were astounded at the sheer number of crime figures who were dues-paying members. Frank Costello was seen meeting there with Catena. Jerry and others held regular meetings at the Club in the "gold room," a room with a gold carpet that only the inner circle could access.

Law enforcement was interested in the club's finances, so along with the State Alcoholic Beverage Commission, they investigated the club. They found that the club was licensed under a fictitious name, never had a bank account in the company's name, and its name was not on any of the property records.

They also discovered that Englewood was the site of a regular card game that Jerry and, sometimes, his brother Gene attended. The men would gather in the club and play gin rummy, bridge, pinochle, and Hollywood gin. As expected, a significant amount of money was involved. The games could get quite competitive and expensive for the loser. Business was never discussed during the game. If something needed to be addressed, the wiseguys would use the men's locker room and have someone watch the door to ensure they were alone.

Jerry did well enough at golf to be treated like any other golfer when he was at the country clubs. Times were changing on that front. The exclusivity of the old-school clubs that once prevented Italians and Jews from joining were giving way to more welcoming, open clubs, where guys like Catena and Zwillman could join. Changes were happening in Jerry's other life as well. The underworld of the 1950s was going through a period of evolution. And some of the men stuck in the past were about to be left behind.

6

Changing of the Guard

The body of Willie Moretti lay splayed across the floor of Joe's Elbow Room in Cliffside Park, New Jersey, on the afternoon of October 5, 1951. Just a few minutes before, Moretti talked in Italian to lunch companions, unaware that his days were numbered. As the five men chatted amicably, a waitress walked into the back to grab the guests some menus. When she was out of sight, shots rang out. Moretti was hit in the right side of the face and right chest. The men ran out of the restaurant, and Moretti fell face up on the black-and-white checkered floor, blood quickly pooling under his head.

The main reason cited by mobsters for the Moretti hit was related to his testimony in the Kefauver Committee hearings. Moretti contracted syphilis when he was younger, and the disease was slowly robbing his mental faculties. He was becoming increasingly talkative, and there was a real fear he would start spilling details about not only his criminal operations, but others as well. In later years, the FBI would listen to wiretaps as mobsters discussed how Moretti was killed and that they would have preferred him to be taken out more privately. Nevertheless, Moretti's killing was seen as a mercy killing for a sick man. But there was, of course, a deep level of self-preservation behind the decision to take out one of the top capos in New Jersey.

In the aftermath of the Moretti killing, Costello appointed Vito Genovese to the underboss slot. Costello and Genovese had known each other for many years, having worked together during Prohibition and having come up in the ranks under Lucky Luciano.

Moretti's death also left his crew rudderless. Frank Costello said he wanted Jerry to take over Moretti's crew. Jerry obliged, becoming the capo of a large group of capable soldiers. He also became "boss" over his brother Gene. While that may have chafed some siblings, Gene was okay with his big brother taking over as his capo. Their relationship did not suffer. It brought them closer, as Jerry started to treat Gene more as a confidant than a soldier underneath him.

This was Jerry's time to show his leadership acumen. He had risen up quickly through the ranks of the crime family. In less than eight years, he went from a non-made associate to a capo, leapfrogging many older crew members. But such was the confidence and trust that Costello had in Catena, allowing him to take on a responsibility like that. Having it be Moretti's crew was an additional challenge due to the size and scope of the crew's operations. Moretti had one of the largest crews in the crime family. In addition to Gene Catena, the now-Catena crew had Jerry and Gene's longtime friend and golf buddy, Pete LaPlaca; Carmien Battaglia, a former member of the defunct Newark crime family who moved over to Luciano in the late 1930s; Angelo "Gyp" DeCarlo; Richie "The Boot" Boiardo (which may have chafed Boiardo a bit); the Catena's Newark associate Charlie "the Blade" Tourine; and over twenty other made guys, in addition to hundreds of associates.

In January 1953, Jerry Catena met with other high-ranking crime family members from New York and New Jersey at La Martinique, a restaurant owned and operated by Gyp DeCarlo. The restaurant, on Route 22 in Mountainside, was frequented by local politicians as well as gangsters, making it a favorite spot for law enforcement to set up surveillance. Advertised as having a "living room atmosphere" serving the "finest in Italian-American cuisine," La Martinique was a favorite dining spot for Catena. But that didn't stop DeCarlo, Catena, and others from using it as a favored meeting spot. Catena also frequently met with Longie Zwillman and Richie Boiardo at the restaurant.

A few days after the La Martinique meeting, on January 15, 1953 Gene Catena was caught up in an indictment for income tax evasion that had its origins in law enforcement's investigations into a floating craps game. A "floating craps game" was as it sounds, a craps game that moved from location to location to avoid surveillance by the police. Oftentimes, it worked, but other times, not so much.

He was indicted with two other members of Catena's crew, William Rega and Angelo "Gyp" DeCarlo. Eugene was accused of evading over $67,000 on income taxes from his involvement in the running of floating craps and dice games in South Plainfield, New Jersey. All three men were also accused of running floating craps games in Miami. The charges against all three were eventually dismissed in 1956.

The early years of Jerry's reign as capo were fairly uneventful from his perspective. His name appeared in the newspapers more for golf tournaments than anything criminal. The FBI was barely keeping tabs on the Mafia at this point. So Jerry stayed out of the way and kept growing his legitimate and illegal businesses.

He also moved his family into a two-story, 4,300 square foot home in South Orange with a private tennis court in the back. The corner lot, in a toney area of the town, was a considerable upgrade from the small apartments that Jerry grew up in. It was one block over from the South Mountain Reservation, a huge public park with trails and a zoo. Jerry had made it to the suburbs. With his large family, this house was perfect for them to grow up in.

While Jerry was happy with the way things were progressing, the same could not be said for Vito Genovese. Although Jerry was very fond of their boss, Frank Costello, Vito grew weary of Frank and itched at the chance to expand his influence over the family. He felt that Frank was becoming too much of a socialite, spending his time in swanky Manhattan restaurants and clubs, rather than tending to the needs of the crime family. Vito Genovese was ready to make his move.

The Majestic is a prime example of New York art deco architecture. Constructed in 1931, this New York City-designated landmark at 115 Central

Park West is right across West 72nd St. from the famous Dakota. Costello was not the first crime figure to reside in the upper-class accommodations. Louis "Lepke" Buchalter, an early crime figure in the city, lived at the Majestic in the 1930s.

Early in the evening of May 2, 1957, Costello was out at dinner with Philip Kennedy, a modeling agency head who was friendly with Costello. They had dinner and Kennedy pressed Costello to stay out for drinks. But Costello needed to go back home. He was expecting a call from his attorney about a recent case. Kennedy and Costello shared a cab back to the Majestic. As the cab pulled in front of the building, neither Costello nor Kennedy noticed a car parked nearby. Thomas "Tommy Ryan" Eboli was the driver. With him were Vincent "Chin" Gigante, a one-time boxer and enforcer for the crime family, and Anthony "Jack Panels" Santoli.

As Frank Costello entered the building, Gigante ran up and followed Costello into the foyer. Before Costello could open the door into the lobby, Gigante raised a .32, aiming for Costello's head, and pulled the trigger. As Frank turned his head, the bullet entered Frank's scalp just below the left ear, curved around the back of his neck and slammed into the top of the marble entrance to the main lobby. The bullet ricocheted to the floor, causing no other damage. Gigante turned and ran past the shaken doorman and out into the night. Kennedy, who was about to pull away in the cab after dropping Costello off, told the cab driver to stop and ran inside. Eboli, Gigante, and Jack Panels drove away in all the commotion.

"Somebody tried to get me. Get a doctor," Costello told Kennedy. Costello wrapped a handkerchief around his head. Kennedy hailed a cab, and they went to Roosevelt Hospital. The wound was superficial, not hitting anything vital. Costello was lucky to be alive—and he knew it.

The writing was on the wall. Vito Genovese had made his move. And missed. But he might not miss the next time. Costello was already facing legal issues related to income taxes. To make matters worse, when police questioned him in the hospital after the shooting, they found a piece of paper in his pocket which listed monies that Costello and other mobsters were taking out of the Flamingo casino in Las Vegas. The hits to Costello, no pun intended, kept coming. Frank had had enough. He backed down as boss of the Genovese family and told everyone he wanted out.

After Costello stepped aside, Vito Genovese became the crime family's boss. Genovese then named Jerry Catena as his underboss. The promotion of Jerry Catena was not unfounded. He rose through the ranks to become a capo after Moretti's death. There was another reason, maybe the most important: Jerry was a huge earner with extensive connections. Between his various business interests, control of the Jersey ports, and gambling operations, he was generating substantial income for the family, which meant Vito was receiving a portion. But according to Angelo DeCarlo, Genovese had one reason above all. "He (Vito) told me, he said, 'Ray, this guy's got the key to Las Vegas!'"[1]

When Vito Genovese ascends the throne of the crime family, a couple of other things happen. The crime family itself becomes colloquially known as the Genovese crime family. Its name continues today, although members often refer to the family as the West Side. As mentioned previously, the family was known as the Luciano, or Luciano–Costello, crime family. With Genovese at the helm, federal law enforcement bestowed the names of the families based on the boss situation around this period.

The other thing is that Catena's appointment to the underboss position also elevated the status of the Jewish mobsters affiliated with Catena, including Longie Zwillman. Although they were never able to become "made" members of the Mafia, the Jewish syndicate figures were eclipsed by the rising power of the Mafia after the Prohibition era. With one of their close associates rising in the ranks, their status rose as well.

Now, the Mafia exists like any other organization. Internal dynamics always cause friction. Catena's quick rise didn't sit well with some high-ranking family members. Mike Miranda, for one, felt that the underboss position should have gone to him. He told anyone within earshot that he believed Jerry had bolstered support for his position by offering pieces, or points, of his Las Vegas action to other family members. Miranda was bitter that he was not on that list. But like any other corporate promotion, there are bound to be those who feel slighted at not being chosen. The rank and file had to trust in the decision of the boss.

With his new role, Jerry Catena's crew was handed over to Richie Boiardo. By then, Boiardo lived on a sprawling thirty-acre estate in Livingston, New Jersey. The estate had iron gates in front, was adorned by sculptures and statues, and reportedly made from imported Italian stone. But the most notable feature was the reputed on-site incinerator, which was used to dispose of bodies. Angelo DeCarlo, talking to Anthony "Little Pussy" Russo, a Genovese mobster based in Long Branch, laid out a partial list of the victims.

> Do you know how many guys have been hit up there. Three guys for Tommy Brown (Thomas Lucchese) Neil (ph) Oreander (ph) up at the farm; he hit the guy for Oliver up at the farm. Who'd he hit? He hit Billy (William Caridnale a.k.a. Billy Jenks), there was Johnny, Billy, and Al and his daughter, they hit the daughter there, all of them. He killed a doctor up there.[2]

DeCarlo: I know a lot of guys got hit there. I know.

Russo: (whispering) I must have hit . . . myself . . . guys walking up there like that . . . they'd let themselves in . . . that door, the garage door, behind the door . . . they'd throw them back down there.

DeCarlo: Where?

Russo: Up in the greenhouse. All the way back. All the way up. They got a big hole there—they put 'em in there and burned them.

DeCarlo: What about the big furnace he's got back there?

Russo: That's what I'm trying to tell you! Before you go up there . . .

DeCarlo: The big iron grate.

Russo: He used to put them on there and burn them.

DeCarlo: He's a real nut! He's a sadist!

Russo: A nut! A nut![3]

However, with the Costello shooting fresh in everyone's mind, this was not the time to stir the pot. Genovese's power was absolute, and any dissent must remain at the level of gossip and sharing frustrations with sympathetic listeners. Although some in law enforcement and the media expected a violent struggle for control of the family, the reality was that there were other more pressing issues to address, particularly assessing the intentions of a rival family boss.

Vito set up a meeting with Albert Anastasia, whose family (later known as the Gambino family) was also undergoing some internal strife. Genovese wanted to break bread with Anastasia and clear the air. There were other reasons for this. Genovese feared that Anastasia, who was both close to Costello and had the reputation of being power hungry, might try some type of move against Genovese to enhance his stature in the underworld.

Genovese had some of the same suspicions about Catena. Jerry met with Costello frequently and even socialized with the wives together. It could have been that Genovese didn't think Catena had any ambitions to make a move. And he was likely correct. Catena's understanding of the internal power dynamics of the Mafia was such that he realized he would be better signing off on the move against Costello than try and take sides against Genovese, whose power was clearly ascending. Additionally, in addition to his investments in Las Vegas, Catena had a large enterprise in New Jersey that the New York crews did not interfere with. Why would Genovese throw away something good?

On the morning of October 25, 1957, Albert Anastasia walked into the Park Sheraton Hotel in Manhattan and went into the barbershop for a cut and shave. He settled into the chair as the barber placed a hot towel over his face. Anastasia did not see or hear the two men who walked in and approached him from behind. The shots started. Ten bullets criss-crossed the small barbershop. Two shots hit his left hand and wrist, another puncturing his right hip. Anastasia bolted out of the chair and fell forward, as another bullet hit him in the back. The final shot was to the back of the head.

The two gunmen had their faces covered and in the ensuing chaos of barber and customers screaming and running from the shop, the two assassins fled into the streets. The image of Anastasia, sprawled on the barbershop floor and covered in sheets, is one of the iconic mob hit photos.

While it became clear that Anastasia was killed due to internal family disputes, which allowed the enterprising Carlo Gambino to take the helm of the crime family after Albert was killed, the death of Anastasia was good news for Genovese. One of Frank's staunchest allies was out of the picture, so Genovese could rest a little easier knowing that his spot at the top of the family was now secure. But that security and promise of no reprisals needed to be hashed out with a larger group of mob leaders. They did not need the Anastasia hit to snowball into an all-out mob war on the streets of New York City. The situation could also impact national operations.

Immediately after the Anastasia killing, there was a meeting in New Jersey of the top leaders of the New York families to discuss the killing. It was held at Richie Boiardo's estate in Livingston. According to contemporary informants, the meeting was more of a trial where members of the faction behind the Anastasia killing pled their case in front of the mob bosses. Before the meeting, various New York mobsters met at a restaurant owned by Jerry Catena, where a crew of New Jersey-based mobsters greeted them. These individuals then drove the men to Boiardo's house, two at a time. The meeting lasted through the night until 5 a.m. the following day. The Gambino captain behind the Anastasia hit, Joseph Riccobono, pleaded his case and owned up to the bosses, getting a free pass for himself and the hitmen who pulled the trigger.

Now that the New York bosses were aligned on the Anastasia killing, they decided to call a national meeting of the bosses. It would ultimately be one of the biggest mistakes that the Mafia made.

The small hamlet of Apalachin seemed like a perfect spot to hold the largest gathering of Mafia bosses in history. The meeting was to be held at the country estate of Joseph Barbara, a member of the Pittston-based crime family led by

Russell Bufalino. Barbara lived on a fifty-eight-acre estate in an eleven-room stone house with a caretaker's cottage and a two-story horse barn.

There have been some discussions over the years about whether Barbara was a member of the Buffalo Mafia or the Bufalino crime family. Based on contemporary evidence and some informant statements, it's likely that Barbara was not only a member of the Bufalino family but may have been acting boss at one time, prior to Russell Bufalino's ascension. Bufalino used to work for Barbara, and Barbara was close to many Bufalino family members.

Barbara was known locally as a successful businessman with deep ties to the community. Many in law enforcement, however, viewed Barbara with skepticism. They knew of his Prohibition past and his association with mobsters across upstate New York and Northeast Pennsylvania.

On Wednesday, November 13, 1957, crime figures from around the country began arriving in Apalachin. Barbara and his son contacted several hotels in the area to reserve rooms. During the initial run of out-of-state visitors checking into motels, a clerk at the Parkway Motel called about a bad check unrelated to the mob gathering. Two New York state troopers, Edgar D. Crosswell and Vincent Vasisko, arrived. While investigating the bad check, they observed Joe Barbara reserving rooms for out-of-town guests. The troopers listened from an adjoining room and became suspicious that Barbara's son was reserving rooms for an unknown number of "beverage" people, as he called them, alluding to his father's bottling company located on the town. The troopers drove over the bottling plant and, seeing nothing out of the ordinary, drove up to Barbara's estate and jotted down some license plate numbers.

The next day, Thursday, November 14th, Sergeant Croswell and another trooper, along with two members of the Alcohol, Tobacco, and Firearms (ATF) agency, drove into the parking lot of Barbara's estate. They started jotting down even more license plate numbers. As they started to drive away, they noticed some men running back into the house. According to a maid who was working the party, Barbara's wife told them it was the State Police. Seeing the troopers come up the drive, the mobsters panicked and started to leave all at once. Vasisko later recalled, "It was a misty day. We were in plainclothes, but one of the guys looked up at the road and hollered, 'It's the staties, it's the staties,' and they all started running into the fields and the woods. We had no reason to arrest anybody, they weren't doing anything wrong."[4]

Crowell and other troopers drove back down the road leading to the estate and set up a de-facto roadblock. One of the first cars that was stopped was a 1957 Chrysler Imperial Sedan driven by Russell Bufalino, the mob boss of the Northeast Pennsylvania crime family. Four other men rode along with him in his eighteen-foot-long Imperial Sedan—Joseph Ida, Camden-based mob figure Dominick Oliveto, Vito Genovese, and Jerry Catena. Bufalino later testified that he didn't know the three men and offered to drive them from Barbara's house as a favor. He told investigators that they simply asked him for a ride. Bufalino, like many of the others arrested, basically reiterated that they were at the meeting to visit Barbara and that none of this was planned.

Over the course of the next few hours, troopers not only stopped more cars coming down from Barbara's estate, but also found some men wandering in the woods, and a few that hitchhiked and were picked up by Apalachin locals and driven back to town. In all, fifty-eight men[5] were detained, many brought to the state police barracks in the nearby town of Vestal. Some of the men were questioned, whereas others were just asked for identification. Jerry Catena kept quiet about why he was visiting Barbara and why he was in the car with Genovese and Bufalino.

Although follow-up subpoenas and obstruction of justice charges resulted in little more than nuisances for the men, the revelation that Mafia figures from around the country were meeting to discuss underworld business at a remote home in upstate New York cemented the concept that there was a nationwide organized crime syndicate in operation.

The fallout from Apalachin reverberated across the underworld. The event's publicity catapulted the Mafia to the front page of newspapers nationwide. There was no love lost for the organizers. "That Apalachin and that lousy Steve Maggadino. He wanted to be a big shot up there and show everybody that he could bring everybody up there from all over the county. That (expletive) ruined the whole world. Mooney (Sam Giancana) had the right idea. To hell with those guys."[6]

The FBI wanted to interview Jerry Catena, so they called him in May 1958 to set up a time to talk. Catena, after talking with his lawyer, declined. With the increasing scrutiny post-Apalachin, it was a wise move on Catena's part. However, the FBI was not so easily dissuaded and managed to snare an interview at the office of Catena's vending company in Newark. Catena was cagey, and the information he shared was carefully parsed out. He said little about Apalachin and even less about other topics. The agents asked about some of his associates, including Doc Stacher. Jerry carefully chose his words, stating that "he heard" Stacher was living in California and it had been "a long time" since they spoke.

On the night of February 25, 1959 Longie Zwillman went to dinner with his wife, and Puddy Hinkes and his wife. Puddy later recalled that Zwillman was in an unsociable mood. Longie left the restaurant early, telling his wife he had somewhere to go. He dropped his wife off at home, then drove to Eugene Catena's house. Jerry was in Florida at the time. After talking with Eugene for a few hours, Longie went home. His wife later told police that she woke up around 2 a.m. to find Longie pacing around the house, saying he had insomnia and could not fall asleep. She went back to bed. The next morning, thinking that her husband had gone to work, Mrs. Zwillman went about her morning routine. After a couple hours, she went to their basement.

There she found Longie, dressed in his pajamas, hanging from the ceiling. He had looped a rope through exposed beams and was already long dead by the time she found him. He was dropped down to his knees. She immediately called the family physician, who arrived at the house just after 10 a.m. He came and pronounced Longie dead. The police and medical examiner were called. The medical examiner ruled Zwillman's death a suicide.

Zwillman's funeral took place at the Philip Aptner Funeral Home in Newark the day after his death. The funeral drew a modest crowd of family, friends, curiosity seekers, and FBI agents looking for names and faces. It was a far cry from the lavish gangland funerals of other well-known racketeers, but enough of his contemporaries showed up to make it known how well liked he was in the neighborhood and the business worlds, legit and not. Some of his closest friends couldn't attend. Jerry Catena was in Florida and couldn't make it back up in time. Friends reported him despondent for days after Zwillman's death. Meyer Lansky and others were out of town, but sent regards. A funeral procession of twenty-seven cars took his body to the B'nai Abraham Memorial Park off Route 22 in Union, just next to the Rahway River.

The pressing question was if Longie really did commit suicide, as the medical examiner determined, or if he was murdered. There were erroneous reports of signs of a struggle, pointing to marks on Longie's wrist. But the marks were determined to be from the way Longie tied himself up. There was no sign of any forced entry or evidence that someone else was there that night. Although very unusual, suicides by mobsters do occur. Zwillman was in poor health and on a medicine that allegedly caused depression. His stepson told reporters that Longie had been depressed and that recent IRS trouble and associated court cases had taken their toll.

In the aftermath, Jerry Catena did make it a point to affirm to Zwillman's stepson that he had nothing to do with Abner's death. Zwillman had gone to see Gene earlier that night he died. There was some speculation that perhaps Zwillman told Gene what he was planning.

The death of Longie Zwillman was the end of the old Third Ward Gang. Many of Longie's former gang members had grown out of the street rackets and were running casinos or sophisticated gambling operations. But while Longie was alive, those rackets were ostensibly under him. Now, with Longie dead, the Genovese family moved in quickly to take over what was left. Newark gambling figures like Irving Berlin and Abe Green were now under Jerry Catena. Jerry's close relationship with Jewish crime figures allowed him to move into a leadership role over them, backed by the full force of the Genovese family. And Jerry's natural propensity toward gambling operations made it an easy transition from a business perspective.

The one illegal enterprise that Jerry Catena was never involved with was narcotics. However, that was not true of others in the Mafia, nor even in the Genovese family. One of the great myths is that the mob was never involved in narcotics. The mob was heavily involved in the narcotics racket from the earliest emergence of organized crime. Mob families ranging from New York City to Kansas City to Tampa were engaged in large-scale trafficking and dealing of narcotics, primarily heroin. It became too lucrative a business line to ignore. In fact, one of the first federal law enforcement agencies to start openly discussing the concept of a national organized crime syndicate was the Federal Bureau of Narcotics (FBN). The FBN's efforts to gather intelligence on the Mafia and leading narcotics traffickers was far ahead of anything that the FBI had been involved with, to that point.

On July 5, 1958, FBN agents arrived at Vito Genovese's modest bungalow-style Atlantic Highlands home and arrested the 61-year-old mob boss. Genovese went with the agents without any fuss and was taken into Manhattan for his arraignment. He was not the only one arrested that day. In all, thirty-nine crime figures were part of the massive indictment. Among the others detained were Genovese's driver Vincent "Chin" Gigante, the would-be assassin of Frank Costello, who had been making strides in the underworld since his aborted attempt to take out the Prime Minister of the underworld. There were some other names of note in the indictment, including Carmine Galante, a member of the Bonanno crime family known for his deep ties in the narcotics world, and Bog John Ormento, a capo in the family led by Thomas Lucchese. Nowhere in the indictment was Jerry Catena's name mentioned.

All the men, and one woman, were alleged to be part of a criminal conspiracy to import heroin into the United States over three years from Europe, Mexico, and Cuba. To the prosecutors, Genovese was the centerpiece, although the evidence that he was directly involved in narcotics trafficking was thin. Still, that did not stop the U.S. Attorney from proclaiming that "Genovese was the hub around which this entire conspiracy revolved."[7]

The trial of the fifteen men began in January 1959, and Genovese was, unfortunately, going to trial during a particularly high visibility time for organized crime. With the Apalachin incident, the sensational shooting of Albert Anastasia, and the congressional hearings looking at the mob's influence in labor, all eyes were on the Genovese trial. Although Vito was not directly involved in the street dealings, the prosecution had a witness, a Puerto Rican drug courier Nelson Silva Cantellops. Nelson told the jury how Genovese attended a high-level meeting of the drug ring. It tied Genovese directly to the criminal acts, but some felt Cantellops played up the attendance of Genovese at this alleged meeting of the drug ring to curry favor with the prosecutors in exchange for a favorable deal. But it was hard to dislodge his testimony from the jury's minds.

While Genovese's attorney did not call any witnesses, some of the other defense lawyers did call witnesses to rebut accusations against their clients and their role in the organized drug conspiracy. The trial lasted for thirteen weeks and went to the jury on April 2, 1959. Despite the defense team's efforts, the evidence against the group was overwhelming. After just one day of deliberations, the jury came back and found all but one defendant guilty. Vito Genovese was going to prison. And Jerry Catena was about to be thrust into the top spot, just two years after being appointed underboss.

7

The Acting Boss

Vito Genovese arrived at the United States Courthouse on Foley Square in Lower Manhattan on April 17, 1959; he smiled at the news reporters waiting outside. He was there with fourteen other defendants, each with lawyers pleading their case before the judge about how little time they should do. When Vito's time came, the judge handed him fifteen years in prison and a $20,000 fine. When asked if he had anything to say, Genovese replied, "All I can say your honor, is that I am innocent."[1]

Upon hearing the sentence, Vito's attorneys went to the appeals court in the same courthouse complex. They convinced the appeals court to allow Genovese to remain free on his initial bail from his arrest. Genovese was able to go home. His attorneys worked to have his conviction overturned but were unsuccessful. In February 1960, Vito Genovese surrendered to authorities and was sent to his new home, a federal prison in Atlanta.

Who was running the Genovese family after Vito Genovese went to prison? Jerry Catena was Genovese's underboss. Standard lines of succession in organized crime dictate that the underboss would move into the top position upon the death or stepping aside of the boss. Often, if a boss is imprisoned, the underboss assumes the leadership role on an interim basis, serving as the acting boss. However, by the 1960s, the Genovese family had begun to a tradition of obfuscation regarding the true power behind the family. As would become common in the years that followed, the family did not always adhere to the logical lines of succession.

Some reports had Tony "Tony Bender" Strollo as one of the leaders behind the scenes. Strollo's legitimate enterprises included a vast real estate portfolio and ownership of several nightclubs and bars in Greenwich Village. Strollo was close to Genovese, even named as one of the possible conspirators who set up Frank Costello for the unsuccessful hit in 1957. But other rumors abounded that Strollo was trying to take out Costello and Genovese. There were rumors that Strollo had met with Carlo Gambino, head of his namesake family, and the main rival in power to the Genovese, to set up Vito for his narcotics bust.

Strollo wasn't able to capitalize on his strategic moves. In the underworld alliances can quickly shift, and in Strollo's case, with the newspapers naming him as one of the top powers in the family, Genovese sent word from prison, through Jerry Catena, that Strollo needed to be eliminated.

On the evening of April 8, 1962, Strollo told his wife he was going out for a few minutes. According to his wife, Strollo left their Fort Lee home with another man who had picked him up in a 1961 Cadillac. Strollo was never heard from again. The police continued the search for several months, but it became clear that Strollo would not be found. A few years later the FBI learned at least one version of Strollo's fate, when Harold "Kayo" Konigsberg, a longtime underworld figure in Newark and associate of the Genovese family, told agents the story.

Kayo said that the order to kill Strollo came from Tommy Eboli and Jerry Catena. It was ostensibly because Strollo was dealing drugs, but it may have had more to do with internal crime family politics. Kayo said that the night of the murder, Giuseppe "Pep" Sabato, a capo in the family, took Strollo to the parking lot of a restaurant in Fort Lee, where Eboli and Dom "The Sailor" DeQuarto, another Genovese capo, were waiting in a van. When Strollo arrived, Eboli and DeQuarto killed him. According to Kayo, Strollo's body was likely buried at a farm in upstate New York, although police never found the body, despite Kayo taking them there.

Another version had Richie the Boot involved in the disappearance of Strollo. During a meeting at the Deauville Hotel in Ft. Lauderdale between Boiardo and Chicago Outfit boss Sam Giancana, Boiardo told Sam that Anthony "Little Pussy" Russo killed Tony Bender and intimated that he, Boiardo, was the one who ordered the killing.

Some in the press had Tommy Eboli taking the acting boss position, with Jerry Catena maintaining his role as the underboss. An informer told the FBI that the Genovese family was being led by a gang of four—Eboli, Catena, Philip Lombardo, and Mike Miranda. Another informant named Jerry Catena and Thomas Eboli as the two acting bosses of the Genovese family after the imprisonment of Vito Genovese. Xavier Eboli, Tommy Eboli's son, said that he was told by his uncle Pasquale Eboli that Pasquale was there when Vito Genovese made Lombardo the boss and that his father was the front boss.

But the FBI believed otherwise. An October 1964 memo from the New York City Field Office stated "It is noted heretofore, Thomas Eboli has been described as the 'acting boss' of the Genovese 'family' and Gerardo Catena as the family 'underboss'. From previous information furnished by the captioned informant as well as the information set forth below, there can be no doubt that Gerardo Catena is the 'acting boss' of the 'family' in the absence of Vito Genovese, and Eboli is the number one man under Catena, or 'acting underboss.'"[2]

Pittsburgh informant Abraham Zeid told his FBI handler that "Catena, while Vito Genovese is in prison, is the real boss of the entire United States insofar as gambling and rackets are concerned."[3]

In 1966, the Los Angeles field office of the FBI was working with a federal grand jury to investigate illegal gambling. They noted that two of the subjects of the investigation, Vincent "Jimmy Blue Eyes" Alo and Anthony "Fat Tony" Salerno, belonged to the La Cosa Nostra "family" headed by Jerry Catena of Newark, NJ. FBI agent John Connors, one of the original FBI agents in the Newark Field Office investigating organized crime, also knew Catena was the real acting boss. "The media had Eboli as co-leader. That was inaccurate.

The FBI knew that Catena was running the entire family."[4] He even went as far as to petition the FBI to change their moniker for the Genovese family to the Catena family. That request was unsuccessful.

Even Tommy Eboli recognized that Catena alone was serving as acting boss. Angelo DeCarlo recalled a conversation with Eboli about his difficulties with Gene Catena. "Tommy was hot one night. He told me 'Who the hell is the boss here? Jerry or his brother?'"[5]

Adding to the evidence that Catena was the acting boss is a 1961 FBI report where agent John Connors notes "subject identified as 'Avugad', that is, a member of 'the Commission.'"[6] The Commission was the leadership of the national Mafia syndicate, serving as arbiters of disputes, makers of key decisions, and representatives of bosses of the smaller Mafia families. The Commission was traditionally comprised of the heads of the New York City Five Families, Philadelphia, Buffalo, Chicago, and Detroit, although the membership roster ebbed and flowed over the years.

Another 1961 report from the FBI cites a highly confidential source who indicated that "Gerardo Catena, Newark Top Hoodlum, has been placed on the 'commission' in the recent past."[7] Connors also stated that Catena was the leader of the Commission for a time, noting that the FBI believed that leadership of the Commission was rotated so that any one mobster would not get too much power.

A 1963 FBI report named the current members of the Mafia Commission. "The syndicate as a whole was governed by 'the commission,' made up of the leaders of the larger families. . . . It was believed they vary from 9 to 12 people. In 1963, they were listed as: Vito Genovese, New York (represented by his underboss Gerardo Catena, since Genovese was in federal prison at the time)."[8]

Other sources corroborated Catena's role on the Commission. An FBI wiretap from October 1964 caught New Jersey boss Sam DeCavalcante complaining about the way Catena represented the Genovese family on the Commission, saying that although Jerry was sincere, he was out of his league with the Commission, going so far as to say Catena wets his pants when the Commission meets. DeCavalcante's potshot at Catena was made public in 1969 after the FBI wiretaps were released. Although embarrassing for both men, they obviously smoothed things over as Catena and DeCavalcante were seen together often in Florida in the 1970s and 1980s.

Additional evidence comes from Tommy Eboli, who was caught on wiretap complaining that Catena was not getting consensus from other Commission members.

> I told this guy here (Catena) going back three years ago, Jerry we never went to a Commission meeting that I know of in the past 20 years unless they consulted Chicago and New York and when I say New York I mean us! When they (we) walked in together we were of one mind. They know what they were gonna do. This guy (Catena) not one time did he even attempt to go and see Mooney (Giancana). To talk about when there is a Commission meeting, (you, Catena) should at least let me go over there and say, after you and I get together you can come . . . but he (Catena) is no politician.[9]

Another interesting note is that Catena was now the crime family's third boss of non-Sicilian heritage. The family's founder, Charlie Luciano, was Sicilian, but his successor, Frank Costello, was Calabrian. Many of Luciano's capos, including Vito Genovese and Jerry Catena, were Neapolitan. The Genovese family was always more heavily Neapolitan than the other four New York crime families, who were heavily Sicilian. That's not to say that the Genovese family didn't have members from Sicily. There were several prominent members of the family of Sicilian descent. Jerry Catena's crew, which he inherited from Willie Moretti (born in the Puglia region of Italy), was heavily Sicilian. But of the five families of New York, they stood alone with a strong Neapolitan lineage dating back to the early 1900s when the Sicilian Mafia and the Neapolitan Camorra were separate groups making their way in the New York underworld. By comparison, the DeCavalcante family of Elizabeth, New Jersey, which was close to the Genovese family, was almost exclusively of Sicilian heritage, more specifically, from Ribera in the Agrigento province of Sicily.

Of course, Jerry Catena was born in America, as were many of the next generation of mobsters coming up through the ranks, which meant that the old country origins mattered less. What mattered more was the ability to work together to make money, and Jerry was all about maximizing his opportunities.

After ascending to the acting boss position, Catena was often seen in the company of other notable crime figures. In November 1960, Jerry took a little vacation to Hot Springs, Arkansas. Hot Springs had always been a favorite getaway for organized crime figures, dating back to the Prohibition era.

Catena booked a room at the historic Arlington Hotel, reportedly a favorite spot for Al Capone when he visited the city, as well as Lucky Luciano. Frank Costello, Catena's good friend and former boss, was a frequent guest in the City. While Catena was there he was seen meeting with Owen "The Killer" Madden, a former New York gangster who moved to Hot Springs twenty-five years prior having told NY parole authorities that he would never set foot in the City again. Catena was seen talking with Madden and two unidentified men in front of the notorious Southern Club, a favorite hangout for visiting wiseguys.[10] Madden was still active in the gambling rackets in Hot Springs at that point.

Catena's new position made him more exposed to law enforcement and scheming underworld figures. In early 1963, the FBI learned that a Pittsburgh mob associate was planning on kidnapping Jerry Catena and Maxie Eder, a Miami Beach-based Jewish mobster who was close to both Meyer Lansky and the Genovese family. The plan was to kidnap both men and hold them for ransom, potentially on a boat off the coast of South Florida.

As he had been for many years, Jerry often ventured south to Florida from weeks to months at a time. Although he spent much time in Miami Beach, he eventually settled on Boca Raton as his favored snowbird destination. As usual, Catena spent much time on the golf courses around Palm Beach

County. Gene Catena often let other mobsters, like Meyer Lansky, know which golf course they could find Jerry playing on any particular day.

The orchestrator of the kidnapping plot was Joseph Merola, an interesting character, described by the Miami FBI as a "notorious smuggler, gunrunner, and general no-goodnik."[11] Merola's plan was interesting on two fronts. First, Merola was already talking with the FBI and CIA about anti-Castro activities in South Florida. Merola cut his teeth running guns to Fidel Castro during Fidel's guerrilla war against Fulgencia Batista. Merola was also working with members and associates of the Pittsburgh Mafia, specifically the Mannarino brothers. After Castro took over, Merola started trying to divulge intel about Castro and Che Guevara to the government to help himself out with some legal troubles.

The second was that Merola told his kidnapping plan to a close friend, Abe Zeid, who was also a confidential informant for the FBI. Zeid promptly reported the threat not only to the FBI but also sent out word through the underworld to Eder and Catena. Zeid told the FBI that "for his own personal welfare and safety he intends to contact both Catena and Raymon (Max Eder) in the very near future and advise each of them of Merola's plans and intentions with respect to these alleged kidnappings and shakedowns."[12]

The FBI also indicated, as is their policy, that they would also let Catena and Eder know what they heard from Zeid. According to the FBI, Catena left Miami soon after hearing about the kidnapping plot and didn't return for some time.[13] It was the only time that a specific threat against Catena was uncovered. But his name was not always spoken with reverence, as the FBI discovered from listening to wiretaps that they placed in mob hangouts around New Jersey.

At least early on, Catena's performance as the acting boss was not universally championed. He had a lot of loyal supporters both within the Genovese family and among other mob bosses and underworld figures. Some in the Genovese family, however, felt that Catena was not as hands-on as he should be, leaving many of the organization's members to wonder, aloud, what he was doing with his time. Angelo DeCarlo told Frankie Casino and Alred Toriello in 1964, "Vito's been away four years and I bet I ain't seen this guy five times. What kind of a boss is that?"[14]

DeCarlo also accused Gene Catena of using his brother's position to his advantage, causing consternation among the rank and file of the family, which is interesting considering how DeCarlo ascended to his rank. One of Jerry's early actions as acting boss was to split his old crew, then led by Richie Boiardo, into three smaller crews: one led by The Boot, one led by Angelo DeCarlo, and one led by Jerry's brother Gene.

Tommy Eboli's particularly vocal issues with Catena were all over FBI wiretaps. They reflected a growing discontent with how Catena ran the Genovese family in Genovese's absence. A major sore point between Eboli and Catena was over a nightclub made even more famous by Barry Manilow in 1978, the legendary Copacabana. The iconic nightclub opened in 1940 on the Upper East Side,[15] and was one of Frank Costello's most lucrative legitimate business ventures. In addition to being a massive magnet for celebrities, it was also frequented by mobsters. Jerry Catena was spotted there numerous times in the 1950s.

The club contracted with a company to haul waste from the club, valued at $2,000 a month. There was a dispute between the Gambino and Genovese families over the handling of the waste hauling. Carlo Gambino met with Tommy Eboli to try to work out an agreement, but Eboli, noted as being a hothead at times, apparently did something to annoy Gambino. Carlo referred to it as not showing him the proper respect. With that, Gambino went and complained to Catena about Eboli.

According to Eboli, Catena seemed to side with Gambino, which enraged Eboli. He was caught on a wiretap telling the story to his brother, Pasquale, and Vito Genovese's brother, Michael. And Eboli was not the only mobster being caught on the wire.

Angelo DeCarlo continued to hold court in his restaurant, La Martinique, but his real court was in a barn out back where he ran his operations and frequently met with other New Jersey mobsters. The barn was also a de-facto man cave where mobsters and associates would simply stop by to hang out. Like most guys hanging out with a few beers, they started to shoot the shit, and unbeknownst to them, the FBI had installed an illegal bug to listen to DeCarlo's conversations.

From 1961 to 1965, the FBI recorded hundreds of conversations ranging from political corruption to insights into major underworld events to banal conversations that provided little actionable information. These conversations also revealed that DeCarlo was a serial gossip who never let a chance to talk badly about someone pass. He chronically complained about the family's leadership, how much money he was making, and everything that annoyed him. Most of his associates knew this was how Gyp was, and little of his whining resulted in reprimand or reprisal. Gyp loved to complain. And because of his chronic kvetching, the FBI gained valuable insight into the operations of the Genovese family at that time.

During a discussion between Anthony Russo and Gyp DeCarlo about the possibility that Vito Genovese might get out of prison early, due to some undisclosed plea agreement the government was setting up, DeCarlo wondered how it would affect the men already out on the street. DeCarlo mentioned how Mike Miranda felt about Vito, saying, "Mike—there's some reason why he don't like Vito. I think because he made Jerry the boss." Russo replied that Mike indeed wanted to be the boss after Vito went away. DeCarlo answered, "That's right. He hurt Mike's feelings."[16]

In this same conversation about Genovese's potential early release, DeCarlo quipped about feelings toward Vito Genovese, "Don't think Jerry Catena likes him!"[17] Russo and DeCarlo then talked about Vito's order to DeCarlo that if anyone makes a move against Genovese while he was in prison, DeCarlo would have a hit list of guys to take out, specifically telling Gyp to hit the

Catena brothers "right in the head" if they tried anything. The hit list also included Richie the Boot and his son, Tony Boy. "They're the most treacherous fuckers in the world," Russo told DeCarlo.[18]

One complaint that threaded through DeCarlo, Eboli, and Anthony Russo was that they felt Jerry was aloof and not paying attention to mob business. They weren't used to such a hands-off boss.

Others felt that Catena was too consumed with money, rather than tending to the crime family's needs. "Meanwhile you grind your teeth a little bit, you really press a little bit for something (and all he thinks about) and he comes up with money! (Eboli is astonished at Catena's attitude)."[19]

DeCarlo also let slip that Jerry had not been attending some of the recent Commission meetings, instead preferring to tend to his various business ventures. To DeCarlo, that was a slap in the face to the role that Catena had inherited. DeCarlo accused Catena of being out of touch and not bothering to talk to some of his old friends who were soldiers in the crime family, instead focusing his attention only on his capos and other family bosses. Although this came off as sour grapes, it spoke to the potential for conflict if things were left to simmer.

Another informant laid out what he saw as a potential rift in the family stemming from questions about succession from a conversation he heard between Anthony Russo, DeCarlo. "There was speculation between DeCarlo and Russo concerning a power struggle in the Genovese family between Gerardo Catena, the 'underboss' of the family and his brother Gene Catena who were aligning themselves with Ruggerio Boiardo and Michael Miranda on one side and DeCarlo, Russo, and Eboli on the other side."[20]

In another conversation picked up by FBI bugs, Gyp DeCarlo adds further that Mike Miranda and Catena were appearing to form an alliance in the event that Vito Genovese did not make it out of prison. "Mike figures winning

Jerry over and him, and the Boot. If Vito don't come out, they'll be the bosses. They'll want everything. Forget Tommy Ryan—forget everybody."[21]

An interesting twist in this DeCarlo/Russo conversation was the belief that Jerry Catena and Richie Boiardo still had lingering tensions dating back to the Prohibition era. "Jerry will never be able to trust them. He knows the old man (Boiardo) wanted to kill him years ago." Russo agreed saying the Boiardo had told Russo, "Take Jerry—get rid of all the headaches,"[22] referring to killing Jerry Catena. To hear The Boot say this about Catena is interesting in the context of the close relationship Jerry forged with Tony Boy Boiardo. From the best man at his wedding to a frequent golf partner, Catena kept a close watch on Tony Boy. DeCarlo once asked him why. "I asked Jerry that once, how come you take this kid with ya all over and he said 'I'm doing it for a reason. This old man is afraid of dyin' for what might happen to his kid.'"[23] That comment said a lot about how Catena viewed his obligation not only to the Mafia, but to those close to him. Although he and The Boot had differences that went back decades, Jerry would never let that get in the way of his friendship with Tony Boy. Also, he respected The Boot enough to ensure that if The Boot passed, Tony Boy would be able to thrive in the crime family.

Russo was caught on another wiretap talking about Catena, this time in Miami. Feds were listening to a conversation between Russo and Stefano Randazzo, a one-time Cleveland mobster who transferred to the Tampa family, led at that time by Santo Trafficante Jr. The feds installed a bug inside Ciro's Restaurant, a highly rated dining establishment in North Miami, frequented by mobsters and a favorite haunt of Trafficante.[24] An unknown male at the table with Randazzo and Russo said that he heard Jerry Catena was a jackass. Russo simply replied "yeah."[25]

But perhaps the most heated criticism of Catena's leadership came from Tommy Eboli. He was unhappy with how he felt that the Commission, specifically Carlo Gambino and Tommy Lucchese, were throwing their weight around, especially regarding the Joe Bonanno situation, which was a significant issue with the Commission.

The Bonanno situation is beyond the focus of this book, but it was important to the history of the Mafia in the 1960s. In a nutshell, it was a power struggle between Joe Bonanno and the Commission. Joseph Bonanno, boss of his namesake family, had reportedly plotted to assassinate some of the heads of the Commission, including Carlo Gambino and Thomas Lucchese. He enlisted the help of family boss Joseph Magliocco. Things went south after the Commission was alerted. Bonanno fled to Montreal, leaving Magliocco to take the heat for the failed coup. He was demoted as family boss (Joe Colombo took over for him). The Commission now had Joe Bonanno in their sights. Bonanno returned from Montreal in October 1964, but was kidnapped on October 21, 1964, right before he was scheduled to appear before a federal grand jury.

Bonanno later told reporters that he was kidnapped and taken up to his cousin's in Buffalo. Maggadino was unhappy and, according to Bonanno, threatened to kill him. He later released Bonanno after six weeks. Fearing another hit, Bonanno went into hiding until 1966. But his family was disintegrating in his absence. The Commission met several times to discuss the whole situation, including Jerry Catena. Jerry agreed with Gambino and Lucchese that Bonanno should be stripped of his title and excommunicated from the Mafia.

Eboli felt Bonanno needed to be given the benefit of the doubt and suggested a meeting of the Genovese hierarchy, including some capos, to discuss the matter and decide where the Genovese family should stand. But Catena had gone along with Gambino and Lucchese, effectively shutting out Joe Bonanno. Eboli was not pleased, especially as Catena refused to discuss the machinations of the Commission decision with his family. "They[26] know that this guy (Catena) is a boob! I told him one day Jerry let's get one thing straight. Anything you and I do, Mike Miranda must know. He's got to know.

He's consigliere and he's gonna be consigliere. And he's got to know what's happening in the administration. We can't keep this guy in the dark."[27]

This unhappiness with Catena seeming to bow to Gambino pressure also extended to the fact that Catena had not sought the opinion of Sam Giancana, despite a close relationship between the Chicago Outfit and the Genovese family. "I told this guy here (Catena) going back three years ago, Jerry we never went to a Commission meeting that I know of in the past 20 years unless they consulted Chicago and New York and when I say New York I mean us! This guy (Catena) not one time did he even attempt to go see Mooney (Giancana)."[28]

Eboli may have been venting but he also seemed to think that Catena might not even want the job as boss. And that is a theme that repeats itself in the future—Catena's seeming disinterest in the day-to-day job of a boss, as opposed to his intense interest in his various business ventures. "I said to Benny Lombardo, Benny I tell you and I tell this to Mike (Miranda) too. Then if we told Jerry (Catena), hey Jerry, you find a way to retire over here, this guy I think he would kiss us! He'll be more than happy."[29] Another FBI report from a year later seems to indicate that Catena was already openly talking about stepping aside. Or, at least that's what Eboli was openly discussing. Eboli and Michael Genovese had "discussed possible change in leadership of Genovese family resulting from stated desires of Gerardo Catena to retire from Organization."[30]

Despite the few who seemed continually unhappy with Catena, he had the support of most of his capos and soldiers. Other bosses respected Jerry. He was close with Carlo Gambino and Thomas Lucchese. Catena enjoyed a close relationship with Angelo Bruno, the boss of the Philadelphia Mafia. When he was in Florida, Catena regularly met with Meyer Lansky. He was seen with Santo Trafficante Jr. and members of the Chicago Outfit.

In the greater context, the issues that a few of his underlings had with Catena were not personal. But they also weren't really about business; they had to do with how those around him perceived a mob boss should act. So, how does Jerry's leadership style fit into the generally accepted mold of what a mob boss should be like? It was not similar. Jerry did not carry himself with any arrogance or ego. Jerry ran things more like a CEO who delegated and allowed those around him to manage their own affairs than a straight "do as I say" mob boss. He did not lead like a stereotypical Mafia boss. He didn't lead the way you think a Mafia boss should lead. He didn't instill fear as a rule, only when necessary. Rather, he led through negotiation, allegiances, alliances, and business.

The other aspect regarding Jerry's leadership is that he came up through the underworld, under the tutelage of Longie Zwillman and his guys. These guys informed, formed, and molded the person that Jerry became in the context of not only his activities and approach to the underworld but also his approach to business and leadership.

And, despite the occasional complaints from his underlings, and apart from Genovese's edict to DeCarlo about Catena, there was no power play to remove him. More people spoke of letting Catena retire than taking him out. Indeed, while Vito was still the boss from prison, and had the final say, there could have easily been a coup to take Jerry out of the picture. But there wasn't. His men genuinely seemed to like him.

But the biggest reason people complained behind his back but never made any kind of move was simple: Jerry knew how to make a lot of money. He made a lot of money for Vito. More importantly, his leadership allowed his men to make money. One example was that it was reported that Jerry did not take any envelopes from his guys. This means that Jerry did not demand tribute from his capos and soldiers like other bosses did. Jerry had his own personal rackets and businesses, which he and maybe a few others were involved with. That was his source of income. He did not need to take anything from those below him. He created opportunities that opened up investment and earning avenues for those who worked under him.

Like most businessmen, meetings were a necessary evil. Jerry would have preferred to conduct all his business meetings on the golf course, but that was not always practical. There were times when he would have to schlep out to a social club or an underground casino to meet with other bosses or underworld figures. But what Jerry did not realize, what few mobsters realized, is that more and more eyes were watching them, developing intelligence on their activities, and starting to become more of a nuisance than they had in the past. It wasn't just local cops this time. It was the feds.

8

Eyes on the Wiseguys

They worked pretty well together for as much griping as Eboli did about Catena. Although Catena was the acting boss, he mainly concentrated on the family's operations in New Jersey and Florida. At the same time, Eboli was the de-facto leader of the Genovese family's New York crews. They meet regularly to discuss family business. They often met at diners. Sometimes it was just Jerry and Tommy. Other times, Jerry's brother Eugene would join them. They hit fancy restaurants and greasy spoons. Although Eboli lived in Ft. Lee, New Jersey, his crew was based in Greenwich Village, and Jerry would occasionally cross the Hudson to meet in the City.

We know this now because by the early 1960s, the FBI was everywhere. They had wiretaps and informants feeding them information on a regular basis. Combined with the ever-increasing sophistication of their surveillance, the FBI might have been playing catch-up regarding the inner workings of the Mafia, but they were catching up quick.

Although the Genovese family was spared much internal violence during the 1960s, apart from an occasional house-cleaning, like Tony Bender, there were times when violence naturally broke out. One event in question concerned a noted Newark gambler named James Del Grosso. Del Grosso was, like Catena, an avid golfer. He also, like Catena, enjoyed gambling. He had an arrest record dating back thirty years. Del Grosso managed a sporting club in Newark, the Essex County Hunting and Fishing Club,[1] in the Vailsburg section of the city. The club became a popular hangout for local wiseguys. Carmine Battaglia, a one-time member of the disbanded Newark family who moved under the Genovese, had a gambling operation at the club. The Essex County prosecutor was not such a big fan. "The place itself is a questionable resort. We're investigating overtones which I think may lead to organized gambling."[2]

On the afternoon of January 31, 1963, the bartender and two club patrons came in to open up. When they got there they found the body of Del Grosso lying on his back, with a kitchen knife by his side. He had been hit over the head with a bottle and stabbed five times with a bread knife. Around the body were strewn playing cards and smashed bottles of whiskey. And there was blood everywhere, on the walls, chairs, and tables.

The prosecutor's suspicion about what went on in the Club was not unfounded. However, police were quick to point out the frenetic and spontaneous nature of the killing, not to mention the highly personal aspect of beating and stabbing someone. They told the newspapers later that day they were sure this wasn't a gangland killing.

They weren't entirely correct. It was a gangland killing, but one that was not sanctioned, and one that was both spontaneous and personal. Police heard from some sources that Del Grosso was seen with two people the evening prior. Because by the time his body was found he had been dead for twelve hours, the two people who he was with may have been the last to see him. With that lead, Newark cops started bringing in potential witnesses, which included underworld figures like Biaggio Campisi, a member of a close-knit family-based crime organization that in the coming decades would leave their own mark on the New Jersey underworld.

After hitting some dead ends, police received intel that the man they wanted was Victor Pisauro, a former professional boxer who started his career in the sweet science the same year, 1931, that he started his criminal career. Aligned initially with Anthony Caponigro and his crew, Pisauro later moved under Richie Boiardo. Pisauro and his girlfriend were at the club that evening with Del Grosso. After a few drinks Del Grosso made some advances towards Pisauro's girlfriend. The two men argued and when Del Grosso threatened to kill Pisauro with a knife, a struggle ensued, and Del Grosso was dead.

When it became apparent the police were after them, Pisauro and his girlfriend turned themselves in, although there was a conversation between Gyp DeCarlo (ID'd as Ray in the wiretaps) and Anthony Boiardo (Tony) shortly afterwards that suggested the Genovese family orchestrated the surrender to try and get ahead of the murder charges. The conversation also gave some insight to how Jerry was handling situations like this.

> Ray: What the hell happened? How did Vic (Pisauro) walk in there like that? Did you tell him to walk into Spina (Newark police Director Dominick Spina)?
>
> Tony: We set it up Ray.
>
> Ray: Why did he make a statement that he did this more or less?
>
> Tony: Because the girl took the whole rap.
>
> Ray: Well, yeah, according to (County Medical Examiner) Albano, she's the one that did.
>
> Tony: He didn't hit him on the head.
>
> Ray: But he's going to be an accessory. He'll wind up with a bit.
>
> Tony: Oh yeah.
>
> Ray: Who squealed on him? How did they know he was there?
>
> Tony: They had him nailed, fingerprints and all. Then Carmine (Battaglia) went around screaming about it.[3]

DeCarlo then talks to Tony about how Richie Boiardo went down to Florida to talk with Jerry Catena about the Pisauro situation and how Battaglia and the Philadelphia Mafia family's Newark crew exacerbated the situation. They had issues with how close Battaglia was with Tony "Bananas" Camponigro and how Jerry's handling of Bruno was not as hard-lined as DeCarlo would have liked.

Tony: No. The Boot grabbed a hold of Jerry down there.

Ray: Oh, down there.

Tony: He talked to Jerry and Jerry sent word to Bruno (Philly Mafia boss).

Ray: It's about time Jerry told Burno to have his men mind their own business.

. . .

Tony: I tell you The Boot was down in Florida and he grabbed Jerry (Catena). He said "Jerry give the word and I'll call up to knock them down."

Ray: Where do these guys come in with us? How do these guys in the other mob come in here and want to know what's going on with us? I only wish Vito (Genovese) was out of prison even if it's two months. Of course Bananas is hanging on by a string.

Tony: You know Angelo Bruno sent word to Jerry that he'll straighten out Bananas and he won't get out of line.

Ray: If Vito was out Angelo Bruno would never have got made a boss. The real reason Jerry favored it is that he (Bruno) buys all his machines off Jerry.[4]

Pisauro and his girlfriend were both indicted for the murder of Del Grosso, although both were ultimately acquitted at trial, after they proved to the jury that the murder was self-defense.

So why did this murder of a club owner by a low-level member of the Boiardo crew create such a headache? So much that Richie the Boot flew to Florida to meet with Jerry Catena to ask Catena if they needed to dole out reprisals, ostensibly to Pisauro? One reason was that Pisauro was suspected of killing a witness to a shooting involving Tony Boy Boiardo, and either The Boot was trying to protect Pisauro from law enforcement reprisals as a favor, or he thought that if faced with a substantial prison sentence, then Pisauro would talk with authorities. Another reason was that the Del Grosso murder and ensuing publicity spurred the creation of a grand jury to dig into illegal gambling operations in Essex County. The grand jury was called by the Essex County Prosecutor Brendan T. Byrne, who was described by mobsters as a man who could not be bought.[5]

This was not good news for Jerry Catena. The grand jury was not only looking into illegal gambling, but the connection between social clubs, illegal gambling, and liquor licenses. This was a way in for law enforcement to force the closure of clubs that were identified by the grand jury as epicenters of gambling. The grand jury was convened in February 1963, and within two months, it handed out its initial set of indictments primarily related to gambling activities. Charges centered on illegal lotteries, keeping a gambling establishment, and bookmaking.

That summer the grand jury reported that they found Essex social clubs that were not political, fraternal, or religious in nature were almost exclusively formed as fronts for illegal gambling. They recommended formal licensing of social clubs, enhanced wiretapping of suspected clubs, formation of specialized gambling units within local police departments in the County, and a semipermanent grand jury that met exclusively to deal with organized crime.

The grand jury called several witnesses in for questioning, including Gyp DeCarlo, Tony "Bananas" Caponigro, one-time Catena employer Jake "Mohawk" Skuratofsky, and bookie Irving Berlin. Subpoenas were also sent out for Jerry and Eugene Catena and the Boiardos.

But things were about to get worse. Not only for Catena and the Genovese family, but also for the Mafia. In late September/early October 1963, a Genovese family soldier named Joe Valachi testified before the U.S. Senate's Permanent Subcommittee on Investigations of the U.S. Senate Committee on Government Operations. The Subcommittee was investigating organized crime and Valachi became their star witness. For the first time, the general public was given a firsthand account of the life of a mobster who lived through some seminal moments in organized crime's evolution in America. Valachi testified as to how he was made into the Mafia, many of its operations, the structure of different families that he came into contact with, and especially information on the Genovese crime family.

The speed and effectiveness with which the FBI collected and processed information were constant topics of conversation in social clubs and hangouts throughout New Jersey.

Sam DeCavalcante (S): I'm not surprised the FBI—

Tony Boiardo (T): No I'm not surprised. I'm trying to let you know how the word got to me what the prosecutor told them. How well informed they are.

Gyp DeCarlo (R): They know who were with and who we ain't with, who the mobs are and everything else.

T: Jerry (Catena) says the jig is up.

R: As long as they can't prove anything, I don't care.[6]

On January 12, 1965, four high-ranking mobsters met at the Villa Capra restaurant in Cedarhurst, Long Island. Frank Manzo, a soldier in the Lucchese family, owned the Villa Capra. Villa Capra was a popular hangout for wiseguys, so it probably wasn't too surprising that FBI agents were staked out that night watching the comings and goings. They were surprised to see Sam Giancana, the boss of the Chicago Outfit, entering the restaurant. He was followed shortly afterward by Carmine Tramunti of the Lucchese family, Tommy Eboli, and Catena. The FBI believed that, despite "a number of lesser lights"[7] attending, Catena, Giancana, Eboli, and Tramunti were meeting to discuss the Joe Bonanno situation.

Giancana was in town to appear before a New York grand jury investigating Joe Bonanno's disappearance. Catena was also subpoenaed for the grand jury and testified for about thirty minutes in late January. Described by the papers as the "big man in the organization," Catena's appearance was short and offered little additional information on Bonanno.

The FBI was also very interested in the Villa Capra meeting. They sub-poenaed the restaurant's owner, Francesco Manza, to testify before a federal grand jury. A month later, Francesco was dropped off at a Queens hospital with facial cuts and a broken ankle. The feds were convinced he didn't fall, but was pushed, then worked over, possibly as a message not to talk to the grand jury.

In February 1965, the FBI received information about a Commission meeting in Miami. Sam DeCavalcante was heading to Florida with Joseph "Bayonne Joe" Zicarelli, a Bonanno family capo who operated in Hudson County, NJ. Sam told Joe that Carlo Gambino was going to meet with them. Tommy Eboli's driver, Dominick Alongi, told Gene Catena that Eboli would not be able to make the Miami meeting. Gene then told soldier Nicholas Belangi to send word to his capo Vincent "Jimmy Blue Eyes" Alo and Meyer Lansky that Jerry could be reached at his place in Boca Raton. The FBI also confirmed that Tommy Lucchese and Joseph Colombo were in Florida.

The next major Mafia sitdown occurred without Catena. Thirteen mobsters met at La Stella restaurant in Queens. The press dubbed the meeting "Little Apalachin." The men gathered for a formal sitdown at around 4 p.m. on September 22, 1966. They did not have a chance to start their meal before police barged in and arrested all, charging them with consorting with known criminals. The men arrested included Carlo Gambino; Joseph N. Gallo, Gambino family member; Anielle Dellacroce, Gambino family underboss; Joseph Colombo, boss of the Colombo family; Santo Trafficante Jr., boss of Tampa; Carlos Marcello, boss of New Orleans; Joseph Marcello, Carlos's brother; Frank Gagliano, New Orleans member; Anthony Carolla, New Orleans member and son of the former NOLA boss.

The Genovese family had the largest representation from the NY Five Families. Tommy Eboli and Mike Miranda hosted the meeting. With them were Anthony "Tony the Sheik" Carillo, Eboli's driver, and Dominick "Fat Dom" Alongi, who was born in New Orleans and a cousin to Frank Gagliano.

As detailed by the sources, the meeting was called to resolve an internal leadership dispute between Carlos Marcello and Anthony Carolla in the New Orleans family.

Police were tipped off and raided the restaurant before much could be discussed. It was a good thing that Catena did not show up. Catena let Eboli handle it because it did not deal directly with the Genovese family's local operations, nor was it a major matter between the Five Families.

With the increasing attention of law enforcement on organized crime by the Justice Department under the leadership of Robert Kennedy, some mobsters openly discussed leaving the US entirely to avoid prosecutions. Philadelphia Mafia boss Angelo Bruno was considering a move to Italy and told Jerry Catena that he should also consider moving. Catena acknowledged the potential risk, but told Bruno that a move overseas would be impossible because of his family. He was willing to see how things unfolded.

Despite the looming threat from the law, Jerry Catena's operations were riding high during the 1960s. In addition to the massive income from gambling operations and unions, Catena also brought in significant income from his legitimate businesses. Catena's legitimate business empire only expanded after he was grilled about his business ventures at the Kefauver hearings in 1950. It was one of the most varied and lucrative of any Mafia figure before or since.

Jerry Catena speaking in front of the McClellan Commission 1959.

Jerry's birthplace in Newark. Photo courtesy of the author.

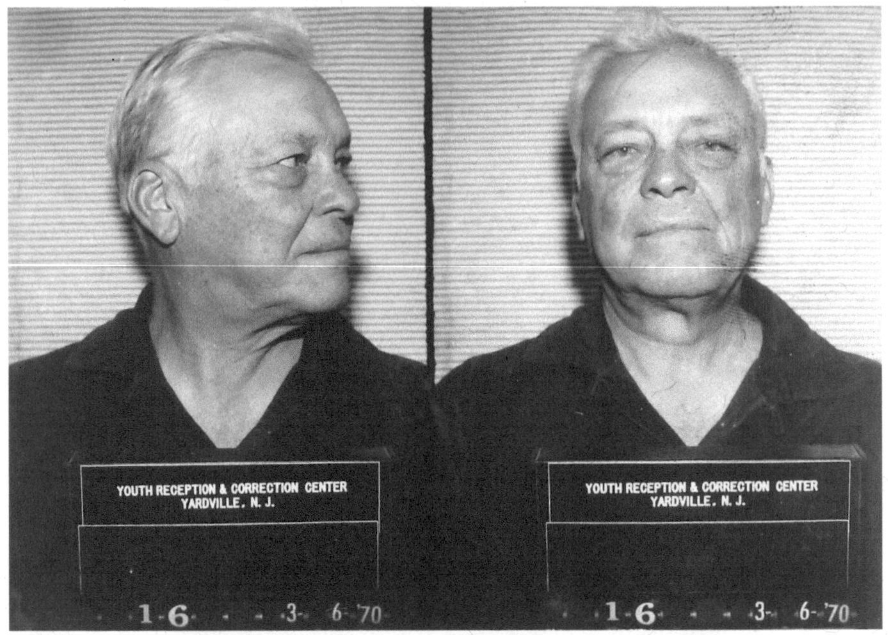

1970 mugshot at Yardville. Photo courtesy of NJ State Commission of Investigation.

Catena entering the Trenton federal courthouse to testify in front of the SCI in 1970. Photo courtesy of the author.

Catena escorted to the Trenton federal courthouse in 1970. Photo courtesy of United Press International Telephoto.

Postcard from the opening of the Fremont in Las Vegas. Photo courtesy of the author.

Matchbook for Public Service Tobacco during the time Catena was part-owner. Photo courtesy of the author.

Another photo of Jerry Catena in 1970. Photo courtesy of NJ State Commission of Investigation.

Catena family residence in 1930, Newark. Photo courtesy of the author.

Jerry in his happy place—the golf course.
Photo courtesy of Eugene Giufurta.

Runyon Sales's New York City office. Photo courtesy of the author.

Site in Brooklyn where Tommy Eboli was gunned down on July 16, 1972. Photo courtesy of the author.

The Majestic apartments, on the Upper West Side, where Frank Costello lived. Photo courtesy of the author.

Bullet mark in the Majestic lobby from one of the shots fired at Frank Costello on May 2, 1957. Photo courtesy of the author.

Eugene Catena (2nd from left) and Johnny "Coca-Cola" Lardiere (2nd from right). Photo courtesy of Eugene Giufurta.

Jerry Catena (far right), Eugene Catena (front left), and Angelo "Gyp" DeCarlo (behind Eugene, cigar in mouth). Photo courtesy of Eugene Giufurta.

Late 1970s chart of the Genovese family. Photo courtesy of Union County Prosecutor's Office, Detective Bureau Intelligence Unit.

9

The Companies of Catena

As mentioned previously, one of the sticking points with Catena's rule was that he often seemed aloof and out of touch to his capos and soldiers. In some ways, as Catena himself had stated, he didn't need, nor particularly want, to be boss. Still, Genovese had decreed that Catena rule in his absence, and Jerry, despite his misgivings, understood the politics of La Cosa Nostra enough to take on the job handed to him.

But another reason that Jerry didn't necessarily need the headaches of leadership of the Genovese family was that he was already quite successful in his various legitimate business enterprises. Sure, the joke that most wiseguys considered themselves "legitimate businessmen" has become something of a punchline. But in Catena's case, it's true.

Jerry Catena was known as a very good, astute businessman. In fact, Jerry may have made more money from his legitimate investments than from his involvement in the Mafia. Catena likely achieved the one dream that so many mobsters before and after had: to turn their illegal enterprises into legitimate business successes. Very few ever achieved that, whether through bad luck, poor business decisions, or law enforcement intervention, which ended their ambitions.

It's not a stretch to say that Jerry Catena may have been one of the more successful entrepreneurs in organized crime. In many ways, Catena acted more like a CEO of a major corporation than what people think of as a traditional mob boss. He was incentivized by money, by making the best deals, and by working at some of the firms where he held an interest. As he ascended the Mafia ladder, Catena occasionally went to the office wearing a suit and briefcase in tow.

His record of business ownership dates back to his years working under Longie Zwillman in the post-Prohibition era. Along with Longie Zwillman, Catena owned interests in the Muzak Corporation, a favorite company of Zwillman's. Muzak Corporation was an outgrowth of the wired music model created by its predecessor company, North American Company (which itself was purchased by Warner Bros.). By 1954, when the Muzak Corporation came into being, Zwillman and Catena both had financial interests in the firm, which also expanded into a franchise model. Yes, the dons of New Jersey were instrumental in the creation of elevator, office, and dentist office instrumental music that, interestingly, still exists in 2025 under the Mood Media brand.

Correlated with his interest in Muzak, Catena also owned a piece of Chatham Electronics in Newark. Chatham was not a fancy company. They created industrial and transmitting tubes for radios. The factory was located on Washington Street in the Third Ward, right around the corner from one of Zwillman's clubs and Catena hangouts, the Casablanca Club.

When the business lines of a prominent mob figure comes to mind, home improvement is generally not among them. But for an entrepreneur like Jerry Catena, any business that could be successful was of interest to him. He witnessed the post-Second World War boom, which brought thousands of new homes and developments across New Jersey and the entire country. With all the new homes, and rising economic fortunes, and the growing popularity of backyard leisure time, what better business to be in than aluminum awnings? Yes, the acting boss of the Genovese crime family was, for a time, the president (in paper at least) of Tren-Metal Inc. of Trenton. This company manufactured aluminum awnings for homes, whose predecessor firm Catena also had a financial interest in, Kool-Vent Metal Awning Company. Tony Boiardo also had a financial stake in both awning firms.

Kool-Vent ads were common in the newspapers during the 1940s and 1950s. Advertising themselves as "nationally famous" and able to make their customers' homes up to twenty degrees cooler in the summer, Kool-Vent's success enabled it to expand across the state. After changing to Tren-Metal, they debuted the Solar-Vent Ventilated awning, giving the homeowner "complete ventilation and diffused light throughout."[1] Suburban comfort was what Jerry Catena was selling.

In 1958, a grand jury was convened in Mercer County to investigate the business ties of some of the New Jersey-based Apalachin delegates. The County prosecutor specifically mentioned examining the ties between Jerry Catena and Tren-Metal Inc. of Trenton. The prosecutor also alleged that Tren-Metal installed metal awnings at the Apalachin home of Joseph Barbara before the ill-fated meeting in November 1957.

Jerry was also involved in the food industry. Pisa Sausage Company was a sausage manufacturer in Paterson. Jerry and Gene both held an interest in the company and were leveraging their influence to push Pisa Sausage into markets around northern New Jersey. Gene Catena was a broker for the firm. It also helped that the Catena brothers controlled the Amalgamated Meat Cutters Union, Local 464 in Passaic County. In the interconnected world of New Jersey organized crime, the president of Pisa Sausage was Mike Pizzi, son of Frank Pizzi, a high-ranking union member.

One of Catena's more intriguing investments was his involvement in oil and gas leases in Oklahoma. In the early 1950s, it was alleged that Catena owned about 20 percent of Murchison Oil Lease in Oklahoma, operated by Clint Murchison Sr. and Jr. Clint Jr. later became the owner of the Dallas Cowboys. The ties between Catena and Murchison Jr. were not as unexpected as one might think, especially because of overlapping interests and associates among Catena, Murchison, and other mob figures. Murchison himself had investments in Havana well as ties to organized crime figures in Dallas, like Joe Campisi. His closest underworld relationships were with associates of New Orleans mob boss Carlos Marcello and members of the Gambino crime family in New York.

Although it is not clear how long Catena held his interest in the oil leases, his involvement with other companies was more transparent. One of them was Marcal Manufacturing. Marcal was founded in 1932 by a Sicilian immigrant in Elmwood Park, New Jersey. By the 1950s, Marcal was one of the top paper products manufacturers on the East Coast. Catena was not only listed as vice president, but he was also reported to have a stake in the company that ranged from 20 percent to 25 percent.

Some of Jerry's corporate investments were of small firms whose histories have been lost to time. These were Newark-based firms like CPC Truck Rentals, Higgins, and University Products Company. Another Newark-based firm that became a lucrative investment for Jerry was People's Express, a trucking company that served the nearby Port Newark, where Jerry began his working career as a laborer.

People's Express was located in the Ironbound section of Newark, not far from where Jerry was born. People's Express was purchased by Jerry's longtime golfing buddy Phil Dameo on June 1, 1946. Phil told Jerry about his idea for buying the trucking company and how he was looking for investors during a golf game at the Knoll golf course. The initial investment in getting People's Express up and running was $40,000. Catena wrote three checks to Dameo for $22,000, owning almost half the company. Two other shareholders were subsequently brought in.

In 1950, during the Kefauver hearings, Dameo was asked about Catena's involvement with People's Express and whether he knew where Jerry was ducking his subpoena.

The Chairman: What does Mr. Catena do there?

Mr. Dameo: He comes and goes.

The Chairman: He goes, apparently.

Mr. Dameo: Apparently.

Catena was also questioned during the Kefauver hearings about his involvement in People's Express. As usual, he was a bit tight-lipped about specifics.

Mr. Halley: How did you happen to get into People's Express?

Mr. Catena: Mr. Dameo invited me in.

. . .

Mr. Halley: And what were the circumstances?

Mr. Catena: He just invited me in, if I wanted to own part of the business.

Mr. Halley: He needed money, didn't he?

Mr. Catena: Well, he needed my part of the money.

People's Express benefited from Jerry's close ties to the various unions around the Port, especially Teamsters Local 560, a haven for Genovese crime family influence. Anthony "Tony Pro" Provenzano was the longtime head of that local. With the backing of the Teamsters, People's Express became a hugely successful trucking company, with a fleet of trucks working across New Jersey and New York.

In 1950, the U.S. Senate began an investigation into People's Express and the timing between union difficulties at Port Newark and a business proposition for People's Express to take over a mothballed truck terminal at the Port. People's Express made an unsolicited bid to use the truck terminal for their operations. This came on the heels of Teamsters refusing to handle goods at the Port. The Senate saw this as coordination between the Teamsters to refuse pickups at the terminal and People's Express's bid, which promised the Port Authority that they knew how to work with he union. That was, of course, because Jerry had multiple inroads into the union and could leverage their practices at the port to benefit his business interests. In the end, however, the Senate investigators dropped their inquiry. They called the Teamsters' actions and the People's Express bid simply coincidental timing.

Phil Dameo was a respected businessleader who was also very active in charities. Dameo was one of the largest benefactors of the Boys' Club of Newark. Starting in 1942, Dameo raised tens of thousands of dollars for the club, even as his own business career began to take off. On July 1, 1963, the Long Branch-based newspaper *The Daily Record* lauded Dameo with an article outlining his charitable contributions. But he knew who his partner was and how to leverage that relationship to the firm's advantage.

Andy Aldi Jr. recalls walking in on his father, Phil Dameo, and Catena as a kid in People's Express offices. Jerry, Phil, and his Dad were sitting in Phil's office, surrounded by big piles of cash. When Andy Jr. saw the money, his eyes opened wide. His father saw him and hustled him out of the room quickly.

Catena's investments also extended into restaurants and bars, common businesses for mob figures to invest their money in. He owned the Silver Hall, a nightclub on Broad Street in Newark. Catena purchased the three-story building that housed the club in 1947. The Silver Hall was located a few doors down from his brother Frank's bar, the Old Colonial Inn.

Frank Catena opened the Old Colonial Inn the weekend of October 6–8, 1950. Described as a genial host, Frank entertained guests and oversaw the restaurant's operations. His brother Jerry was a frequent guest at the Inn. While both the Silver Hall and Old Colonial were hangouts for local gangsters and political figures, the Old Colonial Inn found itself in the crosshairs of law enforcement on multiple occasions. In one case, reminiscent of the *Goodfellas* scene where Henry Hill brings a rack of fur coats into the Bamboo Lounge, a local union boss at Port Newark was demanding Russian furs from ships unloading at the Port. They stored some of the furs at the Old Colonial Inn, where the union boss was able to pick them up.

The Old Colonial was known as a mob hangout, so it was unusual when the restaurant was robbed in September 1961. Two white men overpowered and tied up Paul Altieri, who was working at the restaurant that night. They told

Altieri to make sure and identify them as black when the police came. They robbed the Old Colonial of over $3,000. Paul was so shaken up that he passed away less than two months later. The robbers were allegedly caught, not by police.

Another restaurant endeavor of Jerry's was The Arch in Short Hills, New Jersey. The Arch was owned by Andy Aldi Sr., Catena, and Phil Dameo. Phil and Jerry owned the building and leased it back to the restaurant, through the Cada Realty company, a real estate venture that Catena formed with Dameo. A fourth partner, Sylvio Orlando, who served as the general manager and maître d', came from Italy and once ran a restaurant on Lake Como.

The Arch opened in 1957 and was described as "THE sumptuous dining spot in this area" and "worthy of some of the best dining spots in the East 60s in NYC."[2] With rave reviews like that, The Arch was a popular destination for diners from across northern and central New Jersey, which may have surprised Catena. The restaurant became incredibly successful and was packed all the time.

The Arch's reputation as a hangout for organized crime figures also helped it fill the reservation book.

When I was in high school, my friend and I wanted to take these two girls we knew out for dinner. I said, "Why don't we go to The Arch?" So we all get dressed up and head over to the restaurant. We're sitting there and one of the girls leans over to me and says "I heard gangsters owned this place." A few minutes later my Dad walks in and I told the girl, "I think that's one of the gangsters there." He then walks up to the table and I said "hey Dad." The look on her face.[3]

While Catena did come in occasionally, he was not at all hands on, although his presence was felt enough to keep things running smoothly.

One night I was with my father when he was doing the books at the restaurant. He calls me over and says "come here and look at this." He says that they are supposed to make a liquor profit of 75% but that month was only showing 25%. The revenue was consistent with prior months. To my father this meant one thing. It means the bartender was stealing from them. So my father tells me, "he doesn't know who he's stealing from." My father had a talk with the bartender. The next month, the liquor profit was 130%.[4]

Catena's name was conspicuously absent from the restaurant's official shareholders list. In 1972, when The Arch applied for a retail consumption license from the township of Milburn, Andrew Aldi Sr., and Phil Dameo's names were prominent, but there was no mention of their other, silent partner. Later that year, Sylvio Orlando died, and The Arch continued until closing in 1975.[5]

Some of Jerry's legitimate companies also bled into illegal activities. Such was the case with an interlocking network of vending companies that emerged in New Jersey in the mid- to late 1940s. Four of the six companies were tied to Jerry Catena. The first was L&C Amusements. Catena, along with Willie Moretti, Joe Adonis, and Adonis associate James "Piggy" Lynch, was listed as an employee of this firm in the late 1940s. Headquartered in downtown Newark, L&C was incorporated in 1947 and served to launder profits from dice game operations in Bergen County. Lynch later testified as a state witness confirming the L&C was set up solely to handle monies from carpet joints that offered craps. Carpet gaming halls were more extravagant businesses with plush carpets, hence the moniker. One of the main carpet joints operated by Catena and the L&C set was the Costa Barn in Lodi.

The carpet joints were investigated by state law enforcement, and although Adonis and Moretti were wrapped up in the case, Catena was not indicted as part of the investigation. Usually, when a mobster is not indicted with fellow co-conspirators, it leans toward cooperation with the authorities. However, in Catena's case, his involvement was more on the L&C side, overseeing the company's operation, rather than direct hands-on involvement in the gambling operations.

The other firms tied to L&C and Bergen County gambling were PLA Trading Corporation, General Trading Corporation, and G&R Trading Co. G&R was founded in 1945 by Anthony Guarini, an associate of Catena and Moretti who operated gambling games in Fort Lee and Lodi. Joe Adonis was also a member of G&R. From April 1945 to April 1946 alone, Catena cleared $51,054.27 from G&R, far above the average 1946 family income of $2,600.00. PLA, General, and G&R were set up to handle monies from sawdust joints. These casinos were strictly bare bones operations, the opposite of the swankier carpet joints.

One of the other partners in G&R was James "Niggy" Rutkin, an old friend of Catena's from his bootlegging days. Rutkin, like many others, transitioned from illegal alcohol sales to legal alcohol sales after Prohibition ended. He was a former partner of Joseph Reinfeld and, in the post-Prohibition era, founded Brown Vinters,[6] along with Doc Stacher and Longie Zwillman, an importer for various whiskeys and liqueurs. After hearing about how profitable the gambling operations were, Rutkin approached Catena about becoming involved with L&C. Rutkin needed some help due to some past failures when he tried branching out into gambling on his own. He later told the Kefauver Committee how he and Catena connected.

Mr. Halley: Well what was the reason for going to Catena?

Mr. Rutkin: I don't know. I figured he could help me out, that I was not capable, I suppose.

Mr. Halley: What did he say?

Mr. Rutkin: Because I had tried the gambling business once before. And it was a failure.

Mr. Halley: Where did you go see him first?

Mr. Rutkin: I used to see Jerry quite frequently in Newark.

Mr. Halley: Where did you first discuss it?

Mr. Rutkin: I believe in a barbershop in Newark, on Branford Place.[7]

Catena also managed some of the businesses that Longie Zwillman left after his death. One was a parking lot company, Kinney Parking Company, founded in 1945 by Zwillman associate Emanual "Manny" Kimmel. Longie was a financial investor in the company. Rumor has it that Kimmel purchased parking lots to facilitate his numbers racket, noting that cars coming and going from a parking lot would not attract attention from law enforcement. Kimmel also used lots he owned in New York City as spots where gamblers could meet, park, and take chauffeur-driven cars into Bergen County to visit one of the many gambling houses run by the mob. Also, from a business point of view, parking lots made sense in Newark, a densely populated city lined with row houses and businesses. Parking was at a premium, especially with the rise in popularity of the automobile.

After Zwillman's death, Catena took over his interest in the company. It's unclear when Catena sold his interests in Kinney, but it would likely have been before Kinney merged with three other companies, forming Kinney Service Corporation, which went public in 1962.

The early 1960s brought Jerry some additional business deals. In 1963, an informant told the FBI that the owner of a Newark trucking firm was investing money for Jerry and his brother Gene in the United Equity Life Insurance Company out of Chicago and a manufacturing firm in West Virginia.

Above all other business lines, Jerry Catena continued investing heavily in the vending machine industry. One of his companies even had the contract for vending machines in the Newark Police Department and had the Department's Public Relations Director on its payroll, prompting an investigation by the grand jury. They noted,

We have a lack of full confidence in the Newark Police Department's enthusiasm for a crackdown on the underworld. Nowhere has our attention been focused on any policy statement by the police department vigorously attacking organized crime. This is especially disturbing in light of testimony indicating that the Public Relations Director of the Police Department, one Harry Rosen, is also on the payroll of Automatic Merchants, one of a complex of vending operations dominated by Gerardo Catena, who has been widely reputed to be a syndicate leader in New Jersey.[8]

For all the success in his business ventures, there would be one deal that Catena would be tied to through the next two decades. It was a deal that radically transformed the world of vending and coin-operated machines, legal gambling, the fortunes of two cities, and brought us Gen-X'ers the joy of playing *Pac-Man* and *Space Invaders* at the mall arcade.

10
Bally

When *Space Invaders* arrived in the United States in the spring of 1978, it marked the beginning of what became known colloquially as the Golden Age of Video Games. The simple shooter-style game quickly became popular worldwide. Developed and manufactured in Japan by Taito Corporation, *Invaders* was distributed in the United States by Midway Manufacturing, a Chicago-based subsidiary of Bally Gaming. Buoyed by the success of *Space Invaders*, Bally-Midway[1] reached out to other Japanese video game manufacturers and in 1980 introduced the iconic *Pac-Man*, followed in 1982 by *Ms. Pac-Man*. Within three years, Bally-Midway set the template for millions of Gen X-ers' nostalgic memories of pumping quarters in the arcade machines in shopping malls and pizza shop side rooms. Between its pinball machines and arcade games, Bally-Midway became the dominant name in arcade attractions, much as it had done in the world of slot machines. But Bally-Midway owed its legacy to Bill O'Donnell, an enterprising young salesman with a vision for the future, and Jerry Catena.

William "Bill" T. O'Donnell was born on the north side of Chicago on September 26, 1922. Like many young men of his generation, O'Donnell enlisted in the United States Marine Corps in 1943 and served through the end of the Second World War. After the war ended, O'Donnell returned to Chicago to find work. He got a job as a postal worker. Still, a cousin, who happened to be a bookmaker for a local businessman and a gambler, Raymond Moloney, suggested Bill would be an ideal candidate to work for Raymond. Using his connection as the guy who controlled Raymond's gambling bets, Bill's cousin got Bill a job.

Raymond Moloney owned a company, Lion Manufacturing, that manufactured pinball and bingo games. Lion Manufacturing was located on Chicago's northwest side. Lion was part of a business ecosystem in Chicago, centered on coin-operated games. There were manufacturers of the games themselves, manufacturers that made the parts for the games, artisans who designed the games, and distributors who shipped the games. This vertical integration of companies enabled Chicago to become dominant in the coin-operated games and jukebox industries.

As expected, the competition between the various manufacturers was fierce. Everyone was trying to capitalize on the exploding popularity of coin-operated games, and whoever came up with the next big idea was sure to grab market share from their competitors. Lion gained a market advantage over their competitors in 1932 with the introduction of a new game called Ballyhoo. The Ballyhoo game differed from its contemporaries primarily due to one thing: it was colorful. According to the lore, Moloney was walking down the street in Chicago when he passed a newsstand and "something catches his eye. A satirical magazine, very popular in that time period, called *Ballyhoo*. And he's taking a look at the, I believe, December 1931 issue . . . and it's got this very colorful cover design."[2]

In addition to taking the game's name from the magazine, Moloney created a subsidiary company, Bally, to manufacture that game and other pinball machines. To clarify, Lion Manufacturing Company was the parent corporation, and Bally Manufacturing was a subsidiary of Lion. And Bally was a trade name of Lion. Over time, the colloquial name became known as Bally.

The Ballyhoo game was an immediate success. Supporting the idea that people were attracted to colorful and shiny things, Ballyhoo's unique design stood apart from its rather drab competition. In 1932 alone, Bally sold over

50,000 Ballyhoo machines. With the money coming in from the success of the Ballyhoo game, Bally soon branched out, specializing in a variety of coin-operated machines, including some used for gambling. By the 1940s, Bally was one of the biggest pinball manufacturers in the Midwest and had distributors across the United States.

Initially in the purchasing department, Bill O'Donnell had a knack for sales. He caught Ray Moloney's eye, and Ray allowed him to join the sales team, a role that O'Donnell embraced. Bill rose quickly in the department, becoming a sales manager by the mid-1950s. His colleagues knew him as a nice guy, who always looked people in the eye. He was a charismatic straight shooter with a penchant for the vending business. In his new position, he aimed to strengthen relationships with Bally's various distributors throughout the county. One of the first was Bally's distributor for the New York metro area, Runyon Sales.

Runyon Sales was well-known in the vending industry by the mid-1950s. Runyon was founded in Newark in 1938 by Barnet "Sugie" Sugerman, known as Sugie. His partners were Abe Green and Doc Stacher, although Stacher preferred to remain behind the scenes. Runyon was initially located at 123 W. Runyon Street in the Lower Clinton Hill section of Newark, hence the company's name. The original location suffered a fire in the late 1940s and was subsequently relocated a few blocks away to a larger facility on Frelinghuysen Avenue in the early 1950s.

Runyon Sales also had an office on 10th Avenue in the Hell's Kitchen neighborhood of New York City, which they opened in 1946. That stretch of 10th Avenue was known as Pinball Row for all the vending companies that lined the streets. Sugerman and Abe Green owned the building and leased out offices to other firms in the industry,

Runyon not only sold Bally machines but also had a full selection of jukeboxes, pinball machines, and various parts and accessories for a variety of coin-operated games and music players. It was one of the largest distributors in the country and they regularly advertised in *Billboard* and *The Cash Box* magazines. Sugie and Abe Green were well respected in the field and details of their appearances at trade shows and conventions were often featured in *Cash Box.*

Runyon Sales was also involved in several charitable activities. They often partnered with local and national non-profits to run innovative promotions for the time. In February 1954, Runyon installed a jukebox in the lobby of a theater in Morristown to promote the Rita Hayworth movie, *Miss Sadie Thompson*, a 3D romantic comedy. The jukebox, in the lobby for two weeks, had songs from the movie. All the proceeds from the jukebox went to the American Cancer Society.

Jerry Catena invested in the firm around 1951, buying out Doc Stacher's interest in the company. Jerry worked at Runyon's offices, sitting with Abe Green in a private office behind the switchboard operator. However, his name never appeared in any press releases or advertisements for the company. He visited the office frequently to assist in overseeing the company. However, he rarely allowed other mob figures to meet with him there, maintaining the appearance of a businessman at the forefront. Catena told his capos "that he wanted others in his regime to stay away from his place of business."[3] He saved business meetings for the golf course, where he also played on the Runyon Sales team, competing in local tournaments.

One major meeting occurred at Runyon's New York City office. In 1964, Catena hosted a sit-down with Tommy Eboli, Thomas Lucchese, Carmine Tramunti of the Lucchese family, and Carlo Gambino. The meeting was to discuss the Joe Bonanno situation. The Lucchese family was trying to figure out a plan to hit Joe Bonanno and was looking for assistance from the Genovese family. Tommy Eboli told Catena that if it came down to hitting Bonanno, the Lucchese family couldn't do it, so the Genovese family would handle things.

Although Catena was careful to keep his Runyon investment from becoming public knowledge, law enforcement later investigated these ties. In 1959, the McClellan Committee grilled Catena about his interests in Runyon. Like much of his testimony at the hearing, he invoked the Fifth Amendment frequently, although he did answer some basic questions about Runyon.

The Chairman: What is your business?

Mr. Catena: Runyon Sales Co. of New Jersey.

The Chariman: Runyon Sales?

Mr. Catena: Runyon Sales Co. of New Jersey.

The Chairman: What does this company do? What business is it in?

Mr. Catena: Vending machines.

. . .

Mr. Kennedy: When you speak of vending machines, what kind of vending machines does Runyon have?

Mr. Catena: I respectfully decline to answer that question on the grounds that it may incriminate me.

Mr. Kennedy: Is it all kinds of coin machines Mr Catena?

The Chairman: Do you manufacture or sell them?

Mr. Catena: Vending.

The Chairman: I know they are vending machines, but does your company manufacture them or operate them?

Mr. Catena: We operate.

. . .

Mr. Kennedy: What kind of machines are they? Could you tell me that?

Mr. Catena: Well, I will identify them.

Mr. Kennedy: Thank you.

Mr. Catena: Mostly jukeboxes.

Mr. Kennedy: Mostly jukeboxes?

Mr. Catena: Yes.

Mr. Kennedy: Any other kinds of machines?

Mr. Catena: We have games. We have kiddy rides, and cigarette machines.

Mr. Kennedy: How many jukeboxes do you have, approximately?

Mr. Catena: I would say 800.

. . .

Mr. Kennedy: Who are the officers?

Mr. Catena: Mr. Sugerman and Mr. Green.

Mr. Kennedy: Mr. Sugerman and who is the other?

Mr. Catena: Mr. Green.

The omnipresence of Runyon extended across New Jersey. When Runyon put their machines in your business, it was assumed that you would continue to use their machines, without question. One tavern owner in Princeton had a dispute with Runyon over cigarette vending machines in his bar, The Savoy Place. The bar wanted to put their own cigarette machines in the tavern and word got out. The owner was summoned to a sitdown with Sam DeCavalcante, who lived in Princeton. He asked the owner "Did they ever approach you and tell you that you took one of Jerry Catena's spots? . . . Call Abe Green. Say 'Listen I made a mistake. Some friend of yours made me understand that.'"[4]

Runyon also operated the World Wired Music service out of the Runyon offices. World Wired was similar to Muzak. Catena and company set up a studio in the Runyon building. They played background music records, and the music was hardwired into restaurants and bars. The Tavern restaurant, a favorite haunt for Longie Zwillman and Catena, was one such location that World Wired Music served.

Meanwhile, as Runyon expanded its presence across the New York metropolitan area, back in Chicago, a seismic event shook up Bally. Raymond Moloney died from a sudden heart attack on February 26, 1958. Raymond did not have pre-existing health issues, so he did not have a will or a clear line of succession for Lion and its subsidiaries, including Bally. Because of that oversight, Lion and Bally were put in a trust administered by a local Chicago bank. The trust established a board of directors and appointed Bill O'Donnell to serve on the board.

In early 1960, the trust appointed Ray Moloney's two sons to run the company. Since Raymond's death, the company had started to flounder. His sons believed that with a recent repeal of a law allowing the manufacture of slot machines, there was a wide-open market for them. Many of the Nevada casinos still had Second World War-era machines that were now almost twenty years old. The opportunities to serve that market with new machines were enticing to the sons. They saw it as the only way to salvage the firm. But the bank did not see it that way.

To the bank, getting into slot machines was getting involved with organized crime. They were wary of investing in manufacturing machines that would end up in mob-run casinos in Vegas and the backrooms of mob-run bars and restaurants. The bank told the sons that they would have to get the company right sized and profitable, but without slot machines. The company continued to take on debt, and its traditional coin-operated business failed to match the firm's previous success. Time was up, and in 1962, the bank decided to liquidate. To the bank, it made more financial sense to sell off Lion's assets, including its subsidiary Bally, and pay off creditors.

By 1962, the trust was moving forward with its plan to liquidate Bally and exit the coin-operated machine business. O'Donnell saw this as an opportunity. He loved the business and knew it could succeed if taken out from under the thumb of the trust. O'Donnell also agreed with Raymond's sons that slot machines were the way forward. He wanted to buy the firm, but did not have the necessary capital. Knowing that the bank overseeing the trust would not lend the money, he went out searching for other lenders. He was met with the same cold shoulder from all the banks he approached. They all felt the same as the trust, slot machine manufacturing was risky, and the association with organized crime was not something the banks wanted.

After those failed attempts to find financial backers, he turned to Runyon. Abe Green flew to Chicago, and over dinner, he and O'Donnell discussed the potential purchase. Abe flew back to New Jersey and talked with Sugie and

Catena. They were interested but wanted to meet with O'Donnell to get a feel for how he was going to run the company, and also to see what risks there were from this investment. O'Donnell was anxious to get the deal moving. The company's sale was moving ahead, and O'Donnell did not want to lose out on this chance. "Bill contacted my father and asked him to make an appointment for Bill with Jerry Catena to personally discuss the deal. Bill flew out of Chicago and came to Runyon. Within two hours, Jerry was in on the deal. He saw that it was impossible to lose money."[5]

Years later, O'Donnell told anyone within earshot that he had no idea that Runyon was tied to the mob and he maintained that he never knew who Catena was. Still, based on the above quote by Myron Sugerman, other contemporary accounts, and the general background of how the Bally deal came together, it's clear that Bill O'Donnell knew what he was getting with the Runyon partnership. O'Donnell needed Catena and his connection to not only make the deal work financially, but to put the company in a position to become successful. It was one thing to pick up the pieces of the failing Bally operations, but turning that into a successful business again could be an uphill battle.

Abe, Jerry, and Sugie thought about other potential partners to bring in on the deal. The three of them did not have quite enough capital to purchase Bally outright. They needed some partners. With the implicit approval of O'Donnell, Catena and Green brought in a group of investors that would fundamentally change the gambling and coin-operated business in not only America, but the world. That's a bold statement, but the supporting facts are there. Jerry Catena, acting boss of the Genovese crime family, was at the center of one of the most significant deals in gaming industry history.

One of the first things that the nascent investment group did was to form a corporation to manage the deal. Catena, Green, Sugerman, and O'Donnell formed K.O.S. Enterprises, incorporated in New Jersey. They next went about finding those additional investors. They did not have to search too far.

One of the first investors that Catena brought into the Bally deal was Sam Klein, a vending machine executive who once co-owned the Beverly Hills

Club, a gambling establishment operated for the Cleveland mob. Klein knew Abe Green and Sugerman through the vending machine industry. Klein owned the Stern Vending Company in Cincinnati. When looking to sell in the 1950s, Klein was introduced to Lou Jacobs of Emprise, a company that was heavily involved in sports stadium and arena concessions. Klein sold to Emprise and solidified his relationship with Lou Jacobs, whom he suggested to Catena as another investor.

Lou Jacobs had an interesting background with ties to organized crime figures in Detroit. Louis loaned $256,000 to members of the Detroit Mafia to gain control of the Hazel Park Race Track. Jerry Catena later introduced Louis to Joe "The Wop" Cataldo, who wanted to partner with Louis to finance the purchase of a racetrack in upstate New York. Cataldo was a former protégé of Tony Bender Strollo. He also owned a nightclub in Greenwich Village, where he lived.

In a 1972 *Sports Illustrated* story about the Jacobs family and Emprise, it was alleged that Louis M. Jacobs backed a $1,000,000 bank loan to facilitate Catena's purchase of Bally, providing Catena with some flexibility in his ownership position. Catena told Jacobs that he had the money but that he'd rather do it this way for tax purposes. It also further cemented the close ties between Catena and Emprise. Jacobs also brought in one of his business associates, Frank Prince, as an investor.

With Klein and Jacobs on board, Catena reached out to another business associate, Irving Kaye, who was best known for his custom pool tables. Irving Kaye's business, Kaye Manufacturing Company, was in the same building as Runyon's New York City office.

The way the Bally deal was structured was when Catena and his investors acquired Lion Manufacturing's assets, they transferred the shares to Emprise Corp as collateral against a $4 million loan that Emprise procured for the full purchase of Lion Manufacturing. In essence, Emprise secured the financing for the purchase, pushing Catena's involvement further behind firewalls. On paper, Catena was simply a shareholder. Catena received an 8 percent stake in the company, or more precisely, he was entitled to one-third of the shares of Green and Sugerman, as per a written agreement.

The final financing of the Bally deal came via a loan that O'Donnell structured with the Teamsters Central States Pension Fund. At that time, the Fund was used as much to finance the construction of mob-linked casinos in Vegas as it was to fulfill its fiduciary responsibility to the pensioners who received fund payouts. This use of the Fund as a slush fund for Teamsters leaders, including Jimmy Hoffa, drew attention from the Justice Department, which worked for years to purge the Fund and the Teamsters of organized crime influence.

K.O.S. Enterprises now owned Bally for the purchase price of $1.2 million. The first order of business was to oust the Mooney sons from any role in the new company. The company ownership was split as follows:

- William O'Donnell—250 shares

- Sam Klein—333 shares

- Frank Prince—333 shares

- Emprise—334 shares

- Barnet Sugerman—250 shares

- Abe Green—250 shares

- Irving Kaye—250 shares

- Separate agreement with Catena and Green/Sugerman—Catena owned 166 shares

Several interesting observations can be made regarding the Bally deal. The first was that Catena chose not to look for investors within the Genovese family. He could have easily talked up the idea to Richie Boiardo or Angelo DeCarlo. He could have extended the opportunity to Eboli or Genovese. But he chose not to. Instead, Jerry reached out through his connections in the vending machine business and the Jewish underworld figures he had established. There were no other Italians involved in the Bally deal. This was all Jerry and his associates from outside the "corporation."

This was again an extension of Jerry's approach to business and crime. He knew the legitimate and connected vending machine businessmen were better suited for this deal for one simple reason—they could make it work. Jerry didn't need help from the crime family in the business sense. And if he were to bring in, say, Angelo DeCarlo or The Boot, would they drain the company's funds? Would they have the patience to develop and enact a business plan to bring Bally back to relevance and success in the coin-operated field?

Another observation is Jerry's business-minded approach to structuring his involvement with Bally. He didn't put in all of his money, for one. He also selected specific individuals who would contribute financially and bring value to the company from a strategic perspective. This was the resurrection and reformation of a company that was on top, but now found itself outside looking in.

But Catena did not let all of his vending machine contacts into the deal. Abe Green, Kaye, and Sugie had a longstanding relationship with Dave Stern of Royal Distributors in Elizabeth, New Jersey. Royal also distributed coin-operated games, vending machines, and jukeboxes. Stern and Sugerman had a friendship that went back decades, having been introduced to each other by Charlie "The Blade" Tourine. Sugie thought Stern would be an excellent investor in Bally. Catena, however, saw it differently. He never told Sugie why he did not want Stern to join the Bally deal. He had his reasons.

One other item of note is the lack of participation in the Bally deal from Chicago crime figures. Bally's main office was located at 2640 West Belmont Avenue in Chicago, having relocated there from smaller quarters on Ravenswood Avenue in 1935.[6] The location was ideal for shipping units to both Las Vegas and the West coast, as well as servicing the East Coast markets. What's interesting from an organized crime perspective is that Bally never had a strong relationship with the Chicago Outfit, despite being located right in the heart of the Outfit operations. Its strongest links were with Catena and the Genovese family. That's not to say that there weren't rumors that Catena made concessions to Chicago representatives, such as Sam Giancana and Tony Accardo, to maintain peace, especially as they were all upper-echelon members of the Commission.

Bally's new leadership and infusion of capital came at an opportune time, especially in Illinois. The state rescinded its ban on slot machine manufacturing in 1963, paving the way not only for Bally to resume building slot machines in Chicago, but for them to bring in new advancements that would take the industry to new heights.

While the ban was in effect, many casinos in Las Vegas were using machines with rudimentary technology. Most of the slot machines that were in operation in the early 1960s, dated back to the post-Second World War years. They were worn out, not very flashy, and were only able to handle small payouts due to the mechanical tube system that could only keep a small amount of coins to dispense when a payout was triggered.

One of the innovations Bally developed was an electronic hopper system that revolutionized the gambling industry. "Instead of a mechanical machine with twenty coins, now it could spit out 200, 500 coins. People who never played slot machines before now would. Guys would go to tables and give wives coins to play the slots. This changed everything."[7]

Mickey Wichinsky, a Bally distributor in Las Vegas (who later became a celebrated casino executive and owner of various gaming companies), invented the electronic hopper. Mickey was close to Catena. His nephew was married to one of Jerry's daughters. Mickey was also friends with Doc Stacher, paving the way for him to move into the Las Vegas market and become Bally's chief connection to the casinos there. Mickey owned Bally Sales Corporation of Nevada, located on South Highland Drive in Las Vegas. Wichinsky would dabble on his own time to create new machines and developed a prototype for the electronic hopper. Bally's initial attempts to gain approval from the Nevada Gaming Commission proved fruitless, so Bally and Wichinsky started selling the machines overseas, in the UK.

The first hopper game, and one of Bally's earliest successes, was the Bally model 742A, known as the Money Honey. It was one of the games that jump-started Bally in the slot machine market. One of the hurdles, though, was getting the new machines into Las Vegas. With the prospect of having to upgrade many of their machines, the casino bosses were initially hesitant to dive right into the Money Honey machines. Enter Abe Green.

Jerry Catena dispatched Abe Green to Las Vegas with one goal: to persuade the casinos to start buying the Money Honey machines, and in large quantities. Abe had an ace up his sleeve, a longtime friendship with entertainer Dean Martin. At this time, Dean Martin was at the height of his fame in Las Vegas, performing with the Rat Pack and in his headline shows. Dean took Abe around to all the casino contacts he had, in addition to the ones that Catena knew, and between them, they were able to get the orders rolling.

More orders also came in from a Bally distributor in Reno, who replaced some of the casinos' old machines for free. They told the casinos that if they were not satisfied, Bally would replace them free of charge. When the casinos saw how popular the Money Honey machines were, they accelerated the replacement of the old technology. This was the push that Bally needed to become the dominant force in the slot machine market.

Barnet Sugerman did not live long enough to see the fruits of Bally's success fully. He passed away at the age of 64, on April 12, 1964.

After my father died in April 1964, Catena bought out his shares from my mother. He gave her a good deal. After she died the FBI came by wanting to close out my father's file. They told me "the rumor is that your mom got a lousy deal and got screwed." I told them it wasn't true. Catena took care of her. After the feds came I went over to see Abe Green and Jerry. I told them that the FBI were asking questions. Catena just said "really? How's your mother? How's the family? Give her my love." That was it.[8]

Catena paid Sugie's widow $17,500 for Sugie's 250 shares in Bally.

After Sugie's death, Runyon's ownership was split between Abe Green and Jerry Catena. It continued to operate as a successful business. Barnet's son Myron went to work at Runyon. He recalled one night in the mid-1960s when Catena summoned him to Runyon's office. When he arrived, Catena told him that he was to meet someone at an Italian restaurant in Fort Lee. When Myron arrived, he was greeted by Tommy Eboli and his brother Pasquale "Patsy." They introduced Myron to three other men, all young guys from Naples.[9] "I remember it was an election day. Tommy Ryan had the restaurant serve wine to all the diners in coffee cups, compliments of Tommy Ryan Eboli."[10] The three men from Naples were there to buy Bally machines from Runyon, through Myron.

Eboli had a financial interest in the deal as well. Myron discovered this when he was summoned to a diner a short time after arranging for machines to be delivered to Naples. Tommy and his brother Pasquale were at the restaurant. He immediately tore into Myron, suggesting that the machines were second-hand and not worth the cost. Myron knew the machines were brand new but he suspected this was more about sending a message to Jerry Catena. Eboli knocked down the price he was going to pay for the machines. Myron had no choice but to accept. He immediately left that meeting and went and saw Jerry. Catena listened intently but did not offer up his take. He knew deep down that this was Eboli strutting, another indication of the sometimes uneasy relationship between Catena and Eboli.

Around the time of Sugerman's death, Abe Grene, Irving Kaye, and Catena were investors in a firm that manufactured and distributed Scopitones. The Scopitone was basically a video jukebox, a precursor, in a way, of MTV. Music videos would play on the small screen with accompanying music through the jukebox mechanism. Invented in France, the Scopitone came to prominence in the United States for a brief period during the mid-1960s.

Like Bally, the Scopitone deal was a tangled web of interconnected mobsters and legitimate businessmen. In 1963, a theatrical agent named George Wood saw the Scopitone in Europe and wanted to license and distribute the machines in the United States. A deal was worked out with Runyon Sales to handle distribution. Wood worked for the William Morris agency and realized that the Scopitones they were importing only had French pop music videos. Wood knew they needed American content. They also needed to manufacture the machines in the States and load them with films produced directly for the machines. Wood and his agency would take 10 percent of production fees for each of the short films. It was a risk, but one that Wood was willing to take. Manufacturing and production were beyond the scale of the deal between Wood and Runyon. They needed something bigger.

That something bigger was Scopitone Inc. Alvin Malnik, a successful Miami Beach-based businessman and philanthropist, founded Scopitone Inc. to take over Runyon's distribution deal, expand it nationwide, and manufacture machines in the United States to be filled with American-developed videos. Malnik was a close associate of Meyer Lansky. Malnik also brought Vincent "Jimmy Blue Eyes" Alo and Joe Cataldo, soldiers in the Genovese crime family, into the company. They owned one-half of Scopitone Inc., while Green, Kaye, and Catena (in a hidden ownership role) owned the other half. Green and Kaye also brought in Al Miniaci and Maurice Uchitel. Maurice was the owner of the El Morocco Supper Club in New York and the Eden Roc, one of Miami Beach's most fashionable hotels and a regular hangout for Meyer Lansky, among others. Jerry Catena was also seen at the Eden Roc on occasion.

Miniaci owned Paramount Automated Industries, a vending company based in New York City, and had various business connections with Runyon Sales. Alfred was also considered by authorities as an associate of the Genovese crime family, noting his friendship with Jerry Catena and Frank Costello. Miniaci was linked to Costello through his vending companies and also reported ownership of underground gay bars in Greenwich Village. Most notably, Miniaci was having dinner with Frank Costello the same night that Costello was shot.

When Scopitone Inc. was formed, the company eyed Tel-A-Sign, a Chicago-area manufacturer of advertising signs that was ripe for a takeover. This would give Scopitone Inc. a domestic manufacturer. In the spring of 1964, Malnik oversaw the sale of Scoption stock to purchase Tel-A-Sign.

After the Genovese family-backed conglomerate moved in and took over Tel-A-Sign, they pushed out some of the firm's previous investors, including heavyweight boxing champion Floyd Patterson and noted attorney Roy Cohn.

By January of 1965, Tel-A-Sign had manufactured 500 Scopitones and had plans for expanding production to over 10,000. In 1966, with over 1,000 Scopitones in bars and restaurants across the country, the stock prices of Scopitone and Tel-A-Sign rose. But trouble was brewing on the federal front.

The Securities and Exchange Commission had convened a grand jury to investigate Scopitone and Alvin Malnik. When news of the grand jury's investigation broke, the investors bailed, and Scopitone's stock plummeted. Malnik, Alo, Cataldo, Green, Kaye, and Catena got out with their profits intact. When authorities finally closed in, Jimmy Blue Eyes Alo was the one who took the brunt of the feds' attention. In the 1970s, he was convicted of obstruction and sentenced to five years in prison for the Scopitone deal. The company itself folded in 1969.

The Scopitone deal was different than Bally in some ways, chief among them being Catena's involvement. Federal authorities were certain Catena had money invested in the company that he was filtering through Green and Kaye as well as the initial deal with Runyon. The other difference was that in this case, Catena was in a deal that involved other members of the Genovese crime family. Both of those differed from how he handled Bally. It was clear that Catena did not have the same passion for Scopitone as Bally. And maybe he had the foresight to understand the Scopitone product itself was only a passing fad.

But while Scopitone fizzled out, Bally was surging. O'Donnell wanted to take the firm public. He saw that as the next logical step to fund their growth and bring Bally into the mainstream of gaming companies. The one big stumbling block to that plan was the fact that Jerry's name was on the ownership papers as a major shareholder. In order to meet the requirements from the regulatory agencies, Catena's name would draw increased scrutiny. And Catena saw the outside pressure on Bally as his profile continued to rise.

To that end, Catena sold his shares of Bally to Bill O'Donnell on July 2, 1965, for what was reported to be $175,000. Jacobs followed suit the following year, selling his shares back to Kaye, Klein, Green, and O'Donnell. However, many on both sides of the law believed that Catena maintained a hidden interest in Bally through Abe Green, and that his close association with O'Donnell and Sam Klein kept Catena informed about Bally's business direction. And that direction only went up.

By 1968, Bally was producing more than 90 percent of all the slot machines used in Las Vegas casinos. Bally machines were also placed in bars and taverns across the US, often in areas with laws against gambling machines. In the illegal gambling world, Bally's machines alone were part of a "big, multimillion-dollar business. We know that 80 to 90 percent of these machines nationally come from the Bally Manufacturing Company. . . . We know that the average weekly gross of each machine is $100, with half the profit going to the distributor . . . this means a gross income of $5,200.00 per machine, per year."[11]

While distancing itself from Catena, O'Donnell made a questionable decision in hiring Dino Cellini, a casino operator and frequent associate of Santo Trafficante Jr. and Meyer Lansky, to oversee their expansion overseas. Cellini, who grew up in Steubenville, Ohio as a close friend of Dean Martin, had experience running casinos in pre-Castro Havana. When the mob left Cuba in 1959, Cellini ran casinos for Meyer Lansky in the Caribbean before taking his casino acumen to England. Cellini's relationship with Lansky also pointed to relationships within the Genovese family, including Catena. Cellini was banned from operating casinos in the Bahamas in 1965 and in the UK in 1967. Consequently, he redirected his efforts to bring Bally to underserved countries and regions, wherever he could sell a machine.

Cellini wasn't as much of a deal breaker for O'Donnell as Catena. Dino's name, although associated with organized crime figures, was getting cleaner by the year as his reputation as a successful casino operator grew, especially in Europe. Having Dino Cellini associated with Bally was a big "get" for the company, at least in O'Donnell's eyes. Now it was time to go public.

In preparation for taking the company public, O'Donnell changed the official company name from the Lion Manufacturing Corporation to Bally Manufacturing Corporation in 1968. It was around this time that Bally purchased Midway Manufacturing,[12] its main competitor, which was also headquartered in the Franklin Park neighborhood of Chicago. Midway became a subsidiary of Bally, and as noted earlier in this chapter, rose to prominence a decade later with the advent of the video arcade era.

In March 1969, Bally went public. It was a fantastic turnaround for a company that had just five years prior been struggling to get back on its feet. It had now become a force in the gaming industry, the vending machine business, and the coin-operated gaming sector. Less than two months after going public, an incident occurred at Bally's headquarters in downtown Chicago.

At 12:48 a.m. on the morning of May 5, 1969, an explosion shook the Bally factory. Witnesses saw a flash of light outside the front doors, then an explosion which shattered windows up and down the block. Chicago police discovered that sticks of dynamite were set off outside the building. It was never revealed what the motive was, though most news accounts mention Bally's ties to organized crime. The incident was quickly forgotten, and Bally pressed forward into the new decade.

Would Bally be where it was in 1969 without Jerry Catena? The answer is a resounding no. Could we credit Jerry Catena with setting the stage for the late 1970s and early 1980s arcade game phenomenon? Does Jerry Catena bear partial responsibility for Pac-Man cereal and the Saturday morning *Pac-Man* cartoon show? That would be a stretch.

The success of Bally was partially due to the work of Bill O'Donnell and his vision for the company's future. However, Catena's investment, and his ability to attract outside investors, were instrumental in enabling Bill O'Donnell to take Bally to the next level in terms of success, providing it with the capital to acquire additional companies and expand its offerings of coin-operated games and slot machines. Like many of his other successful legitimate business enterprises, Jerry was laser-focused on building a successful business, sometimes to the detriment of his "day job" as acting boss of the Genovese family in the 1960s.

Another reason for Bally's success was Catena's connections in Las Vegas. When he sent Abe Green to Vegas to persuade the casinos to buy the new electronic hopper machines, the longtime connections Catena had set up years prior paid off. Starting in the 1940s, Catena saw the desert oasis as another business opportunity waiting to be seized. Along with Longie Zwillman and Doc Stacher, Catena spearheaded to New Jersey's influence in Sin City, one that paid dividends for decades.

11

The Vegas Combine

The public perception of the mob's involvement in Vegas starts with Bugsy Siegel and ends with Anthony Spilotro. Bugsy is viewed as an essential founder of Vegas and the start of the mob's rule, whereas Spilotro and his reign symbolize the end. Along the way, some names mentioned are one-time bootlegger Moe Dalitz, Chicago Outfit members like Marshall Caifano, and a smattering of Midwest and West Coast gangland figures. But the reality was Las Vegas attracted a broad cross-section of investment from the underworld, especially gangsters from New Jersey. Their investments and hidden ownership guided some of the more successful casinos of the "golden era" of Las Vegas. But like anything looked at through the rose-tinted hues of nostalgia, the truth often reveals darker aspects of that time that are easily glossed over.

The notion that the mob created Vegas is, partially, a myth. They didn't make the city or build the infrastructure that allowed it to grow. That being said, this oft-repeated line that shows up in many features about the city has some elements of truth. From the start of legalized gambling in March 1931, organized crime figures found Vegas to be an attractive location to set up operations. Some saw Vegas as a legal outlet for their talents as bookmakers and operators of underground casinos, as well as managers of talent. Some, like Siegel, were missionaries in that they saw what was already being done and built up on it, bringing the sawdust floor gambling bars and taverns into the post-Second World War vacation age. Some saw it as an attractive target for their criminal proclivities. And others saw it as a mix of all the above.

Jerry Catena was heavily involved in Las Vegas, and along with Longie Zwillman and Doc Stacher, this pervasive New Jersey influence in some of the most popular casinos of the time is rarely acknowledged in many of the popular conversations about the role of the Mafia in Vegas history. Like many others, Catena, Zwillman, and Stacher saw the opportunities to make significant money in the nascent desert oasis, which by the early 1950s was already becoming a must-see tourist destination, attracting millions of tourists a year by the end of the decade. With that, there was a need to build bigger and better hotels and casinos, which necessitated investment from people outside the city with the means to bring in fresh capital. The days of sawdust joints were over. Vegas was primed and ready for the second half of the twentieth century.

The mob in the early years of Vegas was, in the words of UNLV professor Michael Green, not that exciting. They approached this city in the desert with legal gambling as a pure business venture. They were businessmen who wanted to fly under the radar and not draw unnecessary attention to themselves. Such was the case with Longie Zwillman, who first came out to Las Vegas in the late 1940s to look for opportunities. Zwillman's close ties to Meyer Lansky and Bugsy Siegel were his impetus for venturing west. And he was sure to bring his partners out with him.

Another of the great myths is that the desert outside Vegas is littered with graves of mobsters and others who ran afoul of the guys in Vegas. In reality, the mob in Vegas, during those early years, were not into violence for the sake of violence. That would have drawn too much attention to them, especially because Vegas at that time was relatively small. The metro area's population tripled from 35,000 in 1950 to just under 100,000 in 1960, which was much smaller than many of the cities where the mobsters came from.

The rise of Las Vegas also paralleled the mob's casino interests in Havana, Cuba. Some Vegas casino operators, like Wilbur Clark (who ran the casino for Meyer Lansky at the Hotel Nacional), flew back and forth between the two cities, sharing dealers and pit bosses, and bringing their expertise to both. It was the same for mobsters. Some of the major investors in Cuban casinos also had investments in Las Vegas, including Zwillman, Stacher, and Catena.

By the early 1950s, Havana had become a mecca for the Mafia. Although organized crime figures, from New York to Tampa, had interests in Cuba that dated back to the Prohibition era, the mob's real height of influence and investment there was the 1950s. It was a chance to expand their spheres of influence to a friendly government just out of reach of American law enforcement. The FBI believed that Catena had a financial investment in the Hotel Riviera, known primarily as Meyer Lansky's magnum opus. This was going to be THE hotel in Havana, and they hoped to shape the future of the mob in Cuba.

In February of 1959, Catena appeared before the McClellan Committee and was grilled by Robert Kennedy on Jerry's interests in Havana and Las Vegas. Catena was less than forthcoming.

> Mr. Kennedy: Do you have any interest in Cuba?
>
> Mr. Catena: I respectfully decline to answer on the grounds that it may incriminate me.
>
> Mr. Kennedy: Have you set up or established any gambling casinos, or have any interest in any of the gambling casinos?
>
> Mr. Catena: I respectfully decline to answer on the grounds that it may incriminate me.
>
> Mr. Kennedy: How about Las Vegas? Have you any interests in any gambling casinos?
>
> Mr. Catena: I respectfully decline to answer on the grounds that it may incriminate me.

Investigations showed that Catena was financing investments in Cuban casinos from the proceeds of his Las Vegas operations. That all came to an end when Fidel Castro took over in 1959. Fidel closed the casinos, and many mobsters fled back to the US. Although Castro reopened casinos, American tourism ground to a halt and the mob's investments were lost. One informant told the FBI that he heard Catena, Zwillman, and Stacher lost a combined $4 million.

Post-Havana, mob figures increased their investments and presence in Las Vegas. With the expansion of gaming, increased law enforcement attention fell on some casino investors and operators. They started hearing Catena's name pop up in the news about some of the popular resort hotels. There were a lot of stories.

An informant told the FBI that Catena, Stacher, and Zwillman controlled the Sands and Horseshoe casinos. Another reported that "Catena, Richie Boiardo, Angelo 'Gyp' DeCarlo, Vincent Alo, and Sam Giancana, all mob leaders, were said to own pieces of the Horseshoe, Fremont, and Sands in Las Vegas."[1] One informant relayed that Catena, Gyp DeCarlo, and Anthony Boiardo received a regular "shipment of money"[2] from the Sands, Fremont, and Horseshoe casinos. Yet another informant told the FBI that "almost all of the gambling casinos take their orders from Meyer Lansky and Joseph 'Doc' Stacher."[3] Wherever the authorities looked, Jersey crime figures were there. After the death of Zwillman, Catena took over Longie's shares in some of the casinos and was thought to have "indisputable authority over the disposal of profits ad the employment of persons in critical positions."[4]

The Fremont was the primary casino where Catena, Zwillman, and Stacher had a significant presence. Located on Fremont Street in downtown Las Vegas, the Fremont Hotel and Casino was opened on May 18, 1956. The hotel towered over the cityscape. It was the first downtown high-rise. It was also the tallest building in Nevada at the time. The fourteen-story building cost over $6 million to design and construct. With over 140 guest rooms, a health club, and even a radio station (KSHO-TV) headquartered in the hotel, the Fremont was the height, no pun intended, of Vegas resorts downtown, as they tried to compete with the burgeoning Strip properties.

The Fremont was overseen at the time by Ed Levinson, a one-time gambling figure who had a close relationship with Meyer Lansky and Moe Dalitz. Levinson operated gambling enterprises in Detroit, Kentucky, and South Florida before relocating and investing in Las Vegas, where he became one of the original investors and casino managers of the Sands casino on the nascent Las Vegas Strip. With additional investors and a Teamsters Central States Pension Fund loan, Levinson started designing the Fremont Hotel in 1954.

Levinson was an interesting character in his own right, easily inserting himself into local politics. He had ties to various characters who moved around the edges of national politics at the time, like lobbyist Fred Black. Despite Levinson's affinity for politicians and influential business associates, he had a particular disdain for law enforcement, especially the FBI, which seemed to be watching Levinson's activities at the Fremont. He once told a Las Vegas City Commissioner that he thought one particular FBI agent who had questioned Levinson was "a no good s.o.b." and that Levinson "had him in a chair one time and I let him up. The next time I get him in chair he is not going to get up."[5] The FBI construed this as a threat, bringing even more heat on Levinson.

Levinson and some partners also invested in the Horseshoe Club across Fremont Street. At the time, the Horseshoe was owned by Joe Brown, who took it over from Benny Binion due to Binion's impending federal prison sentence. By 1957, Binion was out of prison but unable to get a casino license due to his felony conviction. He was still involved with the Horseshoe, but Brown was the owner on paper. Brown's health declined, so he decided to sell to the Fremont Hotel ownership team. Harry "Spinach" Coppersmith was reportedly sent to Las Vegas by Catena to oversee some of his investments. Coppersmith was set up in the Horseshoe.

Another partner in the ownership of the Fremont was Lester Sigelbaum, a Philly-born Miami resident who moved to Vegas to work in the gaming industry. Like Levinson, Sigelbaum was heavily involved in the gaming industry and comfortable associating with the various underworld elements. Sigelbaum also leveraged his political contacts into various business interests in the Washington D.C. sphere, including Levinson and ties to lobbyists and lawyers.

Edward "Eddie" Torres had an interest in the Fremont as well. Eddie was just at the start of his career in the gaming industry. He would eventually become the head of several casinos on the Strip and downtown Vegas. Torres was connected to Levinson and Sigelbaum in oil fields in Ohio and racetracks. Sigelbaum and Levinson were also partners in the Exchange and Investment Bank of Geneva, Switzerland. Their connections to the Swiss banking scene connected with Meyer Lansky's interests in Geneva and Jimmy Hoffa's associates.

Jerry Catena was in the middle of a complex web of relationships and associations. These were the business connections that Catena thrived on. He didn't waste his time working with lower-level employees or bothering with any street rackets in Vegas. Catena was playing at a higher level, and Vegas was the right kind of town to do that.

The skim was the main moneymaker for organized crime in Las Vegas then. What was the skim, exactly? The skim, in essence, was the theft of casino proceeds before that money was recorded in the casino's books. During this time, when operators were dealing with coin-operated machines and cash at the table games, there was little to no tracking of how much money was exchanged on the floor. The Gaming Commission was not keeping tabs on the money; rather, they were more interested in ensuring the casino was not cheating customers and that the games were on the up and up. This lack of oversight of the money flow allowed organized crime to quietly divert millions of dollars from the casino's coffers to their own pockets.

The skim was based on the amount of money coming into the casino. The more people came through the doors, the more money the mob could skim off the proceeds. That led to some of the amenities and customer service practices that symbolized the fabled golden era "when the mob ran Vegas." Like most nostalgia-drenched beliefs, there is a recurring theme in this age of mega-resorts controlled by public corporations who are often accused of nickel-and-diming customers that things were better when the gang ran the casinos. That belief stems from the general practices back in the day. The main goal of a casino is to keep the gambler playing. To the mob, wanting to maximize their skim, the longer a player sits, the more money they lose. So you offer free food, free drinks, tickets to a show, a free room for the night, transportation to the airport, and other, more carnal, favors.

Legend has it that Benny Binion was the first to introduce comps to casinos, but the mob had been running illegal gambling palaces and back-room card games for decades at that point. They honed the art of customer care and collection. They brought that acumen to Las Vegas. Another thing they brought was the idea that games should be honest. One of the early gambling issues that nearly cost the mob their interest in Havana casinos was the rampant cheating at many of the hotels. Meyer Lansky spearheaded the effort in Havana to clean games up, which translated over to Las Vegas by not only the mob and their operator associates but also from the founding of the Casino Control Commission in 1959.

When run right, casinos rake in substantial sums of cash. The mob tried to steal as much as they could without attracting the attention of gaming regulators or the FBI. Whether it was coins or cash, when the money came off the floor, it went to a counting room in the back of the casinos. There, the mob had two sets of books set up to track the money. They took the skim off the top, then recorded the remainder as the casino's profit. A few times, the skim takers were a bit aggressive, and they couldn't make payroll. They had to send money back on the floor to run through the table games and slots, back into the counting room.

From the counting room, the bag men would take the skim out, literally walking right out with hundreds of thousands of dollars in bags to be distributed across the country, depending on who was in charge of the skim at certain hotels. At the height of the skim in the 1960s, families from New Jersey, New York, Chicago, Detroit, St. Louis, and Kansas City had their hands in the till. But some of the largest drops were sent to Jerry Catena and Meyer Lansky. Couriers were dispatched to Miami and Newark's delis, restaurants, and back rooms to deliver the money that stayed in the States. The rest was stuffed into luggage and flown overseas into Swiss bank accounts at the Banque de Credit.

Catena and his partners, especially Meyer Lansky, worked with some of the casino operators to ensure maximum return from the skim. At the Fremont, Levinson and Ed Torres were caught on tape discussing the possibility of issuing dividends to Catena and Lansky to reduce the amount of skim coming from the Fremont Hotel operations. In 1966, the FBI Los Angeles field office began an investigation into illegal gambling, focusing on fellow Genovese mobsters Vincent Alo and Tony Salerno. They noted in a report to the grand jury that Catena was receiving regular payments from the skim at the Fremont Hotel.

An FBI informant described a meeting where Levinson and Torres packaged up the skim for delivery to Meyer Lansky and Catena. "At this meeting, approximately $123,500 was packaged for delivery to Meyer Lansky in Miami, Florida. $42,500 of the above sum was scheduled for delivery to Gerardo Catena in Newark, New Jersey. According to the informant, the package of money would be shipped directly to Florida, divided, and Richard Kornick would then take the sum due to the Catena group and deliver it to unknown parties in New York City, New York."[6]

Gyp DeCarlo was overheard on a wiretap discussing how Catena alone received over $150,000 a month from all the Vegas skim action he was involved with. DeCarlo also made an interesting comment that further illuminated the intertwining relationship between Catena and Jewish organized crime in the wake of the death of Longie Zwillman. DeCarlo asserted that it was his belief that upon Zwillman's death, Catena, Doc Stacher, and Meyer Lansky split up Zwillman's extensive holdings in Vegas among the three of them, not bringing in anyone else to share the spoils.

The Horseshoe was another valuable skim operation, also tied to Ed Levinson. Levinson's group sold their 65 percent interest in Horseshoe back to Benny's son Jack, who had started buying back stock in Horseshoe after being granted a casino license in 1961. Levinson was overheard on a wiretap saying that at the time of the sale in 1964, the skim was over $700,000 a year, much of that going to Catena and Lansky.

In the early 1960s, the FBI began an operation known as Vegmon (Vegas Money) that sought to uncover the methodology utilized by the mob to skim money from the various Vegas casinos where they had influence. By then, the skim was already netting the mob a significant amount of money, especially Catena. "Jerry's share was all for him, and it was millions,"[7]

Catena had been getting some skim from his Vegas interests for almost twenty years. In the 1940s, Kartzman's Deli in Newark served as a drop spot for Longie Zwillman's Vegas profits. Documentary filmmaker Michael Weissman interviewed the owner of Kartzman's who recalled a regular delivery of two boxes of cash. Zwillman would come in and pick up one, and Catena would pick up the other. Zwillman and Catena's bagman for their Fremont skim was a New York City theatrical producer who arranged entertainment for many of the casinos and hotels in Vegas. He would bring cash to the deli on his return to New York.

The Sands skim was initially under the control of Frank Costello, through the involvement of Doc Stacher. After Costello's shooting and subsequent retirement, control moved to Vito Genovese, then to Jerry Catena. This was confirmed by an informant who told the FBI that he overheard Sands owner Carl Cohen say that Catena had control over the New York portion of the casino's skim. The FBI was also tracking Cohen. In September 1963, Cohen was overheard planning a trip to New York City to meet with Catena, among others, to discuss future plans for The Sands.

Stacher was hands-on when it came to protecting his investments in the Sands. He was protective of the men who were aligned with him. One was a

Newark gambler named Charles Turner, who was sent to Vegas back in the early 1950s. "Abner Zwillman, Joseph Stacher, and Jerry Catena combine sent Charles Turner, Aaron Weisberg, and Myron Friedman to Las Vegas, to look after their interests."[8] Catena had Turner move over to the Sands to work with Carl Cohen. Turner received a 2 percent stake in the casino to help oversee things on behalf of Catena and Stacher.

One time, Carl Cohen was frustrated with Turner and fired him. When Doc Stacher found out, he was incensed. He arranged a meeting at the Sands with Cohen and "nearly tore Cohen apart verbally and asked Cohen who in 'hell' did he think he was to fire a man like Turner? He was then instructed to go to Turner, get down on his knees, and apologize."[9] Cohen did apologize and put Turner back on the payroll.

Jerry Catena was not the only Genovese member active there. Gyp DeCarlo outlined, to the ever-listening FBI, his position in the Desert Inn and the Stardust. He said that the Cleveland mob held fifty-five points in the Desert Inn and sixty points in the Stardust and that they received about $120,000 from all their points combined, as their take from the skim. He calculated each point's value as worth $1,800 in the skim. DeCarlo also had a 2 percent interest in the Horseshoe and received about $2,000 a month from Gene Catena, DeCarlo's share of the Horseshoe skim.

Gyp DeCarlo also lamented that he was persona non grata in Las Vegas, likely due to his profile in the underworld in New Jersey. He was asked not to go out there, but evidently his name was tossed around by others to gain clout.

Don't you think I'd like to go to Vegas? I got strict orders to stay out of Vegas. Everybody else has been to Vegas but me. And my name is shot around in Vegas more than anybody's. Every jerk that goes out there from around here uses my name. They don't use Jerry Catena's. They're afraid to use Jerry Catena's.[10]

Unaware that the FBI was wiretapping him, it's perhaps a small bit of luck for the mob that DeCarlo stayed out of Las Vegas at that time. The FBI would have certainly gained even more insight into the inner workings of the skim and other underworld operations.

DeCarlo also gave information that even into the 1960s, Jerry Catena and Meyer Lansky were taking money from the original mob casino, The Flamingo. This was supported by FBI intel that Catena had shares in a number of casinos including The Flamingo, from which he was receiving up to $48,000 a month.

> DeCarlo: Jerry's got an income bigger than anyone around, except Meyer Lansky. Meyer owns more in Vegas than anybody—than all of ours put together. He's got a piece of every joint in Vegas. They were over in New York about a week ago, I hear, Jerry and Meyer, and Blue Eyes (Vincent Alo). They were cutting up the pie from that joint out there—the joint that they're robbing all the money out of What's the name of it?
> Russo: The Flamingo?
> DeCarlo: The Flamingo, that's it![11]

The Genovese family was aware that the feds were looking into the skimming operations. One way the FBI traced the skim was marking money in some of the casinos, then tracing to see where that money showed up.

> The last money they gave us they said "don't spend this money around, go and change it someplace." We gave it to Panels[12] to put in the craps game and take the other money out of the crap game. That's how close they're trying to check us—if I went in a bank and got small money for, say $3,000 of twenties, and the whole $3,000 showed up in a bank here in Orange or something. That's what they're looking for. You think they're stupid? They're not so stupid. Intelligence department is very smart.[13]

In September 1963, The Sand's vice president Carl Cohen filed a lawsuit against the phone company, alleging that the company allowed the FBI to install electronic listening devices in the Sands. In an internal FBI memo from September 9, 1963, the feds lamented, "The use of microphone coverage in criminal intelligence cases is one of our strongest weapons against organized crime. It is disgraceful that leaks to the hoodlums have imperiled the use of this technique. We cannot afford a further leak."[14]

Ed Levinson tried the same tactic, suing the FBI for $4.2 million, charging them with invasion of privacy for installing a listening device in the Fremont. The feds noted that Catena was still one of the hidden owners and taking in a substantial "salary" from the skim.

In May 1967, federal authorities caught up with some of Catena's skim handlers, including Ed Levinson and Edward Torres. They were charged with conspiring to skim money from the Fremont and Riviera casinos. Nowhere in the indictment did it mention Catena. However, it was apparent from FBI comments that they believed there was a significant organized crime influence over the operation of the skim. From their perspective, this case could open the door to further inroads against the mob in Las Vegas.

The case against Levinson, Torres, and the others started a couple of years prior when a federal grand jury convened to investigate the gaming industry. They interviewed over a hundred witnesses, including Frank Sinatra. They ended up indicting Levinson and Torres. But Levinson knew where they received the information about the skim at the Fremont. It was from an illegal wiretap. Levinson sued the FBI.

After agreeing to enter a no-contest plea to the skim charges and pay a $5,000 fine, Levinson dropped the lawsuit against the feds. Torres and the others had all the charges against them dismissed. Jerry Catena must have breathed a sigh of relief. The skim was still on, and Torres moved on from the Fremont and became president of the Riviera, on the Strip.

Catena was also tied to the newest casino resort on the Strip. The opulent Caesars Palace opened on August 5, 1966. The day before, however, bad publicity spread courtesy of an article in *The Chicago Sun-Times*, which was picked up by wire services and appeared in newspapers nationwide. It was alleged that Sam Giancana, New England Mafia boss Raymond Patriarca, and Jerry Catena each owned 10 percent of the casino. The report went on further to add that Catena was getting at least $100,000 monthly from his portion of the skim. This revelation caused the Nevada Gaming Commission to dig into matters. After two weeks, they investigated the claims and still had not concluded. But the rumors persisted, especially because Caesars was built with the Teamsters' loan.

Although Vegas continued to be a moneymaker for Catena, he also had to deal with his crime family business back in New Jersey. Even as a successful and legitimate businessman, Jerry Catena was about to encounter an issue with one of his brother's businesses that broke one of the mob's mythical rules: they only kill themselves.[15]

12

Best Sales

Eugene Catena was one of Jerry Catena's closest confidants. One frequent topic in wiretapped conversations of Genovese family members in the 1960s was how much influence Gene had with Jerry. They all agreed that Jerry delegated a lot of business decisions and negotiations, especially with labor-related matters, to Gene. He, however, did not enjoy universal acclaim from his fellow underworld compatriots. Gene flat out rubbed some in the Genovese family the wrong way. "I can't stomach his brother at all. Jerry, I can stomach a little because he never took me too much, but the other rat, I can't even stomach him. . . . If you ever hung around Gene for three months you gotta dislike him. You gotta hate him."[1]

Eugene took over Jerry's crew when Jerry was appointed acting boss after Genovese's incarceration. He made the rounds introducing himself to other mob bigwigs in New Jersey, even speaking to Sam DeCavalcante, "I'm a caporegime who's always available. My people know where to find me or where or how they can reach me."[2]

Some of Gene's top soldiers included his longtime friend Johnny "Coca Cola" Lardiere. Eugene and Lardiere were extremely close, shown together in many family photos at social events and spending time with each other's families. The Pecora brothers, Joseph "Joe Peck," Thomas "Timmy Murphy," and Edward, were valued crew members due in part to their extensive ties to unions. Joe Pecora was a secretary and treasurer for Teamsters Local 863 in Newark. Thomas Pecora was the Maintenance Division head of Teamsters Local 97 in Newark, New Jersey. One of the senior crew members was Pete LaPlaca, Willie Moretti's one-time chauffeur, bodyguard, and in-law; LaPlaca's son was married to Moretti's daughter.

Eugene owned Best Sales Company, on Clinton Avenue in Newark, a block across from Longie Zwillman's old headquarters at the Riveria Hotel. Gene and Jerry owned the building, but it was not in their name. A real estate office nearby, operated by James Marsillo, was the owner on paper. Marsillo was integral to several real estate holdings and properties that the Catena brothers owned.

To set up their food brokerage business, the Catenas sought the assistance of Joseph Lordi, a former Essex County prosecutor who now practices law privately. The Catena brothers and Lordi had a longstanding relationship from their days as prosecutors. There was evidence that Lordi was placed in his initial role as assistant prosecutor by the mob, specifically the Catena brothers. In 1961, Gyp DeCarlo was caught on wiretap complaining about how Lordi acted as prosecutor.

> I'll tell you if he (Lordi) sends for me I'm going to tell Jerry that. I'll say, "Now wait a minute, Jerry, you and Gene OK'd this guy." Because Little Joe (Debenedictis, Newark democratic leader) came to me and asked me "Is it alright to put this guy in? Gene and Jerry vouched for him. . . . You know who put him in, Jerry and Gene Catena."[3]

The Catenas used Lordi's role to assist one of their associates in getting a gun permit. When Lordi was on the State Beverage Commission, he brought on a bartender from the Old Colonial Inn in Newark. Gene and Jerry's brother Frank operated the Old Colonial Inn. Frank was also a made member of the Genovese family, although only a soldier. He was relatively under the radar regarding media attention, save for a few mentions. When he was involved in a major car accident in 1965 after hiding some ice and skiing into a concrete barrier, he was identified as a bar owner (he had some minor injuries, but the car was totaled).

The Lordi connection was one of many political ties that Jerry Catena cultivated over the years through his legitimate business interests as well as his back-room golf club meetings. Like his mentors in the underworld, Jerry knew the benefit of good political protection and connections.

Dominick A. Spina, the Newark Police Director, was one such public official under the influence of the Mafia. Wiretaps caught conversations between Gyp DeCarlo (R), Sam DeCavalcante (S), and Tony Boiardo (T) about their relationship and the mob's need for police protection to continue operating.

> T: You know Dick (Spina) asked me "Why don't you and Ray get together and open up"? I said "what is there to open up."
>
> S: You know Tony thirty to thirty-five years ago if an—was even seen talking to a cop they looked to hit him the next day. They figured he must be doing business with the cop.
>
> R: Today if you don't meet them and pay them you can't operate.
>
> T: The only guy I handle is Dick (Spina). Gino Farina and the guys handle the rest of the law. About seven or eight years ago I used to handle them all.[4]

The Catena brothers' influence extended to other members of the Newark Police Department. When Gene received a tip that some of their gambling places would be raided, he reached out to a couple of cops on their payroll. It was too late to stop the raid, but afterwards, one of their in-house officers got rid of all the evidence.

Other politicians that were part of Catena's network of officials were State Police Superintendent Dominick Capello, Hudson County Democratic leader John V. Kenny (who was also close to Bayonne Joe Ziccarelli, a Bonanno mobster who oversaw Hudson County rackets), and Middlesex County politician David T. Wilentz.

Another politician who had close ties to the Genovese family, including Catena, was Hugh Addonizio, who was Newark's mayor from 1962 to 1970. DeCarlo talked about Hugh as well. "I told Jerry I ain't going to see Dick no more for nothing and I ain't going to see Hughey no more for nothing. They're all going to wind up in the can, Dick Spina and Hughey and everybody. Jerry said every human being in Newark knows about what's going on."[5]

In 1961, Addonizio was running for mayor against city councilman Mickey Bontempo. DeCarlo was concerned that Bontempo would split the Italian vote, leaving Addonizio vulnerable to losing. At that point, Catena and a fellow Newark mobster invested thousands into Addonizio's campaign. DeCarlo was able to convince Bontempo to step aside, leaving only one rival for the mayoral election.

DeCarlo pressed the mob for even more contributions. He took money from Tony Bananas Caponigro, Joe the Indian Polverino, William Rega, and Jerry Catena, who ponied up $25,000 for Addonizio. In the end, Hugh won the mayoral election, and for the next eight years, the mob had a friendly face in City Hall. A friendly face in City Hall meant a lot to the mob. There was selective law enforcement, targeting of competitors, and a business-friendly official who could sway important zoning and business license decisions in favor of businesses owned by mobsters.

While the Catena brothers were diving deeper into local and state politics, Gene's Best Sales business was growing. In 1961, William Pieroni, owner of Pieroni Foods Inc., an Italian food company in Massachusetts, owed money to Johnny H. Williams, a.k.a. John Guglielmo, a Revere-based crime figure who was close to Phil Buccola, one-time boss of the New England Mafia family, led by Raymond Patriarca in the 1960s.

Pieroni traveled to Newark and met with Gene in a Newark restaurant. Gene told Pieroni that he could line up several customers for his products, all for 5 percent commission on all sales. Pieroni began visiting Newark regularly, meeting with Gene and others, including Joe Pecora and Irving Kaplan, head of the Meat Cutters union. Pieroni was taken to supermarkets across New Jersey, and whenever he mentioned Gene's name, the managers would place an order. After a few months, Pieroni's company was still on shaky financial ground, and Catena seemed to have moved on to a new customer base. Pieroni was later called as a witness in a probe surrounding Gene Catena and Best Sales, When asked about his meetings with Catena, Kaplan, and Pecora, Pieroni replied, "I don't have enough life insurance."[6] Best Sales moved on from Pieroni, but soon found another firm to work with, the North American Chemical Company, headquartered at 22 Mercer Street in Paterson, New Jersey.

North American and its subsidiary Ecology manufactured soaps and detergents for retail markets. Ecolo-G and Bohack were the two primary brands of detergent manufactured by the North American Chemical Company. North American's president, Nathan Sobol, was introduced to Gene Catena through an old army buddy. Sobol was looking for a broker to help sell their detergents and approached Gene about representing their detergents. After some negotiation, they signed an agreement on October 3, 1963. Generally, the firm signed a contract with a thirty- or ninety-day cancellation clause, but Gene forced them to sign a ten-year no-cancellation contract. Best Sales was going to be paid $2,100 a month for the length of the contract. When pressed by federal investigators about why they chose Best Sales, Nathan Sobol had few answers.

The Chairman: Before you entered into the agreement, did you make any attempt to determine Best Sales Co.'s capability to promote or sell your company's products?

Mr. Sobol: No sir, I did not.

The Chairman: Did you inquire about the number of agents, subagents, or salesmen they had around the country?

Mr. Sobol: No sir, I did not.

The Chairman: Did you ask for the size of their advertising budget?

Mr. Sobol: No sir, I did not.

. . .

Mr. Chairman: Did you ever inspect their financial statement?

Mr. Sobol: No, I did not.

Mr. Chairman: Did you ever look at them?

Mr. Sobol: No, I did not.

Mr Chairman: You never asked to do that, did you?

Mr. Sobol: No, I never did.[7]

There was an issue with the detergents, however. They were labeled phosphate-free, but their chemical combination made them highly alkaline. Quick chemistry lesson—phosphates were traditionally added to detergents to bind with calcium and magnesium ions, basically softening hard water and enhancing the cleaning ability of the detergents. Phosphate-free detergents were introduced in the 1960s and most tested at the time, except for North American Chemical's two detergents, were safe. Both Ecolo-G and Bohack, however, were found "to be toxic, corrosive to intact skin, and the cause of severe eye irritation."[8] They also did not clean that well.

So Gene was stuck with detergent that didn't work well and was potentially caustic. It's unclear whether he knew that or not. Gene knew that he needed to get the detergents into stores and off the shelves. He initially approached local supermarkets in northern New Jersey. By effective persuasion, Gene would get them to stock North American Chemical's detergents. He first reached out to the Pecora brothers and other union contacts in Teamsters Local 863 and the Amalgamated Meatcutters and Butchers Workmen Union, which the Catena brothers had amassed over the years. Gene planned to use unions within the supermarkets to apply subtle pressure to individual stores and regional managers to stock the detergents on their shelves. This would also offer a bit of a buffer between Gene and the union workers.

North American's profits almost doubled in the first year. The local markets, gently persuaded by union members, were sure to keep the orders coming for the detergent, even if the product was substandard and potentially toxic. The managers of these stores knew who was behind the sales push and knew that they had little choice but to comply.

The detergent campaign's initial success delighted Gene. He saw that getting the detergent into a national chain was the way to take things to the next level. He reached out and set up meetings with the Great Atlantic and Pacific Tea company, known as A&P. This was a huge step up for Gene. A&P was one of the largest supermarket chains in the country and would be a huge windfall for North American and Best Sales.

A&P, however, was not sold on the detergents. They did some independent testing and saw that the products did not work, not to mention the potential health effects on users. The supermarket company was not going to put the detergents on the shelf, so Gene was forced to devise a more straightforward method: strong-arming the company into carrying the products. Gene was overheard telling fellow mobsters that he would take A&P down.

Shortly after hearing the bad news from A&P, an A&P store in Yonkers was firebombed. The store was destroyed. At that time, there wasn't much evidence pointing to Best Sales. There were other firebombs, in Peekskill in June 1964 and in Manhattan in August 1964, with a Bronx store bombed right afterwards. The campaign of intimidation and terror was in full swing, but A&P did not change its mind.

Gene also used his union contacts to pressure A&P from another angle. The butchers' union was negotiating a new contract. They put in some new demands, which A&P balked at. The butchers told the company that the union would go on strike if they did not sign the new deal. Catena got the Teamsters to agree to support the butchers' union and not cross any picket lines should the butchers choose to go on strike.

Even with that, A&P still did not budge. Things came to a head in early 1965 with a rarity in the underworld, the targeting of non-organized crime associates for murder. On January 23, 1965, James Walsh was gunned down on a Brooklyn Street. He was shot four times, with .22 and .32 caliber pistols. Walsh was the assistant manager of a store in Brooklyn.

On February 5, 1965, A&P manager John Mossner was shot three times with a .22 caliber gun when he arrived home from work on a Friday evening. The store that Mossner managed, on Southview Avenue in the Bronx, had been firebombed three times. Mossner was getting some groceries from the back of his car when the gunman walked up the driveway and approached Mossner. The gunman fired a warning shot into the garage. Mossner then followed the gunman back down the driveway and the gunman opened fire. Mossner was hit twice above the right eye and once in the head. He fell face down on the driveway. The gunman ran to a waiting car and sped off.

Police initially ruled out a connection between the two murders. But the store fires, coupled with the murders, did not go unnoticed at A&P corporate headquarters. The company reached out to the Justice Department. The FBI did a thorough investigation and came back with the link between Gene Catena, Best Sales, and the pattern of terror targeting the A&P stores.

Robert Morgenthau, New York's U.S. Attorney, brought Jerry Catena to a grand jury to grill him about his ties to Best Sales. Jerry did not want to be associated with the growing issue, and although he only appeared for a few questions in front of the grand jury, that was enough for him. Jerry ordered things with A&P to stop. There were no more firebombs or murders.

The A&P fires were devastating to the company, costing the chain over $1.7 million over four years, extending from Yonkers, Peekskill, Long Island, Mount Vernon, and New York City out to Secaucus, New Jersey. But after the FBI became involved, things stopped. North American Chemical wanted to terminate the relationship with Best Sales, but Gene Catena requested that they pay him $245,000 a year for the length of the contract. North American agreed, likely not wanting to offend Catena after what transpired with the A&P stores.

The Best Sales debacle was very uncharacteristic of how Jerry had conducted business. The killings, the firebombing, this was not the usual MO, which begs the question as to how much Jerry was in the loop as to what his brother was doing. According to his attorney, one of the only times he ever saw Jerry raise his voice was when he chewed out his brother Gene for Best Sales and the ensuing bad publicity. Jerry was livid that Gene let things get so bad. Although Jerry was aware of the deal, it seems he was dealing with other matters and left Gene on his own with Best Sales. Killing store managers with no ties to organized crime was not how Jerry did business. And although Jerry was not directly involved with Best Sales, his name became wrapped up in all the news stories about the company.

In February 1967, after the Best Sales episode, the Justice Department announced a new initiative against organized crime that specifically examined its investments in legitimate businesses. The Justice Department named Jerry and Gene Catena its top two priority targets in New Jersey. But Gene would not be around to appear before any investigative body.

Gene was sick. He was diagnosed with cancer, and it advanced quickly. Gene Catena died on August 2, 1967, and was buried on August 4th in Morris County. Federal agents were outside the funeral services and noted that a couple of cars belonging to Local 464 of the Amalgamated Meatcutters Union of East Orange were at the services. Less than two weeks later, the same cars were present at Gene's daughter's wedding in South Orange.

Mob business does not pause for a funeral. The day before he buried his brother, Jerry was seen at a meeting on Bloomfield Avenue, with Richie the Boot and Joseph "Newsboy" Moriarty, an Irish Jersey City racketeer who operated large-scale numbers operations in Hudson County. In the summer of 1967, Boiardo sold Newsboy his operations in Hudson County. But Jerry was getting increasingly frustrated with Boiardo. The Boot was slowing down but was not giving up his crew and position in the family; Jerry told him to step it up or step down. Boiardo acquiesced. He repurchased his numbers game from Newsboy and told Jerry he would take a more hands-on approach to running his crew. Boiardo, though, was not happy, telling some of his crew that he felt that he "has done enough for the organization over the years and he should now be able to take it easy."[9]

After Eugene's death, his crew was placed under Pete "Lodi Pete" La Placa, a longtime member of the crime family and respected throughout New Jersey. LaPlaca's appointment shifted the crew's seat of power from Newark to Bergen County, back to Willie Moretti's old stomping ground. Jerry had a close relationship with LaPlaca, dating back to their days under Willie Moretti, and trusted that Pete would be a trustworthy and capable leader. Jerry needed capos that he could leave to their own devices. He didn't want to worry about the day-to-day actions of the crews.

During this time, Jerry was part of one of the more unusual mob cases. In September 1967, a Los Angeles grand jury convened to investigate card cheating at the renowned Friars Club of Beverly Hills. The Friars Club, a midcentury architectural gem on Little Santa Monica, was a celebrity hangout known for its poker games. Under the direction of mobster Johnny Roselli, peepholes in the club were used to observe players' cards and relay their hands to others, fleecing some of the celebrity guests for thousands of dollars.

Jerry was among those subpoenaed to testify before the grand jury, which was also investigating organized crime operations in the state. Jerry was not involved in the Friars Club, so there was a sense that he was being brought in to answer questions under immunity that could be used for prosecutors in New Jersey. Jerry flew out to Los Angeles with his attorney, Chris Franzblau. They rented a suite at the Beverly Hills Hotel.

Franzblau explained to Jerry that the Assistant Los Angeles U.S. Attorney would only ask him a few questions that did not cover anything criminal, hence no need for granting immunity. Jerry did not just take the Assistant U.S. Attorney's word. He discussed his strategy at length with Franzblau, who later recalled how methodical Jerry was in his approach to answering the questions. Jerry thought on every decision he made, weighing the risks of not answering the questions versus responding to them and having his answers come back to bite him. Jerry decided to testify. It turned out to be a lot of nothing. Jerry answered ten questions and was out of the court within the hour.

After Jerry's appearance, he and Franzblau returned to their suite at the Beverly Hills Hotel. They were surprised to see Moe Dalitz sitting there when they walked in. Jerry, who had known Moe for years, was happy to see his old friend. Moe asked how Jerry's appearance went and invited them down to the La Costa Hotel and Spa near San Diego, which Moe owned. Jerry and his lawyer drove down and stayed for a few days to golf with Jerry's Bally partner, Sam Klein, and actor Kirk Douglas.

The Genovese family had long had control of Port Newark, one of the busiest ports in the United States. Through control of the Port and its ancillary businesses and the unions that served the Port, the Genovese family brought millions into the family's coffers through labor racketeering, hijacking of goods, shakedowns, as well as offering illegal gambling and loansharking services to the thousands of port workers. Jerry stood out for his influence through the unions and trucking companies that serviced the docks. "Catena wields almost absolute power over unions along Port Newark and Port Elizabeth."[10]

Port and federal officials saw the New Jersey ports as the most valuable racket the mob had. And by targeting the mob's activities there, they believed they could rid the port of mob influence. "The most effective way to assault Catena's organized criminal empire is to eliminate and keep out of the waterfront areas his most trusted underlings who carry on the daily business of policy, bookmaking, and loansharking."[11] However, it would be another decade before a significant operation was directed at the ports. For now, Catena and many of the unions he influenced, like Local 560 Teamsters, led by Anthony "Tony Pro" Provenzano, were integral to the Genovese family's coffers and operated with relative impunity. There were occasional hearings into crime at the ports, spearheaded by the Waterfront Commission of New York. But even that entity was not immune to Jerry Catena's political influence.

In 1968, State Assemblyman C. Richard Fiore, the chair of the State Assembly Committee on Law and Public Safety, found himself under scrutiny when it was revealed that he had personally lobbied the Waterfront Commission of New York to reinstate the longshoreman work permit for Johnny "Coca Cola" Lardiere. Fiore was spotted with Lardiere at the Old Colonial Inn, although he maintained he was only looking out for one of his constituents.

There were some union leaders with whom Jerry had trouble. One way that Jerry could curry favor with both businesses and unions was to work out deals to guarantee labor peace rather than the union going on strike. Usually, the company that was threatened with a strike would pay Jerry a fee for negotiating the deal, and Jerry would kick back some to the head of the local union. One example of a union leader who did not go along with this scheme was the president of the Retail Clerks Union, Local 1262 in Newark. When the new union president took over in 1964, he was often calling strikes "which interfere with the labor peace that the Catena Group has 'guaranteed.'"[12] Jerry used his influence to silently oust the president and install a new one they could control better. And one that would run things quietly without drawing attention.

The Best Sales debacle had given Jerry Catena unwanted press. The last thing he needed was exposure on a national level. That was the last thing any mob boss wanted. In 1967, one of the stranger chapters in organized crime history unfolded. *Life* magazine published an article entitled "Brazen History of Organized Crime." They included a map showing the heads of all the families across the United States. One of the men shown, Joe Cerrito, boss of the San Jose Mafia, was incensed. He had a finely crafted public image as a successful car dealership owner, although underneath that, he was the head of a small crime family. He was outraged that *Life*'s article exposed his criminal position. He took the unusual step of suing the magazine for $7 million. An admirable action on Cerrito's part, to protect his legacy, but an unwise one for someone who was part of a national criminal enterprise.

As the case moved forward, depositions were held. *Life* decided to do two things to needle Cerrito. First, they published an article in the March 15, 1968 issue outlining Cerrito's business and crime ties. Second, their legal team issued subpoenas for several crime figures, including Carlo Gambino and Jerry Catena. This was not good for Cerrito. Even though he was a boss, he had very little power compared to someone like Gambino or Catena. The outside pressure must have been intense. After the first day of deposition, Cerrito's lawyer told the court that his client wanted to drop the case. Catena did not have to make the trip across the country and Cerrito walked away, tail between his legs.

Cerrito's profile in the underworld suffered greatly because of the lawsuit. Jerry was not pleased to have been brought into the middle of this. Jerry had avoided being charged with a crime for over thirty years at that point. However, changes in the law enforcement landscape in New Jersey were about to send waves of panic through the mob, bringing to light alliances between organized crime and politics in the Garden State. More importantly, it would lead to internal disruption within the Genovese family and throughout all seven of the Mafia families that operated in New Jersey.

13

The Real Boss

As 1968 was coming to a close, Jerry Catena continued "in the position of 'acting boss' of the Genovese 'family' during the absence of Vito Genovese who is presently incarcerated."[1] Under Catena, Eboli was still considered acting underboss and Michael Miranda was the consigliere. The capos included Benny Lombardo, Frank "Funzi" Tieri, Vincent Alo, Richie Boiardo, Antonio Carillo, Gyp DeCarlo, Peter De Feo, Cosmo Frasca, Vincenzo Generoso, Pasquale Eboli (who was acting capo for his brother), Thomas Greco, and Rocco Pellegrino. The hierarchy was relatively unchanged over the past few years, save for the death of Eugene Catena.

Despite conversations captured via wiretap showing dissatisfaction regarding Catena's leadership by Eboli, DeCarlo, and others, by the late 1960s, that discontent had fizzled out. Things in the Genovese family were stable, and Catena remained a steadfast leader while Vito Genovese languished in prison. And while Eboli complained that Catena capitulated to the demands of the other NY bosses, at the end of the decade, it did not really matter much. The Genovese family did not lose any ground in rackets or territory. Their leadership structure was constant, and unlike the Bonanno or Colombo families, there was little internal dissension. If there is anything that speaks to the support of Catena, it's that in the face of the complaints and whining from DeCarlo and others, there was never a serious discussion to make a move against Catena. Some of his capos and acting underboss may not have agreed with him on specific aspects of how he handled the family's business. Still, they respected him and the institution of La Cosa Nostra, allowing him to remain in power as acting boss.

However, like any leader of an organization, rapid changes in situations often come up when least expected. For Catena, in the aftermath of the Best Sales debacle and the loss of his brother, things in 1968 were starting to settle down. But then news started coming out of Leavenworth prison regarding the health of Vito Genovese. Vito had settled into prison life, attending mass and passing the time reading. He wasn't as active as he used to be. Decades of smoking had worn down his health. After only a few years in Leavenworth, he was transferred to the hospital wing, with emphysema and high blood pressure. It was clear that with appeals exhausted and his health declining, Genovese was not going to make it out alive. In January 1969, Genovese was transferred to the United States Medical Center for Federal Prisoners in Springfield, Missouri. The end was near.

Vito Genovese died on Valentine's Day, 1969. His funeral was held at the Anderson Funeral Home in Red Bank, New Jersey. Vito's body, clad in a dark gray business suit, lay in a heavily padded casket, the upright cover festooned with an elaborate rosary fashioned from rosebuds. Scarlet draperies served as a backdrop, flanked on either side by a dozen large floral sprays.[2] Outside the funeral home, there were almost as many reporters and police officers as curious onlookers. The newsmen and police were there to photograph the expected show of mob bosses and underlings. But they were disappointed. None of the major mob bosses nor the leadership of the Genovese family showed up for the wake, nor at the next morning service at St. Agnes Church in the Atlantic Highlands.

After the service at the church, the funeral procession drove over the Outerbridge Crossing, through Staten Island, over the Verrazano Narrows, and up to Vito's ultimate internment spot at St. John's Cemetery in the Middle Village neighborhood of Queens.[3]

Within days of Genovese's death, speculation began about who would succeed him. Jerry Catena was the obvious choice. The day after Genovese's death the *Herald-News'* front page headline read "Catena May Get Genovese Crown," already crowning Catena as the heir apparent to the throne. Tommy Eboli and Mike Miranda's names were also floated. Some news reports dismissed Eboli, noting that he was likely not in line due to "a serious cardiac condition, a surly disposition,"[4] and the fact that he was the target of several law enforcement probes. Eboli's popularity within the underworld was a subject that had come up throughout the 1960s on wiretaps, so it was not unlikely that he was looked at skeptically for taking over the top spot. Miranda also suffered from some serious health issues, so his ascension was questioned. Behind the scenes, the powerful Benny Lombardo lurked in the wings.

There was one rumor at the time regarding the boss of the Pittson/Scranton Mafia family, Russell Bufalino. He was driving Catena and Genovese's car when the police roadblock at Apalachin stopped them. William D'Elia, who succeeded Bufalino as boss when Russell passed away in 1994, came out with a book about his life. In it, he claimed that Bufalino was the acting boss of the Genovese family twice. Once after Genovese went to prison in 1959, and again after Genovese died in 1969. D'Elia also states that Eboli was the acting boss post-1959 and that he took over again for Bufalino post-Vito's death. Neither of these scenarios makes much sense, nor is there any evidence from law enforcement or thousands of hours of wiretap surveillance to support any of the assertions. Bufalino was a close ally of Vito Genovese and had ties to other Genovese powers like Tony Provenzano. But nowhere has it ever been recorded that he was acting boss of the family. Besides, simply being the boss of another, much smaller family, it would be highly unusual, if not unprecedented, for Bufalino to rise up and assume control over the vastly more prominent and more powerful Genovese family, especially with such a deep bench of talent.

There was another rumor that was picked up by newspapers after Vito's death, regarding another family boss vying to take control of the Genovese family. On March 1, 1969, fourteen members of the Kansas City Mafia, including the boss Nick Civella, arrived in Miami for vacation. They were met at the gate by FBI agents who handed them a subpoena to appear before a grand jury investigating organized crime. The press reported that Nick Civella and his brothers, Carl and Anthony, were in town for a meeting of top mobsters to determine the new boss of the Genovese family. The press erroneously reported that Carl Civella, Nick's brother, wanted the top job and was coming to town to lobby for the position, but the FBI quickly quashed that notion. "The Kansas City office has received no information to the effect that Carl James Civella is to replace Vito Genovese and it is believed that the information to that effect resulted from the erroneous statements made by the news media."[5]

The odds-on choice was Catena, as he had been the acting boss for the prior decade. Some early signs pointed in that direction. An FBI report stated that Catena would travel on March 1 for a meeting at Willow Springs, AZ, near Tucson. The FBI interpreted this as visiting the exiled Mafia boss Joe Bonanno. They also believed Catena had the backing of the other New York bosses.

According to a Gannett News Service report, federal authorities reported that Catena and other high-ranking members of the Genovese family took a cruise to Haiti in early April 1969, where they formally elected Jerry Catena as the official boss of the crime family. The news report noted that two days after the cruise, "Catena passed the word that he was reluctant to assume sole control of Genovese's rich criminal empire."[6] That was in keeping with Catena's overall ennui regarding being the boss of the family.

It's unclear whether this "Haiti cruise" ever occurred, as there is little official confirmation in law enforcement files. Gannett noted that "authorities were reluctant to reveal details of the cruise to Haiti other than to acknowledge that it occurred. They would not name who was on board, when the ship sailed, or give the port of departure."[7] But the FBI noted that Carlo Gambino was traveling to Miami in late March 1969, as was Tommy Eboli and Buster Aloi. Boss Joseph Colombo was in Puerto Rico and other mob bosses were observed to be traveling down to Florida. It was apparent that the FBI had tapped into their pool of informants to give them details about the cruise, and with the supporting evidence of travel, Jerry's election very well may have occurred this way.

However the official vote happened, it was clear to many that Catena was the boss after Genovese's death. "Since the death of Vito Genovese, the Genovese family has had a number of bosses, namely, . . . Gerard Catena."[8] New Jersey State Police also pegged Catena as Genovese's successor. An FBI report in late 1969 listed Catena as the boss, given the death of Vito Genovese. He was considered the heir apparent to the throne. Another report referenced two capos "in the Genovese Mafia family now headed by Gerardo (Jerry) Catena."[9] One article noted that Richie the Boot Boiardo was identified as "an underboss in the Cosa Nostra mob family headed by Gerardo 'Jerry' Catena."[10] An internal 1970 FBI report discussed Florida-based mobsters, including a Genovese member Emilio "The County" Delio, calling him a member of the Genovese family "operating in the direction of Gerardo Catena."[11] Some later mob figures, like eventual turncoat Genovese soldier George Barone, confirmed to the FBI in the early 2000s that Catena was the official boss after Vito Genovese died.

Authorities also observed an unusual visit to Catena's South Orange home a few weeks after Genovese's death. The FBI saw a middle-aged man, carrying a briefcase and silver-headed walking stick, enter Catena's home. Catena and the unknown man left Catena's home, "entered the vehicle, and drove to Catena's business establishment, Runyon Sales. They ran inside."[12] After fifteen minutes, the two went to Newark airport, where Catena dropped the man off. The man boarded a flight to Las Vegas. This could have been about the death of Genovese, or more likely the pickup of the casino skim. This aligns with the pattern of skim profits delivery. The FBI noted that the Las Vegas division believed Catena's visitor was none other than Catena's old partner at the Fremont, and then president of the Riviera Hotel, Ed Torres, who by that time had an interest in the Riviera on the Las Vegas Strip. This showed that even with Vito barely cold, Catena knew how to keep things running, especially if he would become the official boss.

Catena knew that being at the top of the pyramid made him even more of a target to law enforcement. And he was correct. Law enforcement attention came to a head at the start of 1970 for several reasons. The first investigation was into the alleged influence of the Mafia in the Newark office of the Internal Revenue Service. It centered on allegations that Philip Dameo was gifting IRS agents various items in return for favorable tax treatment.

On January 15, 1969, a Newark IRS auditor requested that IRS agent Patrick Ciambelli retrieve documents related to eleven specific names. These documents were related to a broader investigation into organized crime in New Jersey. The IRS's Organized Crime Division worked with the Justice Department's Organized Crime Strike Force. One of the names whose files they requested on January 15, 1969, was Phil Dameo. The IRS was unaware that three days prior, on January 12, 1969, Ciambelli attended Super Bowl III, between the New York Jets and the Baltimore Colts at the Orange Bowl in Miami, with Phil Dameo.

IRS agent Ciambelli realized that his relationship with Dameo might come to light so a few months later, he went in and explained that he knew Dameo socially. The IRS's Organized Crime Division already had information on the ties between the agent and Dameo. And they had the receipts: December 1968—attended a private party with Dameo at The Arch. January 8, 1969—lunch with Dameo. January 21, 1969—lunch with Dameo. February 19, 1969—lunch with Dameo. February 26, 1969—lunch with Dameo.

The investigation led to the dismissal of several agents assigned to the Newark office as well as the formation of a grand jury in January 1970 to investigate if there was any contact between the IRS and Jerry Catena. Although the grand jury probe did not ensnare Catena, it was not the last chance law enforcement would have at him that year.

Another investigation was out of Florida, where authorities were looking into the ownership of Central Landfill Inc., a company located in Miami Beach. Local authorities heard that the firm had mob connections from back in New Jersey. They discovered that two attorneys who were part of the ownership team of the firm had connections to the Catenas. One, Nicholas Marino, was married to Eugene Catena's daughter, while the other, Alfred Porro, attended that wedding. Authorities monitoring the calls from Catena's Boca Raton winter home noted that Catena called his nephew-in-law several times before the formation of Central Landfill Inc.

Another tie between Catena and Central Landfill was through the firm's president, James Ruzzo. One of Ruzzo's close associates was John DiGilio, then just "a member of the Gerardo Catena 'family.'" He eventually worked his way to becoming one of the Genovese family's most powerful figures in the ports of New Jersey.

This was followed by the revelation that Central Landfill Inc. was associated with a trucking firm from Quebec, Maislin Trucking. Canadian authorities confirmed that Maislin Trucking was a mob-fronted operation and that its public relations man was Vincent Cotroni. Cotroni was the boss of a powerful Calabrian crime family in Montreal that was part of the Bonanno crime family. Cotroni was a frequent visitor to South Florida.

All these revelations about Central Landfill Inc. did not slow down their movement into the waste management scene in South Florida. Before forming Central, Porro lobbied the City Council of Surfside, just up the road from Miami Beach, to operate their landfill. As negotiations, held outside of normal procurement procedures, developed, Surfside politicians became wary of the firm and the way in which the landfill operation agreement was coming to fruition.

Some in the city went ahead with a contract, signing one that gave Central Landfill control of the Surfside's landfill for fifty-nine months. If the contract was for sixty months, it would have to go to a referendum. Catena's name was prominent in the investigative reports, although ties between him and the company were tenuous. Even with information tying the president of Central Landfill to the Genovese family, Catena's name fell out of reports, and his ties to Central Landfill remained unconfirmed.

But while the IRS and Central Landfill investigations posed little threat to Catena, there was another dark cloud on his horizon, the State of New Jersey Commission of Investigation (SCI). In 1968, New Jersey convened the Joint Legislative Committee to Study Crime and the System of Criminal Justice in New Jersey. The committee found that organized crime in New Jersey was expanding and that it was due to "a failure to some considerable degree in the system itself, official corruption, or both."[13]

The committee recommended the creation of the Division of Criminal Justice, a prosecutorial body, and the SCI, an investigative unit smaller than the Division but one that would gather intelligence on organized crime, make recommendations to the Legislature and Governor for policy and laws to combat organized crime, and, most importantly, bring this information to the public. The SCI also had the power to subpoena witnesses and hold hearings. The SCI has published dozens of reports about organized crime in New Jersey and is considered a gold standard in these investigative organizations.

The SCI started its work on January 1, 1969, for an initial five-year term. The first investigations, as expected, concentrated on organized crime. It was initially under the leadership of Andrew F. Phelan, a former U.S. Attorney in Buffalo who cut his teeth on prosecuting organized crime cases targeting the Maggadino crime family in upstate New York. Phelan was appointed Executive Director of the SCI and spearheaded its first actions, which was to subpoena known organized crime figures to testify in front of the Committee and answer questions related to their businesses, income, any insights the SCI could glean about the inner workings of organized crime, the power structure of the families operating in the State, and how the money was moved between illegal activities and the wide array of businesses operated by crime figures.

In June 1969, subpoenas went out across New Jersey. One of the first was sent to Jerry Catena. As reported, Phelan's goal was "the successful exposure and prosecution of Catena." Although Catena was called out, he was aware of the potential difficulties that could arise from being the main target of the SCI. In discussions with his attorney, Catena considered the pros and cons of testifying under immunity or simply keeping his mouth shut and taking his chances with a contempt ruling.

Some crime figures decided to leave town rather than face the SCI, including several of Jerry's soldiers—Tino Fiumara, John DiGilio, Emilio "the County" Delio—who fled to Florida to avoid the subpoenas. Some of Jerry's other contemporaries did appear, including family friend Johnny "Coca Cola" Lardiere, Louis "Bobby" Manna, and the Russo brothers, Anthony and Nicholas.

Jerry discussed his strategy with his attorney before his initial appearance before the Commission. If given immunity, he was simply not going to talk. He knew he risked some jail time for contempt, but Jerry was adamant that he did not want to say a word. Jerry first appeared before the SCI on November 18, 1969 and, as promised, he kept quiet. The SCI was frustrated but they decided to wait and try again.

Catena was called to appear again on February 17, 1970. He arrived at the Superior Court courthouse in Trenton with a gray suit, hat, and a long dark coat. He had been in Florida so he flew up the day before to ensure he arrived at the courthouse on time. He went in front of the Commission and again refused to testify. They asked over eighty questions, but Jerry did not say a word. When he left, a Mercer County Sheriff's deputy escorted Catena to his car to protect him from the hordes of newspaper reporters desperate for a quick snapshot or quote.

On March 4, 1970, Catena was found in contempt of court and "committed until such time as he purged himself of contempt."[14] Catena was sentenced on March 6, 1970, and sent to the Yardville Correctional Center near Trenton.

Jerry was not the only crime figure imprisoned by the SCI's investigations into mob influence. His friend and fellow crime family soldier, Johnny "Coca Cola" Lardiere, joined him. Nicholas "Joseph" Russo was a fellow inmate from the Gambino family. The Philadelphia Mafia boss Angelo Bruno was in, along with two of his top men, then Atlantic City-based mobster Nicodemo Scarfo, and Ralph "Blackie" Napoli.

While Catena was in Yardville, one of his close political allies was facing a reckoning of his own: Newark Mayor Hugh Addonizio. Following the Newark riots of 1967, Addonizio came under pressure from state officials. There were stories of bribes, kickbacks, and general disregard for specific communities in Newark. Of course, the rumors of mob control and corruption were a regular part of the Newark political machine in those days.

Addonizio, who once enjoyed high popularity, was soundly defeated in his June 1970 re-election bid, perhaps because he was under indictment. But more likely, the political winds and demographics of the City changed. Addonizio represented the old era of political corruption. And when the jury returned their verdict on July 22, 1970, Addonizio was suddenly a convicted felon, found guilty of sixty-four counts of extortion and conspiracy. The Newark mob's hold on City Hall was fractured. They lost their political muscle.

During his time in Yardville, Jerry suffered another loss. His brother Frank passed away from a heart attack in November 1971. Frank was supposed to go in for heart surgery but never made it. In the space of a few years, Jerry had lost two brothers who worked with him in the "family business." It was a lot to process.

Many of Jerry's criminal associates were in their prime a decade earlier. But as men in their fifties and sixties in the 1960s became men in their sixties and seventies in the 1970s, time started catching up. Angelo "Gyp" DeCarlo, who had a somewhat complicated relationship with Jerry, was sick. To make matters worse, he was convicted of extortion in 1970 and sentenced to twelve years in federal prison.

In December 1972, President Richard Nixon commuted Angelo DeCarlo's twelve-year prison sentence after only two years. DeCarlo, then 69 years old, was diagnosed with prostate cancer in the hospital. According to a doctor who treated DeCarlo in prison, the cancer had metastasized.

The official story was that Nixon pardoned DeCarlo due to his terminal cancer. One version of the behind-the-scenes machinations involved the prison hospital. According to a doctor at the prison, DeCarlo learned that there was a possibility he could apply for parole on humanitarian grounds, especially as the cancer had spread. One of the prison doctors completed the required paperwork. Not soon thereafter, DeCarlo was freed. DeCarlo supposedly offered to give the doctor who helped with the paperwork a gift of $25,000.

But there are two other versions of what happened. The first featured Frank Sinatra. DeCarlo had a strong relationship with Frank Sinatra (as well as with Frankie Valli—DeCarlo was a character in the musical and movie *Jersey Boys*). Allegedly, Sinatra, on the behest of DeCarlo (through Valli), made a contribution of $100,000 to Nixon, funneled through Spiro Agnew, with whom Sinatra had grown close. The contribution was given to John Dean, who then shepherded a pardon application through the Justice Department to the desk of Nixon. Sinatra then made a $50,000 donation prior to DeCarlo's release.

I was also told a story about Nixon, Jerry Catena, and a little-known Genovese-affiliated gangster named Joseph Nesline based in Washington, D.C. Nesline had longstanding ties to the Genovese family through his friendships with Charlie "The Blade" Tourine, Dino Cellini, and Meyer Lansky.

According to this version of events, Jerry Catena heard in Yardville that DeCarlo's health was declining. Even though by then the transcripts of the DeCarlo wiretaps from the early 1960s had been released, complete with DeCarlo's less-than-flattering proclamations about Jerry's ability as boss and especially toward his brother Gene, Jerry felt that DeCarlo deserved to die at home. Despite their differences, they had worked together for decades, and Jerry respected the ailing gangster.

Catena met with a longtime associate, known as The Greeter, in Yardville prison. He sent the associate to meet with Joseph Nesline in DC. Nesline took it from there. Nesline reached out to Walter Annenberg, a friend of Nixon, U.S. Ambassador to the United Kingdom, and owner of magazines and newspapers. Annenberg's father was Moses Annenberg, who also owned newspapers and the national racing wire service that drew him into the Chicago Outfit and Al Capone sphere. Nesline convinced Annenberg to approach Nixon with the request for a pardon.

Although the last scenario has little backup documentation, a thread among the various stories regarding what really happened with DeCarlo's pardon is that many in the government were skeptical of why Nixon would pardon him. The second is that the FBI investigated all of these claims and determined that DeCarlo's parody was independent of any outside influences; rather, the determination was made inside the administration that he should be granted a compassionate release. Whatever the true story, DeCarlo was released from prison and died in his home in October 1973.

DeCarlo's death was one of many that occurred while Jerry was in Yardville. Things on the street were getting heated, starting in June 1971, when Joseph Colombo, boss of the Colombo crime family, was shot in the head during the Italian Unity Day Rally in New York City. Then Joe "Crazy Joe" Gallo, who battled with Colombo for control of the crime family, was murdered in a sensational rubout outside Umberto's Clam House in Little Italy on April 7, 1972.

The final in the sensational mob hit trifecta occurred during a humid Saturday night in July, just three months after Joey Gallo's killing. Joseph Sternfeld, a low-level Genovese associate, drove Tommy Eboli from New Jersey through Manhattan and into Brooklyn. Eboli would often visit his girlfriend, who lived in the Crown Heights neighborhood of Brooklyn. Eboli may have needed to let off some steam. He had met with Frank "Funzi" Tieri earlier that evening, and they had a big argument. According to Sternfeld, after dropping Eboli off at his mistress's house, he came back around 1 a.m. to pick him up.

Eboli walked toward Sternfeld's Cadillac, who parked a few doors down and got into the car. Then shots rang out from a passing yellow Ford truck. Sternfeld later told police that he ducked under the dashboard when the shooting started, "I didn't see anything, I don't know what happened, I just heard the shots fired."[15] Eboli was hit with a .32 and .22. He managed to stagger out of the car and died on the sidewalk.

Joseph Sternfeld went to Eboli's daughter's house, telling her that he didn't know what had happened and if Eboli was still alive. According to Eboli's son, his sister picked out shattered bits of glass from Sternfeld. The broken car window was from the first two shots that were fired at the car. Tommy's son Xavier told an interviewer that his father "needed better bodyguards. Joe was not really a bodyguard."[16]

Police arrived at the scene, finding a Ford truck with its engine still running abandoned a few blocks away. They also found a stolen 1965 Plymouth with New Jersey license plates, with another M-3 machine gun equipped with a silencer and twenty-four .45 caliber bullets inside the car. The assassins never used it.

Police found $2,077 in Eboli's coat pocket, so robbery was not the motive. To the police, this was a classic gangland hit. The shooters knew where and when Eboli would be at the location. His trademark hat was nowhere to be found. The funeral home where Eboli was laid out, F. Romanelli and Sons in Ozone Park Queens, was awash with local, state, and federal law enforcement, but few mob guys showed up, nor did many come to Eboli's resting place, a cemetery back across the bridge in Paramus, NJ.

Why was Eboli murdered, and did Jerry Catena have anything to do with Eboli's murder? Well, first, even though Catena was no longer the boss, it was widely thought he was approached in Yardville and signed off on Eboli's death.

The why is a bit murkier. The simple answer was that Eboli was not well-liked on the street. Then there is the story that Eboli borrowed $4 million from Carlo Gambino to finance a narcotics deal and was not forthcoming with repayment. Eboli's son maintained that Bennie Lombardo was always close to his father and even visited Eboli in the hospital when he had his first heart attack in 1968. However, after Tommy Eboli's murder, he never heard from Lombardo again, not even condolences. While that doesn't necessarily mean anything on first glance, it does speak to Lombardo's likely knowledge of why Eboli was killed.

One other rumor about the "why" and maybe whether Catena was involved concerned a slip of the tongue on Eboli's part. During a meeting with Benny Lombardo and Gambino capo Jimmy Brown Failla, Eboli commented on Catena, saying that Jerry "didn't know if he was Italian or a Jew." Failla went back to Carlo Gambino and reported what he heard. Gambino brought this to the Commission and Catena, who sanctioned a hit on Eboli.

Whatever the reason, Eboli's death also reignited rumors and suspicions of who the leaders of the Genovese family were. While Jerry was in Yardville, the position of boss in the family, or acting boss as the case increasingly became with the Genovese family, was a subject of some speculation. Catena was considered by some sources to be the official boss, even while in confinement. But other powers on the street figured in leadership positions in various charts and reports from law enforcement.

News reports focused on the usual stories of "dissention" in the Genovese family due to Catena's legitimate business enterprises, and Tommy Eboli's position was one that confused many. With Catena in prison, did Eboli rise to the top spot? Perhaps. According to Genovese turncoat Vincent Cafaro, "In 1972, Lombardo was the boss, 'Tommy Ryan' (Thomas Eboli) was the underboss, and Fat Tony was the consigliere. Lombardo wanted to stay in the background and keep the heat off himself so Tommy Ryan fronted as family boss, while Lombardo controlled things from the background."[17] Other sources speculated that Eboli controlled the family with Catena and Mike Miranda (who died exactly one year after Eboli, on July 16, 1973).

Then there was Frank "Funzi" Tieri, an Italian-born Brooklyn-based mobster who quietly rose up in the Genovese ranks and, like Lombardo, was on good terms with Catena. A 1970 FBI report stated that "Tieri was now the acting head of the former Genovese family, while Gerardo 'Jerry' Catena was in prison."[18] The FBI noted in their 1988 timeline of organized crime presented before the U.S. Senate Subcommittee on Investigations that Eboli "was succeeded by Frank Tieri."[19] But still other sources say that Eboli and Lombardo shared duties after Catena went to Yardville, with Lombardo taking over after Eboli's death. If the Genoveses were known for one thing in the 1970s, it was the obfuscation of the actual boss. There were numerous conflicting accounts of who was at the top after Catena went away in 1970.

Worrying about the family leadership may have been one item that was on Catena's mind during that time, but his businesses were also unattended while he was in Yardville. He kept enough control through intermediaries to have a handle and understanding of where things stood with his various business ventures, from his vending companies to his continued role in Vegas skim operations. But still, being incarcerated hobbled his effective leadership of his various enterprises.

The following account was previously featured in my book *Garden State Gangland*. Still, in the context of a greater understanding of Catena's business-oriented approach and his control of several significant moneymaking ventures, it takes on additional relevance to understanding that even behind bars, Catena was still capable of making things happen, or not.

It's relevant to include here to illustrate Catena's reach, even "behind bars." Myron relayed this story from 1971, while Catena was in Yardville.

When I was in Israel, Doc Stacher, who was living in Israel at the Old Sheraton, ordered me to show up at the hotel for Shabbat lunch. I had no idea why Doc suddenly was turning religious. I found out why. When we were seated, Meyer Lansky walked in and took the empty seat reserved for him next to me. He was a real gentleman who engaged me in lengthy conversations about his affection and admiration for my father and then we talked about the law, history, politics, etc. At the end of the long Shabbat lunch, after all the guests left, Messrs. Lansky and Stacher took me to the end of the lobby where nobody was seated and couldn't listen to the conversation and they proceeded to ask me to give them an update on Jerry Catena concerning his incarceration together with the other who refused to testify and were held in contempt of court. Over a period of time and because of situations which I was involved in, I realized myself that both Meyer Lansky and Doc Stacher were concerned for their flow of funds coming out of Las Vegas casinos (the rake) and that since Mr. Lansky was no longer in control since he fled to Israel to avoid prosecution, it was now Mr. Catena who ruled. It was my own conclusion at the time that this was the purpose of the Shabbat lunch. It wasn't intended to enhance the Sabbath with spirituality and prayer and the singing of Shabbat songs.[20]

It's doubtful whether Jerry turned off any faucets for Stacher or Lansky. He deeply respected both and had been friends with them for decades. But Lanksy was out of the country, and Stacher had made Aliyah in the early 1960s, so neither was close to the action in Las Vegas. And now that Catena was behind bars, it was a legitimate concern. Although Yardville allowed Jerry to meet more freely with visitors and run things he needed from behind the facility's walls, it wasn't the same as him being on the street.

The other issue was the changing nature of the Vegas skim and the players. The men taking millions in the skim in the early 1960s were moving out of the picture. Levinson and Torres had moved on from the Fremont. New players and new casinos became the focal point for the skim. And the players from New Jersey were being replaced by the Chicago Outfit and the Midwestern families. The final nail was the gradual sell-off of formerly mob-run casinos to businessmen like Howard Hughes and, eventually, larger corporations.

It's not clear exactly when Catena stopped being involved with the skim. Obviously, he was still taking money out of Vegas in the early 1970s. But with the rapidly changing nature of the mob's involvement in the skim and the lessening influence of New Jersey by the late 1970s, Jerry's part in the skim could be construed as done, certainly by the early 1980s.

Jerry's time in prison for contempt was keeping his attorneys busy. They filed a writ of habeas corpus with the U.S. District Court. After that was denied they went to the Third Circuit Court of Appeals but met with the same defeat. Catena's lawyers got him out of Yardville for some holidays, so Jerry could at least see his family a few times, not in detention. There was even an Essex County politician who put forward a bill in the New Jersey Senate to abolish the SCI. Dubbed "Jerry Catena's bill" by detractors, the legislation did not advance.

Over the next few years, his attorney took his case to the U.S. Supreme Court. The first time, the Court upheld the ability of the SCI to compel Catena's testimony. But Jerry's legal team, led by Chris Franzblau, was undeterred. They went back to the New Jersey Supreme Court armed with affidavits from Jerry's wife and children and their testimony.

On August 19, 1975, the New Jersey Supreme Court ruled 5-2 that although they disapproved of Catena's continued silence, there was no justification for keeping him in prison. The Supreme Court also overruled their previous decision in June 1974, keeping Catena in prison longer. The Court did not believe additional time behind bars would convince Catena to talk, noting that:

we are not condoning Catena's defiance of the S.C.I. investigation, nor are we subscribing to his reasons for remaining silent, whatever they may be. We hold only that it now appears that there is no substantial likelihood that further confinement will serve any coercive purpose and cause him to testify. Since no legal basis for the continued confinement of Catena exists, such confinement must be terminated.[21]

With that, Jerry, now 73 years old, was free.

His lawyer picked him up from prison and took him to lunch. They then stopped at a tailor shop to buy new suits. Jerry then went back home to his family. He had been away, with small breaks, for five years. It was the longest time Jerry had spent in prison in decades and the first stretch since his marriage to Kay. Now it was time for the next chapter in Jerry's life. Upon his release, he was no longer boss, and his sights were now set on Florida, where he could fade into the background and, most importantly, play a lot of golf.

14

The Shift South

Upon his release from Yardville, Jerry Catena decided to spend more time in Florida. He left New Jersey to spend the winter of 1975–6 in Boca Raton. At least in theory, Florida was an oasis away from the grind of a mobster's life in New Jersey. But Florida was seeing a marked increase in not only traditional organized crime, but the emergence of a drug scene that would, within a few years, eclipse the scope of the Mafia in South Florida. Florida prosecutors and law enforcement expanded their efforts to combat organized crime.

Although drugs were becoming more and more of a focus for law enforcement in the Sunshine state, Florida did set up a grand jury in 1975 to investigate illegal gambling in the state. When he received word that he was one of the crime figures being investigated, Jerry realized it was only a matter of time before they came for him. Catena was subpoenaed in the spring of 1976 to appear before the grand jury. He spent twenty minutes under questioning. Leaving the courthouse with his attorney, he offered a smile and a "no comment" to reporters outside.

In the summer of 1976, Jerry Catena sold his longtime home in South Orange for $155,000. The home, an adjacent lot, and full tennis courts were the last definite link to New Jersey for Catena. Although he had visited and stayed in Florida for long periods of time starting in the 1940s, Jerry was now a full-time Florida resident like many retirement-aged New Jerseyans before him. They moved into the home they had purchased in 1966, located on Cocoanut

Road, nestled on the barrier island just two blocks from the Atlantic Ocean, and across the Intracoastal Waterway from the Royal Palm Yacht & Country Club.

Although the Mafia traditionally stayed primarily in Miami-Dade County, especially cities like North Miami and Miami Beach, by the 1970s, they started moving north to Broward and Palm Beach County. Catena had always favored Boca Raton, having purchased a home in the Exclusive Estates neighborhood, on Cocoanut Road, in 1966. The 3,859 sq ft house was only a few blocks from the beach and nestled in a quiet residential neighborhood. The white stone house itself was barely visible from the road, nestled behind large tropical trees. The backyard had a large fence that kept onlookers from peering. But even though they kept their privacy, the Catenas were well-liked. Neighbors described Jerry as a "very good neighbor, very quiet."[1]

Boca police were aware of Catena's regular visits since the 1960s, when they described him as a vending machine and waste disposal business owner. They kept an eye on him occasionally, noting "We don't have enough men to follow him around, but we make a note in our organized crime file of when he's here and when he leaves."[2] When he and his wife moved to Boca fulltime, a few of the local residents would drive by his house like some emboldened neighborhood watch.

Jerry was spotted making the rounds of some of the usual mob haunts in South Florida, such as Dean Martin's Pub on the 79th Street Causeway in the mob stronghold of North Bay Village, located between Miami Beach and the City of Miami.[3] He lived near many of his business associates Abe Green, Mickey Wichinsky, and Sam Klein.

The Florida Department of Law Enforcement (FDLE) was investigating ties between organized crime and a burgeoning bagel shop in North Miami, the Bagel Nosh. They noted that the restaurant was becoming a frequent hangout for Miami-based organized crime figures. The FDLE noted that the two franchise owners, Leo Vittorio and Thomas F. Quinn, were organized crime associates and each had arrest records. They also indicated that infiltration of the bagel industry was a common target for organized crime, specifically citing reports that Jerry Catena had interests in bagel businesses back in New York.

In Boca, Catena fell into a routine. "Catena golfs every day. He has meetings every day."[4] Jerry frequented the Boca Raton Hotel and Golf Club. He had been a member since the 1960s. He also played regularly at the Boca Rio Golf Club, where he played with various local businessmen and developers.

While Jerry was easing into retirement, a series of mob hits came close to Jerry's circle. On June 1, 1976, Pasquale Eboli, Tommy Eboli's younger brother, left his Ft. Lee home driving his wife's Cadillac. He never came home. On July 13th, police called his family, letting them know that they found Eboli's car in a parking lot, across the street from the Pan-American terminal at John F. Kennedy Airport in Queens. Police confirmed to the newspapers that they suspected foul play. With rising tensions in the underworld in New York City at the time, it was apparent that Pasquale was caught up in some intra-family struggles. Pasquale Eboli was finally declared dead by the Superior Court of Bergen County in February 1984.

It's a decent assumption that Catena was consulted or at least given a heads-up regarding Eboli's disappearance. Although he had never been particularly close with Pasquale Eboli, because Catena weighed in on Tommy Eboli's killing, it would make sense to have looped him into this one. Again, there is no direct evidence or informant reports, but it would be the right thing to do, in a crime family that often adhered to those protocols.

The other murder had nothing to do with Catena, but he was drawn into the aftermath. On July 28, 1976, Johnny Roselli was reported missing in Florida. He had recently met with Santo Trafficante Jr. for dinner. Both men were recently in the news regarding the explosive allegations that the CIA hired the Mafia to kill Fidel Castro in the early 1960s. The allegations turned out to be true, and in addition to Roselli and Trafficante, Sam Giancana's name was also in the mix. All three men were called in front of the Church Committee, a U.S. Senate Committee tasked with investigating CIA activities. Right before Giancana was supposed to testify, he was murdered in his Oak Park home on June 19, 1975. A year later, Roselli, who did testify in front of the Church Committee, was missing. On August 7th, two fishermen in Dumfoundling Bay, located between Aventura and Sunny Isles Beach, found a chain-wrapped, fifty-five gallon drum floating in the water. When they bought it back and it was opened, the body of Roselli was inside. The gases from his decomposing body brought the barrel to the surface.

Following Roselli's murder, FBI agents made the rounds of South Florida mob hangouts and homes. They were shaking the bushes and speaking to whomever they could find to try and get some intel on the murder. While some sources were more apt to duck the feds, Catena was a bit more forthcoming. When agents arrived at his Boca Raton house on October 8, 1976, Catena was initially reluctant to let them inside, instead asking them to wait while he called his attorney. But when they informed him they only wanted to talk about Roselli, Catena let them inside. As usual Jerry was polite and affable, but his information was of little value to the agents. Jerry denied knowing Roselli, saying he only heard the name through newspaper reports.

One other murder that hit close to Jerry was the 1977 killing of longtime Catena family friend Johnny "Coca Cola" Lardiere. Jerry knew Lardiere well, but Johnny Coca Cola was particularly close to Gene, an ever-present part of family get-together photos and dinners. Lardiere was a member of Gene's crew and followed when Pete LaPlaca took over.

Lardiere was pulled in front of the SCI hearings on organized crime in the State, but, like Jerry, he refused to testify even after being offered immunity. He was jailed for contempt in August 1971. According to sources, sometime during the stay at Yardville, Johnny allegedly disrespected Jerry Catena. Supposedly Coca Cola told Catena to "fuck off."

In April 1977, Lardiere was granted a furlough for Easter weekend. The night before Easter, Lardiere checked into the Red Bull Inn, a motel in Bridgewater,

New Jersey. He was allegedly there to meet his mistress. Johnny went into the hotel lobby to get the keys for his room, then walked back out toward his car.

Before he got to the car, a man walked up to Lardiere and pulled a .22. The gun jammed when he attempted to shoot Coca Cola. According to mob legend, Lardiere yelled at the gunman, "What are you gonna do now tough guy?"[5] The gunman then pulled out a .38 and shot Lardiere in the neck, head, and stomach. Lardiere died at the scene.

Whether the apocryphal story of Lardiere telling Jerry to fuck off was true or not, although he was no longer boss, Catena would have most likely been consulted before Lardiere's killing, both as a sign of respect to his personal family's longstanding relationship with Johnny Coca Cola, and also because Jerry was still a high-ranking member as the former boss, even if he was running full tilt toward retirement.

With Catena trying to settle into the background in Florida, his name still appeared in news reports. This time it had to do with Bally. The company was looking to move into the casino market. And while Catena ostensibly sold the shares he owned in the company back in 1965, there was evidence that he still had a hidden interest in the firm through Abe Green and Sam Klein. Catena also owned stock in the Irving Kaye Co. Jerry held on to the stock in Irving Kaye's company until 1971. Irving was fully aware that Jerry had an interest in his firm. And, as a vice president of Bally, Kaye's continued direct financial involvement with Catena brought even more questions up regarding Catena's interest in Bally.

Hearings in 1972 about organized crime infiltration of sports brought back some of Catena's dealings with Lou Jacobs and Emprise. When Lou Jacobs passed away in August 1968, he left Emprise to two of his sons working there. Jeremy Jacobs appeared before the hearings to defend Emprise, and his father's reputation against allegations of continuing organized crime influence. Although he did acknowledge and admit his father did business with crime figures, he adamantly declared that those associations were all in the past and no longer affected the current Emprise, which by the early 1970s employed over 40,000 people across the United States. But when it came to the subject of Jerry Catena, Jeremy became defensive about his father's connection.

It has been alleged that my father had a knowing relationship with Gerardo Catena in Lion manufacturing and that he cooperated with Catena when he sold the shares which he owned. . . . As to this alleged relationship between my father and Mr. Catena, I would like to make part of the record a letter from E.J. Burker Security Inc. the subject of which details Lou Jacobs purposely avoided having a relationship with Gerardo Catena in 1965 when it was pointed out to him that Catena had alleged organized crime connections.[6]

Jeremy Jacobs read from a letter from the security firm that outlined their investigative efforts into Catena, purportedly on behalf of Lou Jacobs, in 1965. Although the firm said that they were asked to investigate Catena's background, this was well after Abe Green and Sam Klein brought Jacobs into the Bally deal. In addition, Jacobs already acknowledged having significant business dealings with members of the Detroit Mafia well before the Bally deal. If he was comfortable with mob figures from Detroit, why would he then be reluctant to go into business with Catena?

Regardless of how Jacobs may have felt regarding doing business with Catena, the company they helped revive was well on its way to becoming one of the giants in the gaming industry. With integrated design, manufacturing, and distribution operations, Bally was ready for the next step. Already a publicly traded company, in 1975 the New York Stock Exchange allowed Bally stock to be traded on the exchange. Within two years, Bally's stock tripled in value.

This was good news for investors in the company, including an entity that had a long connection with organized crime, the Teamster Union's Central States Pension Fund, one of the primary sources of capital for the construction of mob-controlled Las Vegas casinos. The Teamsters' fund purchased shares in Bally in 1968 and lent Bally $12 million in the early 1970s. The architects behind the Teamsters' financial investment in Bally's included Teamsters' president Frank Fitzsimmons and Anthony "Tony Pro" Provenzano, by then a capo in the Genovese crime family.

Bally was eyeing an even bigger prize, their own casino. Shortly after their New York Stock Exchange debut in 1971, Bally applied for a casino license in Nevada. Bally used the fact that it was publicly traded to assure gaming regulators that it was indeed clean. Abe Green had sold his shares based on initial feedback from gaming regulators, who were convinced that Abe was holding hidden shares in Bally for Jerry. Nevada was tightening its casino laws so it would not be an easy process for a firm that drew its seed money from organized crime. And with rumors swirling that Catena still owned an interest in the firm, it was far from a guarantee that the license would be issued.

In Nevada, two bodies oversee gaming: the Nevada Gaming Commission and the Nevada Gaming Control Board. The Gaming Control Board is the regulatory body for the gaming industry. It has five divisions: Administration, Technology, Audit, Enforcement, and Investigations. Members of the Board are considered law enforcement officers. The Commission is a five-member body that ultimately issues gaming licenses to the applicants. If you make it past the Board, there's a better chance that the Commission will issue a license.

Irving Kaye was the first to try and get a license as an operator. But Kaye was denied due to his "numerous business relationships over a period of years with Gerardo Catena, a person of notorious and unsavory reputation."[7] The Nevada Gaming Commission did issue Bally and Klein a probationary license in March 1975, pending an investigation into Bally and whether Klein and other Bally stockholders still had a relationship with Jerry Catena. This was bound to cause issues with Klein. He had kept in regular contact with Catena, even more so since Catena relocated to Boca Raton. Klein lived close by, and the two often golfed together at local country clubs. One of their golf outings was observed by Boca Raton police. They forwarded a copy of the surveillance report to the Nevada Gaming Commission and Gaming Control Board. As far as the Gambling Commission and Control Board went, the optics were not good.

In August 1976, the Gaming Commission informed Klein's attorney that they wished to discuss his relationship with Catena and requested that he appear before the Gaming Control Board meeting in Carson City. Klein, however, was having some heart issues and had his doctor pen a letter to the Commission for his attorney to read. Klein also wrote a letter of his own to Bill O'Donnell and his attorney read that one into record. Klein wrote, in part:

I wish to emphatically state, without equivocation, that I have no association or connection with any reputed organized crime figure.

In late May of 1976, I was informed that Irving Kaye was seriously ill and would like to see and talk to me. I called him at his home in Florida and he informed me that his return to the hospital in New York was imminent. He asked me to come see him. Of course, I readily agreed, and therefore, during the next ten days, I had dinner with him twice, and had arranged a third such affair, which he failed to attend because of illness. Mr. Catena, an old friend of Mr. Kaye's was present on these occasions. During these occasions, Mr. Catena, who is an avid golfer, expressed a desire to play at the club of which I am a member. It was then arranged that he and a physician friend of his from New York would join me in a game one day that week. I did play with Mr. Catena and his physician friend, along with another long time friend of mine who is a fellow club member.

In the course of the game, I did not discuss Bally Manufacturing or any other business affairs with Mr. Catena. I left the club immediately after the game and lunch while Mr. Catena remained behind with other persons.[8]

Despite Klein's continued denials that he had no relationship with Catena, when asked about his golf outings with Catena by the *Miami Herald*, Klein replied, "Catena has always been a gentleman as far as I'm concerned. I'd play golf with him again."[9]

However, in his letter, which his lawyer read before the Gaming Commission, Klein admitted that his actions were deleterious to Bally's future and offered his resignation as vice president. The Board agreed with that and added it to their official order on September 23, 1976. They also ordered that Klein's license be terminated, that Bally would never again employ Klein in any capacity, that Klein sell his 419,000 shares of Bally within four years, and that Klein would pay the Nevada Gaming Commission a $50,000 fine.

After that decision, Klein attempted to regain access to Bally through third-party stock purchases. He made loans of up to $1 million to an associate who, in turn, purchased Bally stock. The SEC started an investigation, noting that Klein also made payments to third-party associates that were used to purchase Bally stock.

The State of Florida was also looking into Bally. The company was looking to purchase World Jai-Alai Inc. Jai alai was a popular sport in South Florida. Originating in the Basque region of Spain, jai alai arrived in Florida by the 1920s. By the 1970s, South Florida's jai alai frontons, the name of the court on which the game was played, were owned by World Jai-Alai Inc. At that time the president was John Callahan, a Boston-based businessman who had ties to New England organized crime. Callahan and his partner were looking to sell World Jai-Alai in 1976. One potential buyer was an associate of Meyer Lansky. Bally also looked at a potential acquisition.

Bally offered $66 million to acquire World Jai-Alai, but the board ultimately canceled the deal due to the negative publicity Bally was receiving regarding the Catena connection, as well as investigations by gaming authorities in Connecticut. The company later sold to a firm led by investor Roger Wheeler. Far from distancing itself from mob influence, World Jai-Alai was being infiltrated by members of the Boston-based Winter Hill Gang and the New England Mafia. When Wheeler found out, he was murdered on May 27, 1981 by members of the Winter Hill Gang, including White Bulger.

It's unclear whether Bally knew of the already-existing organized crime influence on World Jai-Alai, but it is interesting to note that the firm did not sell to a Lansky-affiliated buyer, nor Bally. But a new prize also awaited Bally—the pending legalization of gambling in New Jersey, specifically Atlantic City.

Bally was well-positioned to take advantage of these opportunities. As a firm, Bally was on a tear. They had two Chicago plants, one in Bensonville and one in Franklin Park, which produced pinball machines and arcade games through their Midway subsidiary, which had just started penetrating the American market. The main Belmont headquarters still built slot machines for the Las Vegas market. With Atlantic City coming online, expanding into casinos was a natural move. And Bill O'Donnell was planning to oversee this.

In the fall of 1977, Bill O'Donnell told an NBC news reporter, "Catena never even so much as picked up a telephone and asked me how business was."[10] When the reporter pressed O'Donnell, he replied that Catena had "no interest whatsoever"[11] in the company. In the same news report, there was footage of Sam Klein being questioned by an NBC news reporter. When asked about his relationship with Jerry Catena, Klein angrily retorted, echoing his protestations from his letter to the Nevada Gaming Control Board the year before, "None whatsoever and never has been. And that's just like asking me why did I kill Jack Kennedy or did I know about it. You're causing an innuendo that has no basis in fact to establish something you want to do."[12] It should be noted that the reporter never mentioned Kennedy.

Around this time, Jerry and Abe Green put a Runyon asset up for sale, the phone number. They sold the phone number for $40,000 to another vending operator and rented out Runyon's space on Pinball Row in Manhattan. The building, on 10th Avenue, was owned on paper by Abe Green's son, having originally been owned by Abe and Barnet Sugerman. The new vending operator rented the old Runyon space to Novel, who now took over many of Runyon's routes.

In 1974, Abe's son, Irving, spun the rest of Runyon off into a new firm, called Coin-Op of Springfield, New Jersey. Irving Green let O'Donnell know that Runyon would now be Coin-Op and no longer under ownership of his father or Jerry Catena. This was done to ensure compliance with gaming regulators' concerns about the continued influence of Catena on Bally. However, during his divorce trial, Irving admitted that Coin-Op was just another name for Runyon, suggesting that his father and Catena may have had an interest in the firm. It turned out that Coin-Op had no employees and that its customer was Runyon Sales. In fact, Irving admitted to Bally's general counsel that he spent over 90 percent of his time at Runyon.

As for Novel, when Rudy Giuliani began cracking down on the mob's interests in vending machines as U.S. Attorney for the Southern District of New York in the late 1980s, Novel's owner closed it down.

But as Runyon was fading, Bally was still rising. On February 24, 1978, Bally's Park Place, Inc., a Delaware corporation that owned 82.8% of the stock in Bally Manufacturing Corporation, applied for a casino license to the New Jersey Casino Control Commission. Bally, in turn, applied for a casino service industry license, allowing Bally to supply the casino with gaming machines.

It became apparent that the past ties between Bally and Catena were becoming a sticking point with gaming regulators. They cited a continuing business relationship between Bally and Runyon Sales Inc., which Nevada gaming authorities had expressly forbidden as a condition of Bally's license there. Abe Green still owned Runyon, and even though Jerry Catena "officially" divested himself from the firm in 1970, it was widely believed that Jerry still had an undisclosed interest in the firm.

O'Donnell was trying hard to distance Bally from the past mob influence on the company, at least to outward appearances, in addition to making public appearances and statements to regulators, confirming his support for their actions against mob influence in Bally. But O'Donnell realized that he was becoming the sticking point. Despite his assurances that the mob days were in the past, his role and position as the face of the company were problematic.

The Casino Control Commission ruled 5-0 against issuing a casino license to Bill O'Donnell. However, the ruling did not end Bally's attempts at an

Atlantic City casino. For the Commission to review the application for Bally's Park Place again, O'Donnell would need to forfeit his 6 percent interest in the company.

O'Donnell resigned from his position in Bally in December 1979, paving the way for Bally's permanent presence in Atlantic City. However, O'Donnell continued the legal fight to regain his position in the company. Finally, in December 1982, the New Jersey Supreme Court ruled against O'Donnell, and his attempts to re-enter the business he had built were thwarted.

There is some debate as to whether Catena still had an interest in Bally at that point. His relationships with some of the main players had been frayed and his chief inside men were no longer involved with the company. And with O'Donnell no longer at the helm and Klein out of the picture,[13] Bally moved forward and became a significant force in the casino industry, as well as other areas where it expanded.

As Catena's name continued to appear in newspapers due to his ties to Bally and investigations in Florida, another event led back to Jerry, although luckily for him, it was a tangential connection.

At 1:20 p.m. on October 18, 1977, Ray Ryan got into his blue Lincoln Continental Mark V, in front of the Olympia Health and Beauty Resort in Evansville, Indiana. As soon as he turned the ignition, a massive explosion erupted from underneath and blasted apart the car, sending debris 150 feet in the air and shattering windows in nearby businesses. Ryan was killed instantly.

Within hours, authorities suspected this was a gangland hit, and everyone who knew Ryan thought the same. Ryan made his fortune in the oil business in the 1940s but cemented his legacy in the casinos of 1950s Las Vegas and 1960s Palm Springs. He hobnobbed with movie stars and business tycoons. He also owned exclusive clubs worldwide, including the Mt. Kenya Safari Club in Nanyuki, Kenya.

The exclusive club opened its doors on June 21, 1959 and became one of the most sought-after memberships of any club worldwide. Royal family members of Europe and Saudi Arabia rubbed shoulders with Neil Armstrong and Winston Churchill. But Ray also found space for some of his gambling buddies from Vegas. He gave memberships to Tony Accardo and Sam Giancana of the Chicago Outfit. He also gave membership to Tommy Eboli and Jerry Catena.

Ryan's ties to organized crime got him into trouble twice. First was when Chicago Outfit member Marshall Caifano tried to extort Ryan for $60,000 a year for his protection. Ryan had recently paid off a gambler who accused him of cheating, so the Outfit wanted in on the action. Rather than paying, Ryan went to the authorities and testified against Caifano. During the trial authorities wanted to examine the membership list of the Mt. Kenya Club. They specifically asked to see if Catena and Eboli were still members. Rather than give it to them, Ryan shredded the membership list.

Caifano did spend a few years behind bars, but when he was released, he had not forgotten Ryan's testimony against him. This was the second time Ryan's ties to organized crime got him into trouble. The story was that Caifano wanted to kill Ryan, so he went to Accardo to ask for permission. Accardo eventually relented, but told Caifano that he could not do it in Palm Springs. In the aftermath, Catena's name popped up in a few news stories, but he was not at all involved in the car bombing and had not been associated with Ryan for over a decade at that point.

Jerry was working his way to full retirement, pulling away from day-to-day operations. Now that he was no longer boss, he must have felt some relief that he would not be dealing with the new wave of violence that took over the New York underworld in the mid- to late 1970s. But the suspicions and general unease in some of the crime families eventually worked their way into a situation that needed consultation—the killing of a boss.

The target was Carmine Galante, acting boss of the Bonanno crime family in the absence of boss Philip "Rusty" Rastelli, who was imprisoned. When Galante was released from his own prison sentence, he quickly moved in to take over the top spot in the Bonannos. Galante was heavily involved in narcotics trafficking and surrounded himself with a crew of "zips," a name given to a new generation of Sicilian-born mobsters who worked for the Five Families. The zips were loyal only to Galante. The newspapers fanned the flames, insinuating that Galante wanted to take over all Five Families. Carmine's brazen power moves worried, and likely annoyed, the other families, including the Genoveses.

Galante's days were numbered. FBI sources reported that Aniello "Neil" Dellacroce, underboss of the Gambino family, flew to Boca in early 1979 and met with Jerry Catena for less than an hour, then drove down to Miami to fly out to Tucson, where he allegedly met exiled boss Joe Bonanno. That was followed by a meeting in February 1979 at Jerry's Boca home. With Frank "Funzi" Tieri, Gambino boss Paul Castellano, and Tampa boss Santo Trafficante Jr., this conclave decided Galante's fate. The police investigating the Galante hit remarked about the meeting at Jerry's home where the hit was reportedly planned, noting that "police believe he still holds a powerful advisory position on organized crime's national commission."[14]

Dellacroce was drumming up support from the families' leadership, and although Catena was no longer boss, his opinion and backing of the plan carried significant weight. Dellacroce was also lining up support from within the Bonanno family to take out the boss.

A week after Dellacroce met with Catena, on July 12, 1979, Carmine Galante was gunned down in the spectacular hit on the back patio of Joe and Mary's Italian Restaurant in the Bushwick neighborhood of Brooklyn. The indelible image of Carmine Galante's bullet-riddled body sprawled out on the patio with his cigar still clenched between his lips remains an iconic image in the history of American organized crime.

The aftermath of the Galante hit brought fresh law enforcement scrutiny onto the Mafia nationwide. The FBI, state, and local authorities were working hard to get up to speed on the latest changes in mob leadership nationwide. A new law, the Racketeer Influenced and Corrupt Organizations Act, known as RICO, had the power to enable prosecutors to go after patterns of crime and larger criminal organizations rather than taking out gangsters a few at a time. It also gave sweeping new powers to remove the upper leadership of families. The boss could be charged for overseeing the criminal activities of their subordinates. The RICO Act had been around since 1970, but it was in 1978 that the first RICO trial started.

The 1970s were about to slide into a new decade, and the underworld landscape was about to be changed forever through law enforcement, internal uprisings, and a new generation of mobsters who eschewed the approach that had served Catena so well. Instead, they looked for flashy cars, flashy suits, and flashy wads of cash to show around with little awareness of prying eyes and surveillance vans. Thankfully, this was not a world Jerry would be a part of. His world was returning to basics: family, golf, and a little advice to mobsters needing guidance. The decades of amassing his fortune had paid off.

15

"Retirement"

Jerry Catena's 1979 Florida driver's license photo showed a more relaxed, tanned Jerry. It was clear that retirement, such as it was, was suiting Jerry. He was playing golf, traveling, and getting much-needed rest. He was well-liked by his Boca neighbors. Jerry and his wife drove around in her gray 1973 Mercedes SEL sedan. In 1982, for his 80th birthday, Sam Klein bought Jerry a brand new Mercedes. Although luxurious for the time, it was not outright ostentatious yet still fit in with the late 1970s/early 1980s vibe of Boca Raton. Catena liked the car a bit too much, being stopped several times for speeding through Boca.

Boca during this time was a different scene than the more freewheeling cocaine cowboys of Miami. It was more relaxed and low-key, much better suited to Jerry's lifestyle. He was a man about town, but in the way an octogenarian would be. Catena and his wife enjoyed eating out at the local restaurants and were often spotted at the Top of the Bridge Restaurant, which overlooks the Boca Inlet. He also continued to play golf at the Boca Raton Hotel and Club. Although Catena didn't play golf as frequently, he did find time to entertain friends on the course. Danny Williams, Catena's old golfing partner from the Knoll, often flew down to play golf with Jerry at the Boca Club. They played together into the late 1980s.

Although Jerry was increasingly out of the day-to-day operational aspects of the Genovese crime family, the feds were still watching him. In October of

1980, two FBI agents came to Catena's house for a routine chat. Jerry invited them in for a casual conversation, opening up to them more than he had in the past. He started off by telling the agents, like any good old-school mobster, that his health was not that good. Catena let the agents know that he had a pacemaker. Jerry also recounted a recent cruise that he and his wife took to Italy, where he was able to return to the birthplace of his father for the first time. He even offered up to the agents that he planned to take even more cruises in the future.

When agents asked him if he traveled often back to New Jersey, Catena replied that the FBI knew exactly what he did, intimating that Catena understood he was still a target for them, despite protestations of his "retirement." And he knew the FBI were keeping tabs. He ended the conversation by telling the agents that he was officially retired. Despite that, the FBI noted in their report that "informants in the Newark area identify Catena as the most powerful man in New Jersey rackets today and in control of many political figures and labor on the Port Newark docks."[1] Even if Catena was spending all his time in Boca, and the golf course, his presence back in New Jersey still loomed large.

Some law enforcement reports echoed Catena's retirement claim, at least reflecting the true state of his standing within the family. A Miami FBI field office reference referred to Catena as "the retired boss of the Genovese Family LCN." However, being a retired boss does not imply that Catena distanced himself from his various financial interests in organized crime. Although he was no longer the boss, Catena still maintained a degree of influence in the Genovese family.

A 1981 article in the *Newark Star Ledger* stated that police described Catena as the Genovese family's retired boss and current consigliere. Other law enforcement sources corroborated that position.

Throughout the early part of 1983, the U.S. Senate held hearings into the state of organized crime in the country. When it came time to display those large organizational charts that became the hallmark of many of these types of hearings, Jerry Catena was still near the top, albeit in a different position. "Lombardo presently resides in Florida and due to poor health, he is in semi-retirement. Catena now serves as the consigliere for the Genovese family," noting that "although Catena presently resides in Florida, his financial interests in New Jersey remain extensive."[2] The FBI's chart listed Philip Lombardo as boss and Anthony "Fat Tony" Salerno as underboss.

That same year the New Jersey State Police issued a report stemming from those Senate hearings called *The Structure of Organized Crime in New Jersey*, noting that the Genovese family "operates primarily in the northern and central sectors of New Jersey" and that "Catena now serves as the consigliere for the Genovese family."[3] What's interesting is that Catena did not appear as a consigliere before these mentions.

The Broward County Sheriff's Department, who had a sophisticated and extensive organized crime squad in the 1980s that focused on the growing number of mob figures who were moving to the County, often made it a point to surveil gangland figures who crossed into their jurisdiction. They would occasionally take a trip to a nearby county. They went north to Palm Beach County a few times to question Catena. Most of the time it was routine intelligence gathering. Once, in the mid-1980s, the Newark FBI field office sent a tip for the Broward Sheriff to follow up on, regarding the Hoffa disappearance. Sheriff's deputies interviewed Tony Provenzano at his home in Hallandale and Catena at his home in Boca Raton. "As usual, both were very friendly and cordial but didn't tell us anything."[4]

Catena's associations during that time also gave law enforcement a view into his activities. He maintained close ties with Sam DeCavalcante, the retired boss of the crime family that bears his name to this day. Like Catena, DeCavalcante was ostensibly retired but also served as a de-facto consigliere and was consulted by many mob figures who made their way to his condo on Collins Avenue in Miami Beach. Law enforcement would occasionally conduct surveillance, but for the most part they were concentrating on the next generation of wiseguys that were operating in South Florida. And with older guys like Catena and DeCavalcante,[5] they were rarely in contact with the new crop of mobsters.

His "official" position as consigliere didn't appear to last too long. The following year, the FBI listed the Genovese consigliere position as belonging to Louis "Bobby" Manna. Catena did not appear anywhere in the leadership, nor the list of caporegimes. Catena's absence from the official FBI list of the Genovese family hierarchy was apparently enough for the *Press of Atlantic City* to refer to Catena, in a December 1985 article about mobsters in Florida, as the "late Gerardo 'Jerry' Catena."[6] He had managed to slink away from the spotlight enough to stifle even reporters from investigating his current status. Or they may have just made a mistake. No correction was offered.

The Genovese family itself was changing due to both law enforcement pressures and the passage of time. By the early 1980s, the Genovese family hierarchy was a bit murky, although law enforcement agreed that Benny Lombardo was the true boss behind the scenes. Frank "Funzi" Tieri died in March 1981, and FBI charts post his death place Lombardo in the top spot. But Lombardo's health was in decline, and by 1983 the FBI named the acting boss Vincent "Chin" Gigante, the gunman who tried to take out Frank Costello back in 1957. The underboss was Anthony "Fat Tony" Salerno, although some charts had him as the front boss. Once again, the Genovese family's approach to a strict hierarchical pyramid structure was unorthodox and designed to obfuscate law enforcement.

Like the boss position, the Genovese consigliere spot switched back and forth between names starting in the mid-1970s. Genovese turncoat Vincent Cafaro testified that Bobby Manna became consigliere in 1980 after the death of Dominick "Fat Dom" Alongi. Before Alongi, Fat Tony Salerno was listed as consigliere in addition to several other names, including John "Buster" Ardito. With this in mind, it's possible that Catena was not truly the official consigliere but rather more informally the go-to person around the turn of the 1980s. While the 1983 charts list Catena as the official consigliere, by the following year, that position was occupied by Louis "Bobby" Manna, the Hoboken-based Genovese gangster who spent time with Catena in Yardville. And some informants stated Manna was the official consigliere dating back to 1980.

By that time, Catena had already given so much to the crime family; it's doubtful that he would rise back up in the hierarchy after making the effort to retire with the Commission's blessing. Still, there were many anecdotal stories that guys were still seeking him out on the golf courses of Boca for an informal chat.

If ever there was a good time for Jerry to be without a leadership position in one of the New York Five Families, this was the time. The rising law enforcement and media scrutiny facing the Mafia was reaching a crescendo, buoyed by the RICO Act, which gave federal law enforcement a bold new way to target organized crime as a structural institution rather than individuals for individual crimes. The brainchild of Notre Dame law professor G. Robert Blakey, RICO was a powerful tool that, in the proper context, could be used to decimate the leadership of entire crime families.

In February 1985, sweeping indictments out of the U.S. Attorney's office, overseen at that time by Rudy Giuliani, targeted the heads of all the NYC Five Families. This was an unprecedented attack on organized crime. Never before had so many bosses been named in one overarching indictment. The charges were based on extensive investigations by the FBI. A combination of wiretaps, listening devices, and informants provided more than ample evidence that the five heads of the New York Mafia were part of The Commission and conspired to oversee the operations of the Mafia and associated crimes. With the power of the RICO law, the federal government had the necessary tools to prosecute the sometimes complex racketeering cases by looking at crime patterns in the context of an entire organization, not individual crimes.

The initial indictment charged:

- Paul Castellano—boss of the Gambino family

- Aniello Dellacroce—underboss of the Gambino family

- Gennaro "Gerry Lang" Langella—boss of the Colombo family

- Anthony "Tony Ducks" Corallo—boss of the Lucchese family

- Salvatore "Tom Mix" Santoro—underboss of the Colombo family

- Christopher "Christie Tick" Furnari—consigliere of the Colombo family

- Philip "Rusty" Rastelli—boss of the Bonanno family

- Anthony "Fat Tony" Salerno—referred to as boss of the Genovese family

Over the next year, a few of the defendants died through a mix of natural (Dellacroce) and unnatural causes (Castellano, wiped out in a spectacular shooting in front of Sparks Steak House in Manhattan on December 16, 1985). Some new defendants and charges were added. The trial, dubbed The Commission Trial, was complex, but with the overwhelming evidence against the defendants, it was a tall order for them to mount a credible defense. On November 18, 1986, the jury returned its verdict: All defendants were found guilty of racketeering and conspiracy. Fat Tony Salerno received a sentence of 100 years in prison without parole and a fine of $240,000.

Serendipitously, a week before the jury's verdict in the Commission case, the November 10, 1986 issue of *Fortune* magazine hit the newsstands with a cover photo of Fat Tony Salerno, the ever-present cigar in his mouth. In bold red, the headline read "The 50 Biggest Mafia Bosses." Inside, they had a chart where they ranked Mafia kingpins, measuring their wealth, power, and influence. They derived their information partly from U.S. government hearings and a study prepared for the President's Commission on Organized Crime by Wharton Econometric Forecasting Associates.

Jerry Catena was sitting at number four on the *Fortune* chart. The 84-year-old was ranked above the active bosses of the Gambino, Colombo, and Bonanno families, and every other family boss, save for Chicago.

Was the *Fortune* article accurate? Like any "best of" list, it's subjective mainly regarding opinion and analysis of available facts. As the mob did not disclose financial information to the magazine or do in-depth investigations of individual wealth, ranking the bosses based on money was primarily conjecture. But it may not have been far off in Catena's case. A few years before, the New Jersey State Commission of Investigation estimated Catena's net worth at $10 million, whereas others pegged it much higher. Recall Anthony "Little Pussy" Russo stating that Catena had "more money than God."

The "power" and "influence" metrics were even more subjective. But even taking that into account, the fact that an 84-year-old mob figure who had been out of a leadership position for a decade at that point was still placed ahead of so many others was an indication that even though he was out of the news, Catena's name was still on the minds of law enforcement, as well as underworld figures who were feeding information back to police and the FBI.

In 1987, the FBI updated its chart of the hierarchy of the Gennaro family. Vincent Gigante was at the top, with Bobby Manna as the consigliere and Venero "Benny Eggs" Mangano as underboss. Gigante was likely the real boss behind Salerno and managed to avoid ensnarement in the Commission trial. He was eventually convicted of racketeering in 1997 and died in prison. Manna was convicted of conspiring to murder Gambino boss John Gotti, his brother Gene Gotti, and Irwin Schiff, a mob-connected New York developer, and sentenced to eighty years in prison in 1989. Manna was released to home confinement on compassionate grounds on April 16, 2025.

With the new Genovese regime rising, Catena was no longer on the FBI's mind. Jerry, however, was still on the mind of gaming regulators. In 1987, Bally went before the Nevada Gaming Commission and Gaming Control Board to revise and update their registration with the state. The Commission issued the revision, but buried in the order was a list of times the company must continue to follow to comply with its gaming license. The fifth item listed said "There shall at no time be any direct or indirect business transactions of any nature whatsoever between Bally Manufacturing Corporation and Gerardo Catena, or Abe Green, or any corporation or other business entity controlled by either of them, or in which they, or either of them own beneficially a 5% or greater interest of any class of voting securities."[7]

Bally went before the Commission and Board again in 1993 and despite Catena no longer being involved in Bally, the line item about his involvement was still included. Over the ensuing years, Bally acquired and shed casinos, fitness centers, and theme parks before declaring bankruptcy in 2007. A hedge fund-backed casino company in Rhode Island, Twin River, acquired Bally's Atlantic City casino and the Bally brand during the pandemic in 2020. In 2023, Bally opened a temporary casino in the Medinah Temple in downtown Chicago while it began construction on a $1.7 billion casino on the Chicago River, only four miles from the original Bally location on West Belmont.[8]

In 1988, the U.S. Senate Permanent Subcommittee on Investigations listed Catena as a member of the Genovese crime family, albeit without any hierarchical position. In 1989, the New Jersey State Commission of Investigation released an overview of the current status of organized crime. The Commission, which investigated Catena in their very first foray into organized crime investigation, now did not even list his name anywhere. Catena was finally off the SCI's radar. New Jersey State Police Superintendent Clinton Pagano told the Fort Lauderdale *Sun-Sentinel* in 1989, "I would expect him to give advice to anyone who wants it. A don like Jerry Catena will forever be listened to, because he's survived the wars."[9] In November 1993, the FBI published an updated list of the Genovese crime family. Catena was listed as inactive. It was his last ever appearance on a law enforcement Mafia organization chart.

The last time I saw Catena was at Al Miniaci's house in Ft. Lauderdale in September 1991. His comment to me was "I was just another Chief Operating Officer of a Major Corporation." He also told me that he asked the Commission to let him retire and they gave their permission. A beat after telling me that he said, "forget what I just told you."[10]

Jerry and Catherine sold their longtime Boca Raton home in the summer of 1999 for $550,000. They moved across the state to Punta Gorda, a small city in Charlotte County, on the Gulf coast, to be closer to their daughter. They lived in Bridge Point, a large condo complex on a canal, one block from the mouth of the Peace River. Jerry's time at his new Punta Gorda home was short-lived, though. His health, both physical and mental, was failing.

Gerardo Vito Catena died on April 23, 2000, at the Charlotte Regional Medical Center in Punta Gorda. He was 98 years old. He was cremated and interred at the Royal Palm Memorial Gardens. There was no obituary in the local paper and his passing did not spur any big articles about him or his legacy. He died quietly and peacefully, under the radar.

Jerry Catena was one of the more unique and influential figures in the history of organized crime. He outlived (almost[11]) all of his contemporaries: Vito Genovese, Frank Costello, Carlo Gambino, Tommy Eboli, Funzi Tieri, Benny "Squint" Lombardo, Meyer Lansky, and Doc Stacher. He was the reluctant boss of a crime family, but did it out of his sense of obligation to the organization of which he was a member. His interest lay as much outside the spheres of crime as it did within. He surrounded himself with businessmen and business-smart racketeers. He came up under the mentorship of Jewish crime figures and learned early on the value of treating organized crime like a business. His ability to navigate complex business deals served him well in navigating and negotiating within the complex world of Mafia politics.

He was one, if not the most consequential, mobster in New Jersey history. I hesitate to employ the overused descriptor "powerful" because more often than not, I use that term to describe mobsters who operate through fear and intimidation, brawn over brains. Jerry operated differently. He saw the world differently than most Mafioso. He ran the family through business acumen, not threats. Although some of his underlings and compatriots skewered the way he led, the proof was in the success of the crime family during his reign and the stability that he inherited and passed on. There are very few Mafia figures who, in the middle of being a successful boss, suddenly says, "Hey, I want to retire and go play golf in Florida," and those around him oblige.

Jerry still could have been a hugely successful businessman without the trappings of organized crime. He was also, in some ways, the victim of circumstance. Had he been born later, he would have fit squarely into post-Second World War America's rising business/entrepreneur class. Alternatively, had he not been associated with Longie Zwillman, would he have had the mentorship to bring his natural talents to fruition? It's hard to say, but at the core, Jerry Catena was the last of his contemporaries in the underworld.

At the end of the day, Jerry Catena did what so few others in his profession could achieve: dying a free man, successfully retired from one of the few careers where it's nearly impossible to do that.

NOTES

Chapter 1

1   Currently known as Independence Park.

2   The school was torn down in the mid-1970s and is now the Louise A. Spencer School.

3   Three doors down from the Catena residence was the bar that was the hangout for mobster Charles "The Blade" Tourine in the 1950s and 1960s. Tourine would become a close associate in the coming years.

4   Now known as the Port Newark-Elizabeth Marine Terminal. It's overseen by the Port Authority of New York and New Jersey.

5   Sugerman, Myron. Letter to Author. "An add on about Catena." Email, August 10, 2024.

6   Bellina was 72 years old when he was formally inducted into the Bruno-Scarfo crime family.

7   *Newark Evening News.* "Only Three Smokes, but They Land Twelve in Jail." January 18, 1927.

Chapter 2

1   The Piccadilly was located across the street from what is now the Prudential Center.

2   *The Daily News.* "Seek Slayer of Grant Patterson across Atlantic." May 5, 1930.

3   Of note, the official documents list Catena's first name as Gerard, and he signs his name as that.

4   United States Congress, *Hearings Before The Select Committee To Investigate Organized Crime In Interstate Commerce* Washington, DC, 1951.

5   Stuart, Mark A. *Gangster #2: Longie Zwillman, The Man Who Invented Organized Crime.* Washington, DC: Lyle Stuart, 1985.

6   Ralph's brothers, Anthony "Little Pussy" Russo and John "Big Pussy" Russo, would become made men in the crime family in the coming years. Ralph was murdered in a gangland hit in Pittsburgh in 1936.

7   Ernest Fiumara was the father of future Genovese crime family power Tino Fiumara.

8   The site is now the Winona Lippman Gardens Apartment Complex.

Chapter 3

1   *The Courier-News.* "Is Determined the Mop State, Says Woodcock." September 26, 1930.

2   Staff Writer. "Shore Officer Held in Jury Fixing Case." *Asbury Park Press*, January 24, 1934.

3   Her family couldn't recall the exact showgirl troupe, but Jerry's longtime lawyer believed she was part of the Ziegfeld Follies.

4   SAC, Newark. Letter to Director, FBI. "La Causa Nostra AR—Conspiracy." Airtel, March 7, 1963.

5   Mangano was the boss of what became known as the Gambino crime family.

6   United States Senate: Special Committee to Investigate Organized Crime in Interstate Commerce. "Investigation of Organized Crime in Interstate Commerce, Part 7, New York-New Jersey." U.S. Government Printing Office, 1951.

7   Ibid., p. 651.

Chapter 4

1   Burke, Harry. "Boiardo Wedding Glittering Festival." *Newark Evening News*, May 1, 1947.

2   After his successful stint on the Kefauver Committee, Halley ran unsuccessfully for mayor of New York City.

3   Spelled Katherine in the official Kefauver transcripts.

4   United States Senate: Special Committee to Investigate Organized Crime in Interstate Commerce. "Investigation of Organized Crime in Interstate Commerce, Part 7, New York–New Jersey." U.S. Government Printing Office, 1951.

5   Ibid.

6   Ibid.

7   Ibid.

8   Ibid.

9   Ibid.

Chapter 5

1   *The Star-Ledger*. 1957. "Catena's Neighbors Can't Believe He Has Mob Ties," December 4, 1957.

2   Reid, Ed. *The Grim Reapers: The Anatomy of Organized Crime in America*. New York: Bantam Books, 1969.

3   Rogers, Wendy. "Boca Raton Resident Gangland's 'Mr. Big'?" *The Miami Herald*, March 9, 1969.

4   *The Times Record*. "Aura of Respectaility (*sic*) Shades Reputed Overseer of Mafia Doings," January 6, 1969.

5   Grutzner, Charles. "An Overseer of Mafia, Gerardo 'Jerry' Catena." *The New York Times*, December 19, 1968.

6   Schenker, Jennifer L. "Resurgent Mob Threatens S. Florida, Officials Warn." *The Miami Herald*, September 5, 1983.

7   Connors, Kevin. John Connor's FBI career. Interview by Author, 2024.

8   Aldi, Andy. Jerry Catena. Interview by Author, August 24, 2023.

9   Nagel, Bruce H., and S. M. Chris Franzblau. *The Last Mob Lawyer*. Nashville: Forefront Books, 2025.

10   Smith, Sandy. "A Death in the Family." *Life*, February 28, 1969.

11   Williams, Danny. Jerry Catena and Golf. Interview by Author, October 29, 2024.

12   Ibid.

13   Ibid.

14   Former Knoll caddy. Catena and golf, 2025.

15   *The Star-Ledger*. "Catena Duo Wins at Suburban," June 5, 1950.

16   Associated Press. "Senate Probe Recalls Witness." *The Record*, October 11, 1971.

Chapter 6

1   SAC, Newark. Letter to Director, FBI. "The Criminal Conspiracy." Airtel, January 16, 1963.

2   Federal Bureau of Investigation. "FBI Transcripts of Investigations of William Rega DeCarlo and Others." Federal Bureau of Investigation, 1970.

3   SAC, Newark. Letter to Director, FBI et al. "The Criminal Commission, AR— Conspiracy." Airtel, January 16, 1963.

4   Sherman, William and Matt Sullivan, "Bidder End For Mob House." *The New York Daily News*, 2002.

5   Various sources give numbers between fifty-eight and sixty-two. The official 1958 State of New York report gives the number at sixty-two (or more attendees), sixty detained, and fifty-eight identified from out of town, and fifty-eight questioned. Later, twenty of the men were charged with federal conspiracy charges.

6   Federal Bureau of Investigation. "FBI Transcripts of Investigations of William Rega DeCarlo and Others." Federal Bureau of Investigation, 1970.

7   United Press International. "Nationwide Ring Hit by Indictment." *Lodi News-Sentinel*, July 9, 1958.

Chapter 7

1   DeStefano, Anthony M. *The Deadly Don*. Citadel Press, May 25, 2021.

2   SAC, New York (92-2300). "La Cosa Nostra AR—Conspiracy." New York Field Office: Federal Bureau of Investigation, October 6, 1964.

3   SAC, New York (RUC). "Re Pittsburgh Letter to Bureau, 1/14/64," January 24, 1964.

4   Connors, Kevin. John Connors—Catena. Interview by Author, August 22, 2024.

5   SAC, Newark. Letter to Director, FBI. "The Criminal Conspiracy." Airtel, January 16, 1963.

6   Connors, John H. "Gerardo v. Catena, Bureau File 92-3172." Federal Bureau of Investigation, September 1, 1961.

7   Federal Bureau of Investigation. "Criminal Informants Criminal Intelligence Program." Washington, DC: Federal Bureau of Investigation, June 21, 1961.

8   U.S. House of Representatives: Select Committee on Assassinations. "Investigation of the Assassination of President John F. Kennedy: Staff and Consultant's Reports on Organized Crime." Washington, DC: U.S. Government Printing Office, March 1979.

9   SAC, New York (92-2300). "La Cosa Nostra AR—Conspiracy." New York Field Office: Federal Bureau of Investigation, October 6, 1964.

10   The Southern Club building still stands. As of early 2025 it is the Josephine Tussaud Wax Museum.

11   Gleichauf, Justin F. "Memorandum of Visit to Joseph Raymond Merola." Federal Bureau of Investigation, February 8, 1961.

12   SAC, Miami (92-463). "Joseph Raymond Merola, Aka AR." Federal Bureau of Investigation, April 23, 1963.

13 Merola somehow managed to avoid Catena's wrath and continued to be a figure in CIA-backed anti-Castro plots. Merola died in 1994.

14 Gale, J. H. Letter to Mr. Deloach. "Vincent Alo, Interstate Transportation in Aid of Racketeering-Gambling." United States Government Memorandum, November 2, 1966.

15 The club changed locations a few times over the decades, even closing for a while in the early 1970s. It's currently located at 625 W 51st St. as of January 2025.

16 SAC, Newark. Letter to Director, FBI. "The Criminal Conspiracy." Airtel, January 16, 1963.

17 Ibid.

18 Ibid.

19 SAC, New York (92-2300). "La Cosa Nostra AR—Conspiracy." New York Field Office: Federal Bureau of Investigation, October 6, 1964.

20 Federal Bureau of Investigation. "La Cause Nostra, Bureau File 92-6054." Federal Bureau of Investigation, January 31, 1963.

21 SAC, Newark. Letter to Director, FBI. "The Criminal Conspiracy." Airtel, January 16, 1963.

22 Ibid.

23 Ibid.

24 Ciro's was located less than two miles from Santo's Miami home.

25 SAC, Miami. Letter to Director, FBI. "Anthony Stephano Randazzo." Memorandum, December 20, 1962.

26 Carlo Gambino and Tommy Lucchese.

27 SAC, New York (92-2300). "La Cosa Nostra AR—Conspiracy." New York Field Office: Federal Bureau of Investigation, October 6, 1964.

28 Ibid.

29 Ibid.

30 FBI New York. Letter to Director 2—Encoded. "La Cosa Nostra, AR—Conspiracy." Coded Teletype, April 6, 1965.

Chapter 8

1 The Essex was affiliated with a nearby club, The West End Club, that Del Grosso also managed. The West End had transferred its liquor license over to the Essex in

1962 because it was larger. After Del Grosso's murder, the state beverage commission revoked the license.

2   *The Star-Ledger.* "Murder Called 'Spontaneous.'" February 2, 1963.

3   Volz, Joseph, and Peter J. Bridge. *The Mafia Talks.* Fawcett Gold Medal, 1969.

4   Ibid.

5   Byrne later used that tagline as part of his campaign for governor. Byrne was the governor of New Jersey from 1974 to 1982.

6   SAC, Newark. "La Causa Nostra AR—Conspiracy." Received by Director, FBI, March 7, 1963.

7   *The New York Daily News.* "Gang Probers Call L.I. Cafe Man." February 17, 1965.

Chapter 9

1   *The Star-Ledger.* "Ad for Solar-Vent." May 27, 1956.

2   Schiffman, J. 1968. "Restaurant of the Week." *The Item of Milburn and Short Hills,* September 26, 1968.

3   Aldi, Andy. Catena, Dameo, and The Arch. Interview by Author, August 24, 2023.

4   Ibid.

5   In 1976, Japanese restaurant chain Benihana purchased the building and is still operating in the location as of February 2025.

6   He sold the company to Seagram's in 1940, although he later maintained that he was cheated out of his fair profits, resulting in a tax evasion trial.

7   United States Senate: Special Committee to Investigate Organized Crime in Interstate Commerce. "Investigation of Organized Crime in Interstate Commerce, Part 7, New York–New Jersey." U.S. Government Printing Office, 1951.

8   In Re Presentment of The Essex County Grand Jury. Harry Rosen, Movant-Appellant and Cross-Respondent, V. State of New Jersey, Respondent and Cross-Appellant. (The Supreme Court of New Jersey March 7, 1966).

Chapter 10

1   The subsidiary company became Bally-Midway in 1982.

2 They Create Worlds. "Lion and Bally Manufacturing." Podcast. Podbeam, May 15, 2019.

3 Power, SAC Newark, Thomas A. "John Lardiere." Federal Bureau of Investigation, July 23, 1965.

4 Volz, Joseph, and Peter J. Bridge. *The Mafia Talks*. Fawcett Gold Medal, 1969.

5 Sugerman, Myron. Bally Gaming Deal. Interview by Author, April 24, 2024.

6 Lion Manufacturing was originally located at 310 West Erie St. It moved to Ravenswood in 1933 and to the main facility on West Belmont in 1935.

7 Sugerman, Myron. Bally Gaming Deal. Interview by Author, April 24, 2024.

8 Ibid.

9 According to Myron, two of the men were bodyguards for Lucky Luciano in Naples before he passed. The third was Emilio Palamara, a Camorra associate whose car was discovered abandoned in Naples in 1972. Emilio was never found.

10 Sugerman, Myron. Letter to Author. "Re: Your Tommy Ryan Post." Email, October 27, 2024.

11 Hiltner, George J. "Moylan Asks Pinball Ban." *The Baltimore Sun*, March 13, 1969.

12 In 1978 Midway started licensing Japanese video games and came to be the face of the video arcade explosion of the 1980s with games like *Space Invaders* and *Pac-Man*.

Chapter 11

1 U.S. House of Representatives: Select Committee on Assassinations. "Investigation of the Assassination of President John F. Kennedy: Staff and Consultant's Reports on Organized Crime." Washington, DC: U.S. Government Printing Office, March 1979.

2 Parker, SA M. B., *Nevada Gambling Industry*. Federal Bureau of Investigation, November 16, 1964.

3 Ibid.

4 Ibid.

5 Federal Bureau of Investigation. "Anthony Giacalone, ELSUR," June 10, 1964.

6 Shedd, SA John Edward. "Edward Levinson." Washington, DC: U.S. Government Printing Office, February 14, 1963.

7 Connors, Kevin. 2024. John Connor's FBI career. Interview by author.

8 Parker, SA M. B., "Nevada Gambling Industry." Federal Bureau of Investigation, November 16, 1964.

9 Ibid.

10 SAC, Newark. Letter to Director, FBI. "Angelo DeCarlo, A.k.a. AR." Airtel, March 19, 1962.

11 Ibid.

12 Anthony "Jack Panels" Santoli, a soldier in the Genovese family.

13 SAC, Newark. Letter to Director, FBI. "Angelo DeCarlo, A.k.a. AR." Airtel, March 19, 1962.

14 Evans, C. A. *Carl Cohen, Sands Casino Eavesdropping Suit.* Federal Bureau of Investigation, September 9, 1963.

15 The fact is that there have been many examples of innocent people getting killed by mobsters over the decades, dating back to the early 1900s through the 1990s.

Chapter 12

1 Davis, Leslie. "Moretti Tied to Unsolved Murder." *The Herald-News*, January 14, 1970.

2 Connors, SAC John H. "Newark Airtel to Washington." Federal Bureau of Investigation, December 28, 1964.

3 Eastmond, William. "Lordi, Choice to Curb Casino Crime, Faulted for Efforts in Essex." *Asbury Park Press*, July 17, 1977.

4 SAC, Newark. "La Causa Nostra AR-Conspiracy." Received by Director, FBI, March 7, 1963.

5 United Press International. "Prominent Figures Mentioned in Tapes Released by Judge." *The Millville Daily*, January 7, 1970.

6 Norton, Edward. "Witness Against the Mob Is Missing." *The Record*, October 12, 1971.

7 United States Senate: Committee on Commerce. *Effects of Organized Criminal Activity on Interstate and Foreign Commerce: Hearings before the Committee on Commerce, United States Senate, Ninety-Second Congress.* 1972.

8 United States Senate: Committee on Commerce. *Effects of Organized Criminal Activity on Interstate and Foreign Commerce: Hearings before the Committee on Commerce, United States Senate, Ninety-Second Congress.* 1972.

9 Devlin, John Patrick. *La Cosa Nostra: Newark Division.* Federal Bureau of Investigation, October 3, 1967.

10 State of New York Senate. "Report of the New York State Joint Legislative Committee on Crime, Its Causes, Control & Effect on Society." State of New York, 1970.

11   Associated Press. "Pier Officer Asks Ouster of Mafiosi." *The Morning Call*, June 27, 1969.

12   Connors, SAC John H. *Gerardo Catena*. Federal Bureau of Investigation, May 14, 1964.

Chapter 13

1   O'Neil, Robert G. 1968. "La Cosa Nostra." Federal Bureau of Investigation.

2   Foderaro, Jane. 1969. "Genovese Funeral Puts Red Bank in Spotlight." *The Daily Register*, February 17, 1969.

3   St. John's Cemetery is also the final resting place for John Gotti, Lucky Luciano, Joe Colombo, Carlo Gambino, and many other Mafia figures.

4   Grutzner, Charles. 1969. "Of 9 Mafia Commissioner in 19560, Only 4 Still Remain in Power." *The New York Times*, August 31, 1969.

5   SAC, Kansas City. Letter to Director, FBI. 1969. "Carl James Civella, A.k.a. Corky." Airtel, March 10, 1969.

6   Gannett News Service. 1969. "Mafia Leaders Pick Catena, but He's Reluctant to Serve." *The Ithaca Journal*, April 30, 1969.

7   Ibid.

8   United States Senate: Committee on the Judiciary. 1983. "Organized Crime in America." U.S. Government Printing Office.

9   Associated Press. 1970. "F.B.I.-Taped Conversation Sheds Light on 1962 Gangland Slaying of Strollo." *The New York Times*, January 8, 1970.

10 Norton, Edward. 1970. "Addonizio, Aides Guilty." *The Record*, July 23, 1970.

11 Fortier, Andre N. 1970. "Pasquale Michael Erra." Federal Bureau of Investigation.

12 Federal Bureau of Investigation, Newark Field Office. "Teletype to Director Las Vegas & Miami: La Cosa Nostra, AR—Conspiracy." Federal Bureau of Investigation, February 28, 1969.

13 State of New Jersey Commission of Investigation. 1973. "Report for the Year 1972."

14 Catena v. Seidl (1974) (The Supreme Court of New Jersey).

15 Pace, Eric, "Eboli Chauffeur being Questioned," Archives (*The New York Times*), July 18, 1972, http://www.nytimes.com/1972/07/18/archives/eboli-chauffeur-being-questioned-tells-police-he-didnt-see-killer.html?_r=0.

16   The Gangland History Podcast. 2025. "#40: Interview with Xavier Eboli, Son of Thomas 'Tommy Ryan' Eboli." YouTube. February 11, 2025. https://www.youtube.com/watch?v=pnxW8CoTKrQ.

17   United States Senate, Committee on Government Affairs. 1988. "Organized Crime: 25 Years after Valachi." Washington, DC: U.S. Government Printing Office.

18   SAC, Newark. Letter to Director, FBI. 1970. "Frank Tieri, Aka AR." Memorandum, August 3, 1970.

19   Ibid.

20   Sugerman, Myron. *Interview on NJ Organized Crime*, February 7, 2017.

21   Catena v. Seidl. 1975. The Supreme Court of New Jersey.

Chapter 14

1   Pepinsky, Pete. "Reputed Mafioso out of Jail." *Boca Raton News*, August 19, 1975.

2   Cooke, Peter. 1975. "Mobster Residing in Boca." *The Palm Beach Post-Times*, October 19, 1975.

3   In mid-2024, a luxury twenty-four-story condo development broke ground on the former site of the pub.

4   Cooke, Peter, and Barbara Pusch. "The Westchester Connection." *The Palm Beach Post-Times*, April 15, 1979.

5   Sterling, Guy. "Arrest Ends Long Search for Suspect in Mob Killing." *The Star-Ledger*, March 12, 2007.

6   United States House of Representatives Select Committee on Crime. 1972. "Organized Crime in Sports (Racing)."

7   In the Matters of the Application of Bally's Park Place, Inc. a New Jersey Corporation, For a Casino License and the Application of Bally Manufacturing Corporation, a Delaware Corporation, for a Casino Service Industry License (New Jersey Casino Control Commission March 16, 1981).

8   Nevada Gaming Control Board. "Registration of Bally Manufacturing Corporation, Sam W. Klein. Transcript of Proceedings Hearing," August 26, 1976.

9   Savage, James, and Ron LaBrecque. "Organized Crime Is Entering into Mainstream of Economy." *The Miami Herald*, June 19, 1977.

10   MOBFAX. 2022. "Gerardo 'Jerry' Catena & the Bally Company (1977)." 2022. https://www.youtube.com/watch?v=ZMOxxlV-zG0&list=PLTC3pvZhj74bUaGI-GyOsUQiuiS66B8dX.

11 Ibid.

12 Ibid.

13 In 1995, Klein founded the Sam W. Klein Charitable Foundation and before his death in 2007, donated millions to various causes.

14 McEvoy, George. "Galante Killing Plotted in S. Florida." *Fort Lauderdale News*, August 26, 1979.

Chapter 15

1 SAC, Miami. "Gerardo Catena." Federal Bureau of Investigation, November 10, 1980.

2 Committee on the Judiciary, United States Senate. "Organized Crime in America" Washington, DC: U.S. Government Printing Office, 1983.

3 New Jersey State Police. "The Structure of Organized Crime in New Jersey," 1983.

4 Lamberti, Al. Letter to Author. "Jerry Catena." Email, July 6, 2024.

5 Sam DeCavalcante died in February 1997 from heart issues.

6 Checchio, Michael. "A Better Climate: Authorities Say Scarfo Will Run A.C. From Fla." *Press of Atlantic City*, December 16, 1985.

7 Nevada Gaming Control Board, and Nevada State Gaming Commission. "In the Matter of Bally Manufacturing Corporation (Registration)," April 16, 1987.

8 The new Bally's Chicago is located a block from the corner of Halstead and Grand ave, near some one-time Chicago Outfit hangouts.

9 *South Florida Sun Sentinel*. "The Gangster Next Door." September 25, 1989.

10 Sugerman, Myron. Catena. Interview by Author, April 24, 2024.

11 Abe Green died in December 2003 at 91 years old.

BIBLIOGRAPHY

Acuff, Lloyd. "Jersey Racketeers Become Doves after Truce Feast." *Daily News*, October 8, 1930.

akin214. "Organized Crime in Dallas, Texas, and the Murder of Lee Harvey Oswald." Assorted Musings from an Unknown Historian, December 17, 2018. https:// historicalmusings.com/2018/12/17/organized-crime-in-dallas-texas-and-the-murder- of-lee-harvey-oswald/.

Aldi, Andy. Catena, Dameo, and The Arch. Interview by Author, August 24, 2023.

Aldi, Andy. Jerry Catena. Interview by Author, August 24, 2023.

Apoyan, Jackie. "The Hit That Could Have Sunk Las Vegas." The Mob Museum, May 4, 2017. https://themobmuseum.org/blog/costello-hit-sunk-las-vegas/.

Arougheti, Ilana, Jake Sheridan, and Robert Channick. "Gamblers Welcome Chicago's First Casino as Bally's Opens Temporary Site at Medinah Temple. 'They're Going to Do Fantastic Here.'" *Chicago Tribune*, September 9, 2023. https://www.chicagotribune. com/2023/09/09/gamblers-welcome-chicagos-first-casino-as-ballys-opens-temporary- site-at-medinah-temple-theyre-going-to-do-fantastic-here/.

Asbury Park Press. "Grand Jury Calls Ex-City IRS Aide." January 27, 1970.

Asbury Park Press. "Kool-Vent Ad." April 18, 1950.

Asbury Park Press. "Relative of Chief Held in Rum Ring." November 14, 1929.

Asbury Park Press. "Whitfield Wins, Chance at Title." August 19, 1945.

Associated Press. "'Inside Look' at New Jersey's Crime Evokes Many New Questions." *Asbury Park Press*, August 20, 1969.

Associated Press. "4 Plead Guilty in Jury Bribing Case." *The Morning Call*, March 12, 1934.

Associated Press. "14-Story Hotel Opens in Vegas." *Reno Gazette-Journal*, May 18, 1956.

Associated Press. "Apalachin Tie Asked of Four." *The Courier-News*, February 6, 1958.

Associated Press. "Catena, Smiling, Returned to Jail." *Asbury Park Press*, February 28, 1974.

Associated Press. "Crime Probers Hit O'Dwyer for Laxity." *Press of Atlantic City*, May 2, 1951.

Associated Press. "F.B.I.-Taped Conversation Sheds Light on 1962 Gangland Slaying of Strollo." *The New York Times*, January 8, 1970.

Associated Press. "Four Youths Confess to Scores of Hold-Ups." *Press of Atlantic City*, March 16, 1931.

Associated Press. "Gangland Kills Dry Agent Murder Witness." *The Herald-News*, November 7, 1932.

Associated Press. "Investigation Begun on Charges of Still Operation in Holmdel." *The Daily Record*, December 10, 1941.

Associated Press. "JERSEY GAMBLER DIES; James (Piggy) Lynch, 54, Was Adonis Associate." *The New York Times*, April 23, 1958.

Associated Press. "Jury Decrees 2 Innocent," October 31, 1963.

Associated Press. "Jury Probes Backers of 2 Trenton Firms." *Atlantic City Press*, February 6, 1958.

Associated Press. "Mafia Deal Is Reported." *St. Joseph News-Press*, June 26, 1969.

Associated Press. "Newark Dry Agents Will Be Transferred." *The Courier-News*, June 23, 1932.

Associated Press. "Newark Man Held for Old Murder." *Asbury Park Press*, August 24, 1931.

Associated Press. "Pier Officer Asks Ouster of Mafiosi." *The Morning Call*, June 27, 1969.

Associated Press. "Police Round up Gang Truck Thieves." *The Central New Jersey Home News*, January 18, 1927.

Associated Press. "Riviera Hotel in Las Vegas to Be Expanded." *Reno Gazette-Journal*, July 9, 1971.

Associated Press. "Senate Probe Recalls Wittness." *The Record*, October 11, 1971.

Associated Press. "Skim Charges Laid in Vegas, Grand Jury Indicts Seven." *Reno Gazette-Journal*, May 12, 1967.

Associated Press. "State Grand Jury on Illegal Gambling Meets New Jersey's 'Ex-Crime Boss.'" *The Pensacola Journal*, May 20, 1976.

Associated Press. "Violators of Rum Law Sentenced." *The Morning Call*, November 19, 1932.

Associated Press. "Young Bandits Caught." *Press of Atlantic City*, March 17, 1931.

Austin, William A. "Due Process in Civil Contempt Proceedings: A Comparison with Juvenile and Mental Incompetency Requirements." *Fordham Law Review* 44, no. 5 (1976).

Baum, Captain William J. Letter to Sgt. Adam Carter. "Central Landfill Inc. of Florida." Memorandum, August 27, 1971.

Beer, John. "Dolan, Berrien Lead on Crestmont Links." *Newark Sunday News*, October 5, 1947.

Bennett, Cliff. "Essex Jury Told to Push Crackdown on Rackets." *The Star-Ledger*, October 22, 1963.

Bennett, Cliff. "Jury Finds Pair Innocent of Bartender's Fatal Beating." *The Star-Ledger*, October 31, 1963.

Berger, Jeff. Runyon. Interview by Author, March 5, 2025.

Bergman, Lowell. "Pinball, Slot Machines, and Crime Help Tilt the Attorney General." *Fifth Estate*, July 1974.

Bertucelli, Steven. "Vincenzo Cotroni." Miami-Dade Police Department, Criminal Surveillance Unit, March 31, 1971.

Bertucelli, Steven. Letter to Sgt. Adam Carter. "Information." Memorandum, August 17, 1971.

Birkbeck, Matt. *The Life We Chose*. New York, NY: William Morrow, 2024.

Birkbeck, Matt. *The Quiet Don: The Untold Story of Mafia Kingpin Russell Bufalino*. New York, NY: Berkley Books, 2013.

Blue, Agent, W., J. Derener, and A. Sergeant. "Case No 7-143: Investigation into the Activities of Central Landfill of Florida, Inc." Miami-Dade County, Criminal Surveillance Unit #1, September 22, 1971.

Blue, Agent, W., J. Derener, and A. Sergeant. "Case No 7-143: Investigation into the Activities of Central Landfill of Florida, Inc." Miami-Dade County, Criminal Surveillance Unit #1, October 7, 1971.

Blue, Agent, W., J. Derener, and A. Sergeant. "Case No 7-143: Investigation into the Activities of Central Landfill of Florida, Inc." Miami-Dade County, Criminal Surveillance Unit #1, October 11, 1971.

Blue, W., and L. Huard. "Case No. 7-143." Miami-Dade Police Department, Criminal Surveillance Unit, October 22, 1971.

Boca Raton News. "Real Estate Transactions." July 11, 1999.

Boca Raton News. "Will He Talk This Time?" May 9, 1976.

Bond, Brad. "History of Muzak." Mood Media, July 11, 2022. https://us.moodmedia.com/blog/history-of-muzak/.

Brady, Thomas. "Addonizio and 4 Convicted of Extortion by U.S. Jury." *The New York Times*, July 23, 1970.

Brown, James S. "Law Agencies Eye Dameo for Flirtations with Mob." *Asbury Park Press*, January 2, 1970.

Bruck, Connie. *Master of the Game: Steve Ross and the Creation of Time Warner.* New York: Simon & Schuster Paperback, 2020.

Burke, Harry. "Boiardo Wedding Glittering Festival." *Newark Evening News*, May 1, 1947.

Burnside, Susan M. "O'Key Scolds Chamber for Statement." *The Miami Herald*, June 19, 1971.

Camarotti, Antonio. "The Raleigh: A Landmark Transformation in Miami Beach." Forbes, December 9, 2023. https://www.forbes.com/sites/antoniocamarotti/2023/12/09/the-raleigh-a-landmark-transformation-in-miami-beach/?sh=318d2d043a03.

Cannon, Randall. *Caesars Palace Grand Prix: Las Vegas, Organized Crime and the Pinnacle of Motorsport.* Jefferson, NC: McFarland & Company, 2021.

Cantwell, John Davis. "Cardiologist to the Mafia: Reflections of a Former Prison Doctor." *Proceedings (Baylor University. Medical Center)* 29, no. 3 (July 2016): 346. https://pmc.ncbi.nlm.nih.gov/articles/PMC4900793/.

Capuzzo, Jill P. "Mountainside, N.J.: Natural Beauty and Teardowns." *The New York Times*, June 18, 2018.

Catena v. Seidl (The Supreme Court of New Jersey August 19, 1975).

Catena, Jerry. Roselli. Interview by SA Bert P. Stickler and SA George M. Maloney, October 8, 1976.

Cefkin, Ott, and Mike Hauser. "14 Mafia Leaders Assemble in Hollywood." *Fort Lauderdale News*, March 2, 1969.

Channick, Robert. "Bally's Timeline: From Pinball to Pac-Man, Health Clubs to Casinos, a Colorful Name in Chicago's Corporate History." *Chicago Tribune*, August 11, 2022. https://www.chicagotribune.com/2022/08/11/ballys-timeline-from-pinball-to-pac-man-health-clubs-to-casinos-a-colorful-name-in-chicagos-corporate-history/.

Chatham. "Chatham Electronics; Newark, NJ Manufacturer in USA, Model T | Radiomuseum.org." Radiomuseum.org, 2025. https://www.radiomuseum.org/dsp_hersteller_detail.cfm?company_id=7125.

Checchio, Michael. "A Better Climate: Authorities Say Scarfo Will Run A.C. From Fla." *Press of Atlantic City*, December 16, 1985.

Cherwa, John. "Hubbard's Ties Are Questioned: Horse Racing: Race Track Owner Has Had Associations with Emprise, a Company L." *Los Angeles Times*, January 17, 1991. https://www.latimes.com/archives/la-xpm-1991-01-17-sp-324-story.html.

Civil Action M-113618 Order To Show Cause (Superior Court of New Jersey, Bergen County Law Division February 1984).

Cocchis, Roberto. "L'angolo Giallo." Blogspot.com, February 25, 2025. https://angologiallo.blogspot.com/2022/.

Cole, Robert J. "WJA, Xcor in Fight for Jai-Alai." *The New York Times*, July 26, 1978.

Committee On the Judiciary, United States Senate. "Organized Crime in America." Washington, DC: U.S. Government Printing Office, 1983.

"Congressional Record—Senate, Volume 5884," March 11, 1969.

Connors, John H. "Gerardo v. Catena, Bureau File 92-3172." Federal Bureau of Investigation, September 1, 1961.

Connors, John H. "Gerardo v. Catena, File #93-3172." Federal Bureau of Investigation, September 1, 1961.

Connors, Kevin. John Connor's FBI career. Interview by Author, August 23, 2024.

Connors, Kevin. John Connor's FBI career. Interview by Author, August 23, 2024.

Connors, Kevin. Interview by Author, August 22, 2024.

Connors, SAC John H. "Gerardo Catena." Federal Bureau of Investigation, May 14, 1964.

Cook, Fred J. *Mafia!* Greenwich: Fawcett Gold Medal, 1973.

Cooke, Peter. "Mobster Residing in Boca." *The Palm Beach Post*, October 19, 1975.

Cooke, Peter. "Mobster Residing in Boca." *The Palm Beach Post-Times*, October 19, 1975.

Cooke, Peter, and Barbara Pusch. "The Westchester Connection." *The Palm Beach Post-Times*, April 15, 1979.

Cummings, Charles. "Essex House Was 'a Haven for the Elite,'" 2016. https://knowingnewark.npl.org/essex-house-was-a-haven-for-the-elite/.

Curley, Bob. "McBride, Arcole Medalist, Drops from Tournament." *The Herald-News*, June 15, 1953.

Dade County Public Safety Department. "Daily Bulletin: Classic Pattern of Organized Crime." Miami, FL: Dade County Public Safety Department, June 13, 1968.

Davis, Leslie. "Moretti Tied to Unsolved Murder." *The Herald-News*, January 14, 1970.

DeStefano, Anthony M. *The Deadly Don*. Toronto, ON: Citadel Press, 2021.

Devlin, John Patrick. "La Cosa Nostra: Newark Division." Federal Bureau of Investigation, October 3, 1967.

Downey, Mike. "She's Propelled by Dad's Memory." *Los Angeles Times*, August 16, 2008. https://www.latimes.com/archives/la-xpm-2008-aug-16-sp-olydowney16-story.html.

Dunn, SAC Edward J., and Federal Bureau of Investigation. "Roskill." Washington, DC.: Federal Bureau of Investigation, March 1, 1977.

Durkin, Paul G. "Charles Tourine." New York Field Office: Federal Bureau of Investigation, October 27, 1967.

Eastmond, William. "Lordi, Choice to Curb Casino Crime, Faulted for Efforts in Essex." *Asbury Park Press*, July 17, 1977.

Eboli. "Gerardo Catena—Man as Corporation." Black Hand Forum, October 25, 2021. https://theblackhand.club/forum/viewtopic.php?t=8357.

Eisenberg, Dennis, Uri Dan, and Eli Landau. *Meyer Lansky*. New York, NY: Grosset & Dunlap, 1979.

Ensslin, John C. "The History of Beer in New Jersey: From Colonial Days to the Rise of the Micropubs." North Jersey Media Group, November 13, 2018. https://www.northjersey.com/story/life/food/2018/11/13/history-beer-new-jersey/1126421002/.

Evans, C. A. "Carl Cohen, Sands Casino Eavesdropping Suit." Federal Bureau of Investigation, September 9, 1963.

Farabee, SA Maurice F. "Pasquale Michael Erra, Aka." Washington, DC: Federal Bureau of Investigation, February 12, 1973.

FBI New York. Letter to Director 2—Encoded. "La Cosa Nostra, AR—Conspiracy." Coded Teletype, April 6, 1965.

Federal Bureau of Investigation. "Accurate Detective Laboratories." Washington, DC: Federal Bureau of Investigation, December 1, 1961.

Federal Bureau of Investigation. "Anthony Giacalone, ELSUR," June 10, 1964.

Federal Bureau of Investigation. "Benny Binion, Horseshoe Club, Las Vegas Nevada," November 1, 1963.

Federal Bureau of Investigation. "Criminal Informants Criminal Intelligence Program." Washington, DC: Federal Bureau of Investigation, June 21, 1961.

Federal Bureau of Investigation. "FBI Budget Request—Fiscal Year 1968." Federal Bureau of Investigation, 1967.

Federal Bureau of Investigation. "FBI Transcripts of Investigations of William Rega DeCarlo and Others." Federal Bureau of Investigation, 1970.

Federal Bureau of Investigation. "Findings of the Office of the Inspector General Department of Justice Critical of Forensic Work Performed by Certain Lab Examiners," May 17, 1999.

Federal Bureau of Investigation. "Frank Pizzi; Joseph Sibilia; Garden State Sausage Company—Victim Anti-Racketeering," December 13, 1962.

Federal Bureau of Investigation. "Gerardo v. Catena," June 8, 1959.

Federal Bureau of Investigation. "La Cause Nostra, Bureau File 92-6054." Federal Bureau of Investigation, January 31, 1963.

Federal Bureau of Investigation. "La Cosa Nostra Hierarchy in the United States." U.S. Government Printing Office, June 1985.

Federal Bureau of Investigation. "Newark Airtel to Washington." Federal Bureau of Investigation, December 28, 1964.

Federal Bureau of Investigation. "Thomas Eboli." Washington, DC: Federal Bureau of Investigation, February 26, 1963.

Federal Bureau of Investigation, Newark Field Office. "Teletype to Director Las Vegas & Miami: La Cosa Nostra, AR—Conspiracy." Federal Bureau of Investigation, February 28, 1969.

Federal Bureau of Investigation, Los Angeles Field Office. "Joseph Stacher." Federal Bureau of Investigation, September 12, 1963.

"Federal Register—Extension of Remarks," November 16, 1971.

Federici, William, and Henry Lee. "Tony's Mistress Missing; Cops: Both May Be Dead." *The New York Daily News*, April 17, 1962.

Fessier, Bruce. "Gangsters in Paradise." *The Desert Sun*. TDS, November 30, 2014. https://www.desertsun.com/story/life/entertainment/2014/11/30/palm-springs-gangsters-in-paradise/19040507/.

Finkelstein, Al. "Ex-Con Missing; Search Going On." *The Miami Herald*, February 5, 1960.

Foderaro, Jane. "Genovese Funeral Puts Red Bank in Spotlight." *The Daily Register*, February 17, 1969.

Former Knoll caddy. Catena and golf, February 2025.

Fortier, Andre N. "Pasquale Michael Erra." Federal Bureau of Investigation, March 11, 1970.

Fulsom, Don. "The Mob's President: Richard Nixon's Secret Ties to the Mafia Crime Magazine." Crimemagazine.com, 2020. https://www.crimemagazine.com/mobs-president-richard-nixons-secret-ties-mafia.

Gage, Nicholas. *Mafia USA*. Chicago, IL: Playboy Press, 1972.

Gale, J. H. Letter to Mr. Deloach. "Vincent Alo, Interstate Transportation in Aid of Racketeering-Gambling." United States Government Memorandum, November 2, 1966.

Gannett News Service. "Mafia Leaders Pick Catena, but He's Reluctant to Serve." *The Ithaca Journal*, April 30, 1969.

George, Joseph. "Sift Background of Man Found Murdered in Car." *Daily News*, January 25, 1965.

Gleichauf, Justin F. "Memorandum of Visit to Joseph Raymond Merola." Federal Bureau of Investigation, February 8, 1961.

Green, Prof Michael. Las Vegas and the Skim. Interview by Author, September 18, 2024.

Grutzner, Charles. "An Overseer of Mafia, Gerardo 'Jerry' Catena." *The New York Times*, December 19, 1968.

Grutzner, Charles. "Of 9 Mafia Commissioner in 19560, Only 4 Still Remain in Power." *The New York Times*, August 31, 1969.

Hastings, SA James E. "Michael Coppola, Aka." Miami Field Office: Federal Bureau of Investigation, June 12, 1961.

Heneghan, Daniel. "Exec: Bally Ended Questionable Ties." *Press of Atlantic City*, November 14, 1980.

Hiltner, George J. "Moylan Asks Pinball Ban." *The Baltimore Sun*, March 13, 1969.

historyofhowweplay. "Chicago Legacy: Exploring Bally Manufacturing." The History of How We Play, May 14, 2019. https://thehistoryofhowweplay.wordpress.com/2019/05/14/chicago-legacy-exploring-bally-manufacturing/.

House Select Committee on Crime. "Organized Criminal Influence in Horseracing." Washington, DC: U.S. Government Printing Office, 1973.

Hunt, Thomas. "1946 Havana Mafia Convention Never Happened | American Mafia." Mafiahistory.us, 2018. https://mafiahistory.us/a045/f_havanaconvention.html#n29.

Immerso, Michael D. "Enclaves of Memory." *Newark Historical Society*, May 23, 2019. https://www.newarkhistorysociety.org/images/articles/resources/PDF/Enclaves-of-Memory,-by-Michael-Immerso.pdf.

In Re Presentment of The Essex County Grand Jury. Harry Rosen, Movant-Appellant and Cross-Respondent, v. State of New Jersey, Respondent and Cross-Appellant (The Supreme Court of New Jersey March 7, 1966).

In the Matters of the Application of Bally's Park Place, Inc. a New Jersey Corporation, For a Casino License and the Application of Bally Manufacturing Corporation, a Delaware Corporation, for a Casino Service Industry License (New Jersey Casino Control Commission March 16, 1981).

Ipdb.org. "Internet Pinball Machine Database: Bally 'Ballyhoo,'" 2025. https://www.ipdb.org/machine.cgi?gid=4817.

Irving Kaye Dedicated to the preservation of the legacy of this uniquely American brand. "'Friends' of Irving Kaye—Irving Kaye," July 7, 2011. https://irvingkaye.com/about-irving-kaye/friends-irving-kaye/.

Jacobs, Sanford. "Paterson Firm Linked to Mafia." *The Morning Call*, June 27, 1969.

Janas, Gene. "Lansky Linked to Untaxed Vegas Profits." *Fort Lauderdale News*, June 7, 1966.

Jenkins, Gary. "N.J. Mobster Jerry Catena." YouTube, October 23, 2022. https://www.youtube.com/watch?v=etcU86u3V38&list=PLTC3pvZhj74bUaGI-GyOsUQiuiS66B8dX&index=3.

Justia Law. "Hotel Riviera, Inc. v. Torres," 2025. https://law.justia.com/cases/nevada/supreme-court/1981/12370-1.html.

Justia Law. "Nicholas Delmore, Also Known as Nicholas Amoruso v. Herbert Brownell, Attorney General of the United States, and Raymond G. Hoffeller, Agent in Charge of Immigration and Naturalization Service, Appellants, 236 F.2d 598 (3d Cir. 1956)," 2025. https://law.justia.com/cases/federal/appellate-courts/F2/236/598/440614/.

Justia Law. "United States of America Ex Rel. Gerardo Catena, Appellant, v. Albert Elias, Superintendent of Youth Reception and Correction Center at Yardville, N. J, 449 F.2d 40 (3d Cir. 1971)," 2025. https://law.justia.com/cases/federal/appellate-courts/F2/449/40/241137/.

Justia Law. "United States of America, Appellee, v. Anthony Salerno, A/k/a 'Fat Tony,' Vincent Di Napoli, A/k/a 'Vinnie,' Louis Di Napoli, A/k/a 'Louie,' Matthew Ianniello, A/k/a 'Matty the Horse,' John Tronolone, A/k/a 'Peanuts,' Milton Rockman, A/k/a 'Maishe,' Nicholas Auletta, A/k/a 'Nick,' Edward J. Halloran, A/k/a 'Biff,' Alvin O. Chattin, A/k/a 'Al,' Richard Costa, A/k/a 'Richie,' and Aniello Migliore, A/k/a 'Neil,' Defendants. Matthew Ianniello, A/k/a 'Matty the Horse,' Vincent Dinapoli, A/k/a 'Vinnie,' Louis Di Napoli, A/k/a 'Louis,' Nicholas Auletta, A/k/a 'Nick,' Edward J. Halloran, A/k/a 'Biff,' Aniello Migliore, A/k/a 'Neil,' Anthony Salerno, A/k/a 'Fat Tony,' and Alvin O. Chattin, A/k/a 'Al,' Defendants-Appellants, 974 F.2d 231 (2d Cir. 1992)," 2025. https://law.justia.com/cases/federal/appellate-courts/F2/974/231/437565/.

Kamau, John. "Sex, Gamblers and Mafia: The Untold Story of Nanyuki's Mt Kenya Safari Club." *Nation*, April 5, 2022. https://nation.africa/kenya/news/sex-gamblers-mafia-untold-story-nanyuki-mt-kenya-safari-club-3769416#google_vignette.

Katz, Leonard. *Uncle Frank*. London: W. H. Allen, 1974.

Kiernan, Joseph, and Art Smith. "Boss of 4F Killer Gang Nabbed after B'klyn Hoodlum's Slaying." *New York Daily News*, June 12, 1944.

Kirkman, Edward. "Cosa Nostra Big Three Queried about Parlays." *Daily News*, January 20, 1965.

Kirkman, Edward. "Eboli's Date with Death: Tryst & Ambush." *The New York Daily News*, August 29, 1972.

Kirkman, Edward, and Paul Meskil. "Mafia Boss Keeps a Date with Death." *The New York Daily News*, July 17, 1972.

Konigsberg, Harold. Tony Bender Strollo. Interview by SAS Paul G. Durkin and SAS Charles G. Donnelly. Federal Bureau of Investigation, June 15, 1965.

Koshetz, Herbert. "Bally Agrees in Principle to Add World Jai-Alai Inc. for $66 Million." *The New York Times*, February 5, 1977.

Kroeger, Mark. "Deafening Blast, Debris Startle Many at Death Site." *Evansville Courier and Press*, October 19, 1977.

LaBrecque, Ron. "Organized Crime Figures, Associates in S. Florida." *The Miami Herald*, June 19, 1977.

Lacey, Robert. *Little Man*. Lb Books, 1992.

Lamberti, Al. Letter to Author. "Jerry Catena." Email, July 6, 2024.

Landau, Jack C. "U.S. Names 'Targets' in Mafia Probe." *The Star-Ledger*, January 12, 1969.

Lantigua, John. "Simone 'Sam the Plumber' DeCavalcante." *The Miami Herald*, February 10, 1997.

Legacy. "Sam Klein Obituary (2007)—Boca Raton, FL—the Palm Beach Post." Legacy.com. Legacy, October 25, 2007. https://www.legacy.com/us/obituaries/palmbeachpost/name/sam-klein-obituary?pid=96762086.

Lewin, Tamar. "Slain Gangster's Kin Missing." *The Record*, July 25, 1976.

Life. "A Searching Look at Big Crime." February 23, 1959.

Lubasch, Arnold H. "U.S. Indictment Says 9 Governed New York Mafia." *The New York Times*, February 27, 1985.

Luminello, Patrick. "Tony Strollo's Fate Remains a Mystery." *The Record*, May 2, 1962.

Marshall, Jonathan. *Dark Quadrant*. Lanham, MD: Rowman & Littlefield, 2021.

Mayo, Michael. "Nearing the Finish Line, Still Feeling like a Winner." *South Florida Sun Sentinel*, May 11, 2004.

McCarthy, Robert, Joseph Donnelly, and Jack Smee. "Costello Shot in Ambush at Door of Home." *Daily News*, May 3, 1957.

McDonald, Robert, and John Mallon. "Seek Link in Killing of 2 A&P Managers." *Daily News*, February 7, 1965.

McEvoy, George. "Galante Killing Plotted in S. Florida." *Fort Lauderdale News*, August 26, 1979.

McMeninmen, Robert V. "Willie's Income, Wedding Outlays Didn't Add Up." *Asbury Park Press*, October 2, 1988.

MOBFAX. "Gerardo 'Jerry' Catena & the Bally Company (1977)." www.youtube.com, 2022. https://www.youtube.com/watch?v=ZMOxxlV-zG0&list=PLTC3pvZhj74bUaGI-GyOsUQiuiS66B8dX.

Moran, Emerson. "Darkhorse Frank Tieri Seen Genovese Heir." *The Courier-News*, March 18, 1969.

Moran, Emerson. "N.J. Rackets Boss Called Genovese Successor." *The Courier-News*, April 30, 1969.

Mullin, Edward J. "Crime Probe Pot Boiling." *The Herald-News*, December 31, 1968.

Murray, Leo. "Former 'Ladder Man' Tells of His Work at Dice Games in the Area." *The Morning Call*, March 31, 1954.

Murray, Leo. "Joe Adonis to Take Stand Today as Trial of Winne Continues." *The Morning Call*, April 1, 1954.

Nagel, Bruce H., and S. M. Chris Franzblau. *The Last Mob Lawyer*. Forefront Books, 2025.

Nevada Gaming Control Board. "In the Matter of Bally Manufacturing Corporation (Sam W. Klein)," September 23, 1976.

Nevada Gaming Control Board. "Minutes of the Nevada Gaming Control Board," July 27, 1955.

Nevada Gaming Control Board. "Registration of Bally Manufacturing Corporation, Sam W. Klein. Transcript of Proceedings Hearing," August 26, 1976.

Nevada Gaming Control Board, and Nevada State Gaming Commission. "In the Matter of Bally Manufacturing Corporation (Registration)," April 4, 1975.

Nevada Gaming Control Board. "In the Matter of Bally Manufacturing Corporation (Registration)," April 16, 1987.

Nevada Gaming Control Board. "In the Matter of Bally Manufacturing Corporation (Registration)," April 1993.

Nevada State Journal. "U.S. Slaps $340,486 Income Tax Lien on 'Doc' Stacher." April 23, 1952.

"New Illinois Guidelines Aim to Boost College and Career Readiness." *WTTW News*, 2017. https://doi.org/1002587/c2n_sitewide_300x250_3.

New Jersey Bureau of Vital Statistics. "Marriage Records—1936," 1936.

New Jersey State Police. "The Structure of Organized Crime in New Jersey," 1983.

New York Times News Service. "Do Looks Deceive: Man in the News." *Corpus Christi Times*, December 31, 1968.

Newark Board of Education. "District History—Newark Board of Education," n.d. https://www.nps.k12.nj.us/info/district-history/.

Newark Evening News. "Albert Dansereau Is Elected East Side High's Track Head." June 22, 1922.

Newark Evening News. "Champions of Rotary Loop Rewarded with Footballs." December 6, 1923.

Newark Evening News. "East Side Separate Eleven Loses Only Three Veterans." September 24, 1923.

Newark Evening News. "Guard Fails to Identify Trio Caught by Police as Shot at by Him." July 2, 1925.

Newark Evening News. "Industrial Doings." June 30, 1927.

Newark Evening News. "Industrial Doings." August 22, 1927.

Newark Evening News. "Ironbound Star Joins Scranton." April 9, 1928.

Newark Evening News. "Ironbounds Lose Inaugural, 6 to 4." April 16, 1928.

Newark Evening News. "Only Three Smokes, but They Land Twelve in Jail." January 18, 1927.

Newark Evening News. "Policeman Is Bitten on Hand in Arrest of Trio." October 24, 1924.

Newark Evening News. "Winners of Ironbound Community House Title." October 29, 1929.

Newark Evening Star. "20 Students Start New Strike: Surrender to a 'Strikebreaker.'" October 10, 1912.

Newarkmemories.com. "Longy Zwillman: The Notorious Gangster from Newark's Third Ward," 2021. https://newarkmemories.com/memories/567.php.

newarkmemories.com. "Rise and Fall of Newark Underworld Character during Longy Zwillman Era," n.d. https://newarkmemories.com/memories/592.php.

Newsday. "Elmont Killer May Have Been Burglar." February 8, 1965.

Newsom, SA Milton L. "Joseph Francis Civello, Aka." Washington, DC: Federal Bureau of Investigation, September 29, 1960.

Norton, Edward. "Addonizio, Aides Guilty." *The Record*, July 23, 1970.

Norton, Edward. "How They Live in Bergen and Passaic." *The Record*, August 10, 1970.

Norton, Edward. "Witness Against the Mob Is Missing." *The Record*, October 12, 1971.

Novellino, Tex. "15,000 Try to See Boiardo Wedding." *The Star-Ledger*, May 1, 1950.

Nussbaum, Jerry. "Personally Speaking," May 1, 1956.

O'Neil, Robert G. "La Cosa Nostra." Federal Bureau of Investigation, September 18, 1968.

O'Neil, Robert G. "La Cosa Nostra, Anti-Racketeering Conspiracy." Federal Bureau of Investigation, September 26, 1968.

OC SHORTZ—Organized Crime Shortz. "WORST Mafia BOSS in Genovese Family?" YouTube, May 17, 2023. https://www.youtube.com/watch?v=DDNqS6Myvsw&list=PLTC3pvZhj74bUaGI-GyOsUQiuiS66B8dX&index=6.

Office of the Prosecutor, County of Morris. "Organized Crime, Morris County NJ," 1982.

Oregon Department of Justice, Criminal Justice Special Investigation Division. "The Use of State Regulatory Action against Criminal Infiltration of Legitimate Business," 1978.

Orsbon, R. Anthony. "Immunity from Prosecution and the Fifth Amendment: An Analysis of Constitutional Standards." *Vanderbilt Law Review* 25, no. 6 (November 1972).

Over50Vegas.com. "Binion's Horseshoe 128 Fremont Las Vegas, NV." Over50vegas.com, 2019. https://over50vegas.com/128_Fremont_Binions_Horseshoe.html.

Parker, SA M. B. "Nevada Gambling Industry." Federal Bureau of Investigation, November 16, 1964.

Passaic Daily Herald. "Firemen to Ask Probe of Murder." November 13, 1929.

Patrick J. Ciambelli v. The United States (The United States Court of Claims May 12, 1972).

Pennsylvania Crime Commission. "A Decade of Organized Crime: 1980 Report." St. Davids, Pennsylvania, 1980.

Pepinsky, Pete. "Reputed Mafioso out of Jail." *Boca Raton News*, August 19, 1975.

Perlmutter, Emanuel. "A Key Gang Figure Slain in Brooklyn." *The New York Times*, July 17, 1972.

Pileggi, Nicholas. "Big Money Won't Bank on Atlantic City." *New York Magazine*, February 27, 1978.

Plosia, Les. "Anti-Mafia Measures Aimed at Waterfront." *The Herald-News*, June 27, 1969.

Plosia, Les. "Galante Power Lust Riled Bosses." *The Herald-News*, July 17, 1979.

Poundstone, William. *Fortune's Formula*. Hill and Wang, 2010.

Power, SAC Newark, Thomas A. "John Lardiere." Federal Bureau of Investigation, July 23, 1965.

Press of Atlantic City. "Wage Violator Fined $2,100." January 22, 1955.

Privette, William Heath. "Organized Crime in the United States: Organizational Analogies for Counterinsurgency Strategy." Thesis, 2006.

Raab, Selwyn. "Canadian Gangs said to Seize Major Role in Florida Rackets." *The New York Times*, January 27, 1984, sec. U.S. https://www.nytimes.com/1984/01/27/us/canadian-gangs-said-to-seize-major-role-in-florida-rackets.html.

Reid, Ed. *The Grim Reapers: The Anatomy of Organized Crime in America*. Bantam Books, 1969.

Renner, Tom. "Jewish Power Irked DeCarlo." *Newsday*, January 13, 1970.

Riesel, Victor. "Inside Labor: Federals Learn to Cope with Pattern of Mafia." *The Argus*, January 7, 1960.

Rogers, Wendy. "Boca Raton Resident Gangland's 'Mr. Big'?" *The Miami Herald*, March 9, 1969.

Rowan, Roy, and Andrew Kupfer. "The 50 Biggest Mafia Bosses." *Fortune*, November 10, 1986.

Rudolph, Robert. "Tieri's Death Puts New Boss in Jersey." *The Star-Ledger*, April 6, 1981.

Ryan, Cy. "'No Conclusion' on Underworld Hidden Interests." *Nevada State Journal*, August 18, 1966.

SAC, Kansas City. Letter to Director, FBI. "Carl James Civella, A.k.a. Corky." Airtel, March 10, 1969.

SAC, Miami. Letter to Director, FBI. "Anthony Stephano Randazzo." Memorandum, December 20, 1962.

SAC, Miami. "Gerardo Catena." Federal Bureau of Investigation, March 25, 1980.

SAC, Miami. "Gerardo Catena." Federal Bureau of Investigation, July 9, 1980.

SAC, Miami. "Gerardo Catena." Federal Bureau of Investigation, November 10, 1980.

SAC, Miami. Letter to Director, FBI. "Investigation Concerning Harry Del Prete." Teletype, October 14, 1976.

SAC, Miami. "La Cosa Nostra Index." Federal Bureau of Investigation, October 7, 1980.

SAC, Miami. "Organized Crime Intelligence Unit (OCIU), RICO Intelligence Matters." Federal Bureau of Investigation, June 9, 1983.

SAC, Miami (92-463). "Joseph Raymond Merola, Aka AR." Federal Bureau of Investigation, April 23, 1963.

SAC, New York. Letter to Director, FBI. "Top Hoodlum Program." Memorandum, September 23, 1958.

SAC, New York (92-2300). "La Cosa Nostra AR—Conspiracy." New York Field Office: Federal Bureau of Investigation, October 6, 1964.

SAC, New York.(92-2300)."LCN AR—Conspiracy." New York Field Office: Federal Bureau of Investigation, February 12, 1969.

SAC, New York (RUC). "Re Pittsburgh Letter to Bureau, 1/14/64," January 24, 1964.

SAC, Newark. Letter to Director, FBI. "Angelo DeCarlo, A.k.a. AR." Airtel, March 19, 1962.

SAC, Newark. Letter to Director, FBI. "Anthony Provenzano, Walter a Dorn." Airtel, January 28, 1965.

SAC, Newark. Letter to Director, FBI. "Frank Tieri, Aka AR." Memorandum, August 3, 1970.

SAC, Newark. Letter to Director, FBI. "La Causa Nostra AR—Conspiracy." Airtel, March 7, 1963.

SAC, Newark. Letter to Director, FBI et al. "The Criminal Commission, AR—Conspiracy." Airtel, January 16, 1963.

SAC, Newark. Letter to Director, FBI. "The Criminal Conspiracy." Airtel, January 16, 1963.

SAC Norbert R. Linker. "Criminal Influence in International Brotherhood of Teamsters, Local 560, Union City, New Jersey." Federal Bureau of Investigation, January 15, 1962.

SAC, San Juan. Letter to Director, FBI. "Dino Cellini, Eddie Cellini, Operation Financier." Memorandum, June 28, 1974.

Salerno, Ralph. "CID Agents Ousted after Democratic Leader Arrives at Gangster's Funeral." *The Philadelphia Inquirer*, December 20, 1969.

Savage, James. "Bagel Nosh Chain Linked to Organized Crime Investigation." *Independent*, July 8, 1977.

Savage, James. "Probes Link Crime Figures to Bagel Nosh Restaurants." *The Miami Herald*, June 15, 1977.

Savage, James. "Stock-Deal Probe Brings Conviction of Mafia Figure." *The Miami Herald*, September 30, 1970.

Savage, James, and Ron LaBrecque. "Organized Crime Is Entering into Mainstream of Economy." *The Miami Herald*, June 19, 1977.

Schenker, Jennifer L. "Resurgent Mob Threatens S. Florida, Officials Warn." *The Miami Herald*, September 5, 1983.

Schiffman, J. "Restaurant of the Week." *The Item of Milburn and Short Hills*, September 26, 1968.

Schwartz, David G. *At the Sands: The Casino That Shaped Classic Las Vegas, Brought the Rat Pack Together, and Went out with a Bang.* Las Vegas, NV: Winchester Books, 2020.

Scott, Peter. "Peter Dale Scott Deep Events and the Global Drug Connection Deep Events and the CIA's Global Drug Connection," 2008. https://www.ratical.org/ratville/JFK/FalseMystery/DEaCIAsGDC-PDS.pdf.

Select Committee on Improper Activities in the Labor or Management Field. "Investigation of Improper Activities in the Labor or Management Field. Hearings before the Select Committee on Improper Activities in the Labor or Management Field." Washington, DC: U.S. Government Printing Office, 1959.

Shedd, SA John Edward. "Edward Levinson." Washington, DC: U.S. Government Printing Office, February 14, 1963.

Shropshire, Mike. "Does the Creator of the Cowboys Really Belong in the Hall of Fame?" *D Magazine*, August 24, 2018. https://www.dmagazine.com/publications/d-magazine/2018/september/does-the-creator-of-the-cowboys-really-belong-in-the-hall-of-fame/.

Simpson, Victor L., and Philip Wechsler. "Catena Called Boss of State Cosa Nostra Crime Syndicate." *The Record*, June 7, 1967.

Singer, Commander H. L. Letter to Detective Seargant Chiaventone. "M. Mark Marguiles." Memorandum, August 18, 1971.

Smith, Frank L. "Dino Vincent Cellini." Federal Bureau of Investigation, October 26, 1965.

Smith, Sandy. "A Death in the Family." *Life*, February 28, 1969.

Smith, Sandy. "Skimming Racket Masterminded by Lansky." *The Herald-News*, June 21, 1966.

Soloway, John. "Jersey Business." *The Star-Ledger*, September 18, 1966.

South Florida Sun Sentinel. "The Gangster Next Door." September 25, 1989.

Spaw, Rod. "First to Arrive at Scene Knew Ryan Was Dead." *Evansville Courier and Press*, October 19, 1977.

Staff Writer. "No Clues in Hunt for Eboli." *The Herald-News*, September 9, 1976.

Staff Writer. "Shore Officer Held in Jury Fixing Case." *Asbury Park Press*, January 24, 1934.

Star-Ledger Washington Bureau. "Lombardo: Heir Awaits." *The Star-Ledger*, February 17, 1983.

State of Florida Organized Crime Control Council. "1976 Annual Report." Tallahassee, April 4, 1977.

State of New Jersey. "Certificate of Incorporation of Central Landfill, Inc.," November 3, 1970.

State of New Jersey. "Index of Deaths in New Jersey 1916–1919," 1920.

State of New Jersey. "State Census of New Jersey, 1905." Trenton, NJ: New Jersey State Archive, 1905.

State of New Jersey Commission of Investigation. "21st Annual Report," September 1990.

State of New Jersey Commission of Investigation. "First Annual Report," January 1970.

State of New Jersey Commission of Investigation. "Report for the Year 1971," February 1972.

State of New Jersey Commission of Investigation. "Report for the Year 1972," February 1973.

State of New Jersey Commission of Investigation. "Thirteenth Annual Report," 1982.

State of New Jersey, Office of Administrative Law. "New Jersey Administrative Reports, Volume 11," 1989.

State of New York Senate. "Report of the New York State Joint Legislative Committee on Crime, Its Causes, Control & Effect on Society." State of New York, 1970.

"Steckman–Catena Score; Take Suburban Golf Event by Stroke on Net Card of 125." Nytimes.com. The New York Times, June 5, 1950. https://www.nytimes.com/1950/06/05/archives/steckmancatena-score-take-suburban-golf-event-by-stroke-on-net-card.html.

Sugerman, Myron. Letter to Author. "An Add on about Catena." Email, August 10, 2024.

Sugerman, Myron. Interview by Author, April 24, 2024.

Sugerman, Myron. "Re: Your Tommy Ryan Post." Email, October 27, 2024.

Sullivan, Joseph F. "Napoli Reneges on Pledge to Reveal Mafia Secrets." *The New York Times*, July 27, 1973.

Taplin, R. Clinton. "A Revised 'Who's Who' of Organized Crime." *The Record*, February 17, 1983.

The Cash Box. "Runyon Advertisement." January 31, 1948.

The Cash Box. "Runyon Advertisement." February 27, 1954.

The Cash Box. "Runyon Aids Cancer Fund Drive." February 27, 1954.

The Central New Jersey Home News. "Forsgate pro Honored." October 19, 1953.

The Central New Jersey Home News. "Member–Member Tourney." June 17, 1952.

The Central New Jersey Home News. "Reputed Mafia Leader Cuts Last Jersey Link." August 11, 1976.

The Chicago Tribune. "Knocks Out Windows in N. Side Area." May 5, 1969.

The County Prosecutors Association of New Jersey. "Report of the Task Force on Organized Crime." New Jersey, 1978.

The Courier-News. "Is Determined the Mop State, Says Woodcock." September 26, 1930.

The Courier-News. "Nick Delmore, Sought Three Years in Murder of U.S. Agent, Caught." October 19, 1933.

The Courier-News. "Two Combines Tie for Honors at Local Course." June 2, 1945.

The Daily News. "Seek Slayer of Grant Patterson across Atlantic." May 5, 1930.

The Daily Record. "Man Aids 565 Newark Boys." July 1, 1963.

The Daily Record. "Newark Golfers Whip City Team at Twin Brooks." September 16, 1946.

The Gangland History Podcast. "#40: Interview with Xavier Eboli, Son of Thomas 'Tommy Ryan' Eboli." YouTube, February 11, 2025. https://www.youtube.com/watch?v=pnxW8CoTKrQ.

The Herald-News. "Couple on Honeymoon in London." August 14, 1967.

The Herald-News. "Jerry Catena's Bill." March 3, 1975.

The Herald-News. "Missing Alarm for Eboli Kin." July 24, 1976.

The Herald-News. "No Knowledge of Link between Union, Crime." October 27, 1967.

The Herald-News. "Prosecutor Says Orecchio Case near End." April 9, 1952.

The Herald-News. "Winne Witness Escapes Perjury Investigation." April 1, 1954.

The Jersey Journal. "Ad for Kool-Vent." May 2, 1952.

The Jersey Journal. "Found Guilty of Bad Bank Charge." January 17, 1928.

The Jersey Journal. "Gambling Background Seen in Newark Man's Slaying," February 2, 1963.

The Miami Herald. "Klein Denies Allegations." August 20, 1976.

The Morning Call. "Katz Is Named in Beer Indictment." December 4, 1923.

The New York Daily News. "2 Franks' Pals Bounce Fotogs." May 2, 1950.

The New York Daily News. "Gang Probers Call L.I. Cafe Man." February 17, 1965.

The New York Daily News. "N.J. Cop Faces Quiz on Source of Gang Guns." June 4, 1944.

The New York Times. "Aide to Boiardo is Slain in Jersey." May 21, 1973, sec. Archives. https://www.nytimes.com/1973/05/21/archives/side-to-boiardo-is-slain-in-jersey-chieppa-worked-30-years-for-top.html.

The New York Times. "Barnet Sugerman (Obituary)." April 12, 1964.

The New York Times. "Halley Dies at 43; Ex-Crime Counsel; Former Kefauver Committee Aide Served as President of City Council here Exposed Rackets on TV Lawyer Suffered Reverses in Municipal Post—Lost in '53 Mayoralty Race Proposals Defeated Ran as

'Watchdog.'" November 20, 1956. https://www.nytimes.com/1956/11/20/archives/ halley-dies-at-43-excrime-counsel-former-kefauver-committee-aide.html.

The New York Times. "Nixon Commutes Term of Jersey Mafia Leader." December 24, 1972.

The Newark Evening News. "Ferrone Arrested." December 19, 1952.

The Newark Evening News. "Legislator Interceded for Gambling Figure." December 20, 1968.

The Newark Evening News. "Pleads Not Guilty in Still Operation." May 11, 1951.

The News. "Catena Back, Served by Kefauver Committee." October 23, 1950.

The Record. "Frank Catena Services Today." November 9, 1971.

The Record. "Lordi Hits Story on Mobster Ties." October 21, 1977.

The Record. "Missing Man's Land May Be Sold." December 31, 1976.

The Record. "Paterson Slayer Pleads Non Vult." October 5, 1931.

The Star Ledger. "50 Expected Tomorrow in Morano Golf." August 12, 1947.

The Star Ledger. "Ceres Keeps Golf Post." February 17, 1947.

The Star-Ledger. "3 Witnesses Held in Club Slaying." February 1, 1963.

The Star-Ledger. "A Discussion on the Mob's Help to Addonizio." January 7, 1970.

The Star-Ledger. "Abe Green, 91, Owner of Firms in the Entertainment Industry." December 10, 2003.

The Star-Ledger. "Ad for Solar-Vent." May 27, 1956.

The Star-Ledger. "Catena Duo Wins at Suburban." June 5, 1950.

The Star-Ledger. "Catena's Neighbors Can't Believe He Has Mob Ties." December 4, 1957.

The Star-Ledger. "Ceres, Russo, Caloyers Win Golf Crowns." August 7, 1953.

The Star-Ledger. "Ex-Boxer and Girl Held in Slaying." February 14, 1963.

The Star-Ledger. "Friedman and Catena Win Knoll Golf Title." June 15, 1953.

The Star-Ledger. "Golfers Vie for Essex, Newark Titles." August 5, 1952.

The Star-Ledger. "Jury Hears Witness in Murder Quiz." February 7, 1963.

The Star-Ledger. "More Mafia Tapes." January 7, 1970.

The Star-Ledger. "Murder Called 'Spontaneous.'" February 2, 1963.

The Star-Ledger. "Notice of Application." June 7, 1963.

The Star-Ledger. "Probers Drop Hunt for Longie." August 19, 1951.

The Star-Ledger. "Sylvio Orlando, Restaurateur, 71." March 14, 1972.

The Star-Ledger. "Top Jersey Golfers in Morano Tournament." August 9, 1949.

The Star-Ledger. "West End Club Liquor License Is Revoked." May 5, 1964.

The Times Record. "Aura of Respectaility (*sic*) Shades Reputed Overseer of Mafia Doings." January 6, 1969.

The Times Record. "Hard Times for the Mafia." October 17, 1972.

The United States of America v. Russell A. Bufalino (Southern District of New York June 17, 1960).

They Create Worlds. "Lion and Bally Manufacturing." Podcast. Podbeam, May 15, 2019.

ThrowBackMedia. "Xavier Eboli: After My Father Was Assassinated, We Never Heard from Benny Squint Lombardo Again." YouTube, March 2, 2025. https://www.youtube. com/watch?v=jvUvz0WkXcg.

Tickel, Herman E. "The Criminal Commission, et al Little Rock Division, FBI File 92-233." Federal Bureau of Investigation, April 27, 1962.

Toon, Jason. "Mafia Killed the Video Star: Shoddy Goods 026." Meh.com. Shoddy Goods, from meh.com, by Jason Toon, January 7, 2025. https://shoddygoods.meh.com/p/mafia-killed-the-video-star-shoddy.

Trimboli, Nicholas J. "Utica Renewal Project given Go Ahead Signal." *Syracuse Herald-Journal*, July 25, 1965.

U.S. Census Bureau. "Fourteenth Census of the United States. Newark Ward 10, Essex, New Jersey." Washington, DC, 1920.

U.S. Census Bureau. "Thirteenth Census of the United States. Newark Ward 10, Essex, New Jersey." Washington, DC, 1910.

U.S. House of Representatives: Select Committee on Assassinations. "Investigation of the Assassination of President John F. Kennedy: Staff and Consultant's Reports on Organized Crime." Washington, DC: U.S. Government Printing Office, March 1979.

Union County Prosecutor's Office, Detective Bureau, Intelligence Unit. "Organized Crime Figures Associated with Fort Lee, New Jersey," 1982.

United Press International. "A&P Fire Suspect Charged." *Detroit Free Press*, June 13, 1969.

United Press International. "Catena Faces Jail If He Doesn't Talk." *Courier-Post*, February 18, 1970.

United Press International. "Gambling Board Approves Vegas Hotel License." *Nevada State Journal*, January 26, 1956.

United Press International. "Gangster Slain in Hospital by Pair Who Flee." *The Courier-News*, November 4, 1930.

United Press International. "Killing of Dry Agent in Elizabeth Brewery Raid Indicates War to End between Dry Agents and Racketeers." *The Courier-News*, September 20, 1930.

United Press International. "Las Vegas Gamblers Surrender." *Desert Sun*, May 12, 1967.

United Press International. "Nationwide Ring Hit by Indictment." *Lodi News-Sentinel*, July 9, 1958.

United Press International. "Newark Robbers Tie, Bag Porter." *The Jersey Journal*, September 25, 1961.

United Press International. "Probe Jersey Cosa Nostra." *The Jersey Journal*, February 22, 1967.

United Press International. "Prominent Figures Mentioned in Tapes Released by Judge." *The Millville Daily*, January 7, 1970.

United Press International. "Vegas Gamblers Pay 'Skim' Fines." *Nevada State Journal*, May 28, 1968.

United States Congress: Committee on Governmental Affairs. "Organized Criminal Activities: South Florida and U.S. Penitentiary, Atlanta, Ga." Washington, DC: U.S. Government Printing Office, October 25, 1978.

United States House of Representatives Select Committee on Crime. "Organized Crime in Sports (Racing)," July 1972.

United States of America v. Russell A. Bufalino, Ignatius Cannone, et al. (United States Court of Appeals for the Second Circuit November 28, 1960).

United States Senate: Committee on Commerce. "Effects of Organized Criminal Activity on Interstate and Foreign Commerce." Washington, DC: U.S. Government Printing Office, 1973.

United States Senate: Committee on Commerce. "Effects of Organized Criminal Activity on Interstate and Foreign Commerce: Hearings before the Committee on Commerce, United States Senate, Ninety-Second Congress," 1972.

United States Senate: Committee on Government Affairs. "Organized Crime: 25 Years after Valachi." Washington, DC: U.S. Government Printing Office, April 1988.

United States Senate: Committee on Rules and Regulations. "Financial or Business Interests of Officers or Employees of the Senate." Washington, DC: U.S. Government Printing Office, April 13, 1964.

United States Senate: Committee on the Judiciary. "Measures Relating to Organized Crime." Washington, DC: U.S. Government Printing Office, June 1969.

United States Senate: Committee on the Judiciary. "Organized Crime in America." Washington, DC: U.S. Government Printing Office, March 3, 1983.

United States Senate: Special Committee to Investigate Organized Crime in Interstate Commerce. "Investigation of Organized Crime in Interstate Commerce, Part 7, New York-New Jersey." Washington, DC: U.S. Government Printing Office, 1951.

United States Treasury Department. *Mafia*. New York, NY: Harper Collins, 2009.

"US Congressional Record: 91st Congress." Washington, DC: U.S. Government Printing Office, August 12, 1969.

US House of Representatives Select Committee on Assassinations. "Investigation of the Assassination of President John F. Kennedy." Washington, DC: U.S. Government Printing Office, December 28, 1978.

Valin, Edmond. "Two Informants from Gambino Crime Family | American Mafia." Mafiahistory.us, 2018. https://mafiahistory.us/rattrap/gambinoinf.html#n54.

Valin, Edmond. "Zeid: Pittsburgh Snitch Is Murdered | American Mafia History." Mafiahistory.us, 2021. https://mafiahistory.us/rattrap/infzeid.html.

Van Burskirk, Lt. L. J. Letter to T. A. Buchanan. "Underbosses of the Vito Genovese Family." Memorandum, Miami-Dade Police Department, January 29, 1964.

VanBuskirk, Lt. L. J. Letter to T. A. Buchanan, Sheriff. "Under Bosses of the Vito Genovese Family." Memorandum, January 29, 1964.

videogamehistorian. "Bally Manufacturing—They Create Worlds." They Create Worlds, May 23, 2015. https://videogamehistorian.wordpress.com/tag/bally-manufacturing/.

videogamehistorian. "Historical Interlude: The History of Coin-Op Part 5, Consolidation and Stagnation." They Create Worlds, May 23, 2015. https://videogamehistorian. wordpress.com/2015/05/23/historical-interlude-the-history-of-coin-op-part-5-consolidation-and-stagnation/.

vLex. "United States Ex Rel. Catena v. Elias," 2025. https://case-law.vlex.com/vid/united-states-ex-rel-895559923.

Volz, Joseph, and Peter J. Bridge. *The Mafia Talks*. Fawcett Gold Medal, 1969.

Waggoner, Walter H. "Spina Indicted in Newark as Lax on Gambling Laws." *The New York Times*, July 25, 1968.

Waller, Leslie. *The Swiss Bank Connection*. New York, NY: Signet Book, 1972.

Walsh, Ed. "3 Bigshot Jersey Gamblers Indicted for Tax Evasions." *The Star-Ledger*, January 12, 1953.

Washington News Bureau. "Catena Hides behind 5th 80 Times." *The Jersey Journal*, February 11, 1959.

Weissman, Dan. "Catena May Get Genovese Crown." *The Herald-News*, February 15, 1969.

Williams, Danny. Jerry Catena and Golf. Interview by Author, October 29, 2024.

Zendzian, Craig A. *Who Pays? Casino Gambling, Hidden Interests, and Organized Crime*. New York, NY: Harrow and Heston, 1993.

ABOUT THE AUTHOR

Scott M. Deitche is the author of several books on organized crime, including the critically acclaimed *Garden State Gangland: The Rise of the Mob in New Jersey* and *Hitmen: The Mafia, Drugs, and the East Harlem Purple Gang*. He has also written articles on organized crime for national magazines and newspapers and has been featured on numerous television and news shows. Scott lives in St. Petersburg, Florida.